KU-251-762

Media on the Move

'An original and marketable collection, very well organised and integrated by an experienced and committed editor.'

John Tomlinson, *Director, Institute for Cultural Analysis,*
Nottingham Trent University

Media on the Move provides a critical analysis of the dynamics of the international flow of images and ideas. This comes at a time when the political, economic and technological contexts within which media organisations operate are increasingly global.

The surge in transnational traffic in media products has primarily benefited major corporations such as Disney, AOL-Time Warner and News Corporation. However, as this book argues, new networks have emerged which buck this trend: Brazilian TV is watched in China, Indian films have a huge following outside India and Al -Jazeera has become a household name in the West.

Media on the Move brings together internationally known theorists and regional specialists to examine the alternative media flows against the US-led global flows. Combining a theoretical perspective on contra-flow of media with grounded case studies into one up-to-date and accessible volume, *Media on the Move* provides a much-needed guide to the globalisation of media, going beyond the standard Anglo-American view of this evolving phenomenon.

The book comprises four thematically linked sections:

- Contextualising Contra-Flow
- Non-Western Media in Motion
- Regional Perspectives on Flow and Contra-Flow
- Moving Media – From the Margins to the Mainstream?

Contributors include: Oliver Boyd-Barrett, Arnold S. de Beer, Steven Guanpeng Dong, Myria Georgiou, Nitin Govil, Koichi Iwabuchi, Anandam P. Kavoori, Youna Kim, Antonio C. La Pastina, Musa Maguire, Lisa McLaughlin, Terhi Rantanen, Cacilda M. Rêgo, Anbin Shi, Roger Silverstone, Ruth Teer-Tomaselli, Daya Kishan Thussu and Herman Wasserman.

Daya Kishan Thussu is Professor of International Communication at the University of Westminster in London. His previous publications include *Contra-Flow in Global News* (1992), *Electronic Empires: Global Media and Local Resistance* (1998) and *International Communication: Continuity and Change*, second edition (2006).

Communication and Society

Series Editor: James Curran

Media on the Move

Global flow and contra-flow

Edited by Daya Kishan Thussu

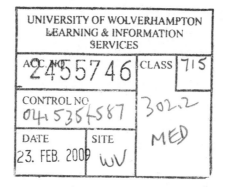

Routledge
Taylor & Francis Group
LONDON AND NEW YORK

First published 2007
by Routledge
2 Park Square, Milton Park, Abingdon, Oxon OX14 4RN

Simultaneouly published in the USA and Canada
by Routledge
270 Madison Ave, New York, NY 10016

Transferred to Digital Printing 2008

Routledge is an imprint of the Taylor & Francis Group, an informa business

Typeset in Baskerville and Gill by BC Typesetting Ltd, Bristol
Printed and bound in Great Britain by
CPI Antony Rowe, Chippenham, Wiltshire

British Library Cataloguing in Publication Data
A catalogue record for this book is available from the British Library

Library of Congress Cataloging-in-Publication Data
Thussu, Daya Kishan.
   Media on the move: global flow and contra-flow/Daya Kishan Thussu.
      p.   cm. – (Communication and society)
   1. Communication, International. 2. Globalization. I. Title. II. Series:
   Communication and society (Routledge (Firm))
   P96.I5T485   2006
   302.2–dc22   2006017712

ISBN10: 0–415–354579 (hbk)
ISBN10: 0–415–354587 (pbk)
ISBN10: 0–203–001230 (ebk)

ISBN13: 978–0–415–354578 (hbk)
ISBN13: 978–0–415–354585 (pbk)
ISBN13: 978–0–203–001233 (ebk)

In memory of Roger Silverstone, 1945–2006

Contents

Tables and figure

Tables

Figure

Notes on contributors

Oliver Boyd-Barrett is Director of the School of Communication Studies at Bowling Green State University, Ohio, in the United States, and holds a joint professorship in the Department of Journalism and the Department of Telecommunications. He has authored and edited many books and articles on international communications media, particularly the major international news agencies. His current research focuses on media coverage of the 'war on terrorism'. His latest book is *Communications Media, Globalization, and Empire* (John Libbey, 2006).

Arnold S. de Beer is Professor Extraordinary in the Department of Journalism, Stellenbosch University, as well as in the Faculty of Law, University of the Western Cape, South Africa. He has written on media in Africa and is the founding editor of *Ecquid Novi*, the South African journal for journalism research. He is the co-author with John C. Merrill of *Global Journalism: Topical Issues and Media Issues* (Pearson/A&B, 2004).

Steven Guanpeng Dong is Assistant Dean and Senior Lecturer of Political Communications, School of Journalism and Communication, Tsinghua University, Beijing. He is also the Director of the Tsinghua-Reuters Programme on Global Journalism based in Beijing. Among his most recent publications are *The Encyclopedia for Spokespersons* (Xinhua Press, 2005) and *Press Conferences and Media Relations for the Government* (Tsinghua University Press, 2005). He is senior consultant for the State Council Departments and a presenter for the national television networks.

Myria Georgiou teaches International Communications at the Institute of Communications Studies, University of Leeds in the UK. Her research interests are in the areas of diaspora, transnationalism, identity and the media. Her latest book is *Diaspora, Identity and the Media* (Hampton Press, 2006).

Nitin Govil is the co-author of *Global Hollywood* (BFI, 2001) and *Global Hollywood 2* (BFI, 2005). He has also published on in-flight entertainment, broadband content distribution, race and television, media piracy and wartime unilateralism, Indian digital media outsourcing, and is co-authoring a book on the Indian film industry. He received his PhD from the Department of Cinema Studies at New York University and recently joined the faculty at the University of California, San Diego, where he is an Assistant Professor in the Department of Communication.

Koichi Iwabuchi teaches at the School of International Liberal Studies of Waseda University in Japan. He is the author of *Recentring Globalization: Popular Culture and Japanese Transnationalism* (Duke University Press, 2002) and editor of *Feeling Asian Modernities: Transnational Consumption of Japanese Dramas* (Hong Kong University Press, 2004).

Anandam P. Kavoori is Associate Professor of Telecommunication at the Grady College of Journalism and Mass Communication, University of Georgia in the United States. He has a PhD in journalism and mass communication from the University of Maryland. He is a specialist in the comparative cultural analysis of media texts, with a special focus on television news. Among his publications are: *The Global Dynamics of News* (Ablex, 2000) and most recently *Media, Terrorism, and Theory: A Reader* (Rowman & Littlefield, 2006).

Youna Kim is Co-Convenor of the MSc in Media and Communications at the London School of Economics and Political Science. She is author of *Women, Television and Everyday Life in Korea: Journeys of Hope* (Routledge, 2005). She holds a PhD from Goldsmiths College, University of London. Her new project *Diasporic Daughters* explores transnational mobility and media consumption of young Asian women in the UK and the USA.

Antonio C. La Pastina teaches at the Communication Department at Texas A&M University in the United States. He holds a PhD from the Radio-TV-Film Department at the University of Texas at Austin. His research interests are on media ethnography; the representation of otherness in mainstream media and its role on diasporic cultures as well as Brazilian media and telenovelas.

Musa Maguire is a PhD candidate in Media Studies at the University of Texas at Austin. His dissertation research examines hybridity in Islamic satellite television. He received his MA in Media and Communication Studies from Goldsmiths College, and a BA from the University of Pennsylvania. In 2004, he was awarded a Fulbright grant for study in Egypt where he is pursuing his dissertation fieldwork as well as working at Huda TV in Cairo, where he hosts the English-language programme, *Ask Huda*.

Lisa McLaughlin is an Associate Professor at Miami University-Ohio, USA, where she holds a joint appointment in Mass Communication and Women's Studies. She has published a number of articles and chapters on feminism, media and the public sphere, and, more recently, on feminism and the political economy of transnational public space and the gender implications of the corporatization of development as this phenomenon has emerged under the auspices of the United Nations. At present, her research concentrates on gender training initiatives that have originated as public–private partnerships brokered through the UN. She is co-editor of *Feminist Media Studies*, an international peer-reviewed journal published by Routledge.

Terhi Rantanen is Director of the MSc in Global Media and Communication programme at the London School of Economics and Political Science. She has published extensively on a range of topics related to global media. Her publications include *The Globalization of News* (with Oliver Boyd-Barrett, Sage, 1998), *The Global and the National: Media and Communication in Post-Communist Russia* (Rowman & Littlefield, 2002) and *The Media and Globalization* (Sage, 2005). She is a founder and editor of the Sage journal *Global Media and Communication*.

Cacilda M. Rêgo is Assistant Professor of Portuguese at the Department of Languages, Philosophy, and Speech Communication at Utah State University. She received her PhD from the University of Texas at Austin and has published on Brazil's Cinema Novo, telenovelas and Brazilian media policies.

Naomi Sakr is Reader in Communication in the School of Media, Arts and Design at the University of Westminster. She is the author of *Satellite Realms: Transnational Television, Globalization and the Middle East* (I. B. Tauris, 2001), editor of *Women and Media in the Middle East* (I. B. Tauris, 2004), and a contributor to recent books on television policy, al-Jazeera, the making of journalists, international news, the regionalisation of transnational television, media reform and governance in Gulf countries. Her principal research interest is media policy in the Arab Middle East.

Anbin Shi is Associate Professor of Media and Cultural Studies, School of Journalism and Communications, Tsinghua University in Beijing. Shi has a PhD from Penn State University in the United States. Among his publications is *A Comparative Approach to Redefining Chinese-ness in the Era of Globalization* (Edwin Mellen Press, 2003). He is also a senior consultant for varied CCTV cultural and arts programmes.

Roger Silverstone was, at his death in July 2006, Professor of Media and Communications at the London School of Economics and Political Science. His most recent book is *Media and Morality: On the Rise of the Mediapolis* (Polity Press, 2006).

Ruth Teer-Tomaselli is a Professor of Culture, Communication and Media Studies at the University of KwaZulu Natal in Durban, South

Africa. Her research interests include the political economy of broadcasting and telecommunications in Southern Africa; programme production on television; radio, particularly community radio; and the role of media in development. She is a member of the Board of Governors of the South African Broadcasting Corporation, and holds an Orbicom Professorship, the World-Wide Network of UNESCO Chairs in Communication.

Daya Kishan Thussu is Professor of International Communication at the University of Westminster in London. He is the co-author of *Contra-Flow in Global News* (1992, published in association with UNESCO); editor of *Electronic Empires – Global Media and Local Resistance* (1998, Arnold, London and Oxford University Press, New York); author of *International Communication – Continuity and Change* (2000, Arnold, London and Oxford University Press, New York, second edition published in 2006), and co-editor of *War and the Media: Reporting Conflict 24/7* (2003, Sage, London), and of *Ideologies of the Internet* (2006, Hampton Press: Cresskill, NJ). He is the founder and Managing Editor of the Sage journal *Global Media and Communication*.

Herman Wasserman is Associate Professor in the Department of Journalism, Stellenbosch University, South Africa. He is a former Fulbright Scholar to Indiana University (Bloomington), deputy editor of *Ecquid Novi*, the South African journal for journalism research and co-editor of *At the End of the Rainvow: Power, politics and identity in the post-apartheid South African media* (2007, Cape Town: HSRC Press) and *Shifting Selves: Post-apartheid essays on Mass Media, Culture and Identity* (Cape Town: Kwela). His research interests relate to the role of the media in post-apartheid South African society, including the use of the new media technologies for social change, the media constructions of identity, and media ethics.

Introduction

Daya Kishan Thussu

Mobility of the media is a key characteristic of the increasingly digitised global communication ecology. In a digitally connected globe, flows of all kinds of information – political discourse, scientific research, corporate data, personal communication and media entertainment – circulate round the world at a speed unimaginable even a decade ago. New information technologies ensure production, consumption and distribution of information in a highly individualised manner, unbounded by temporal and spatial constraints.

As a 'global' Indian and a member of the 'digital' diaspora, I have experienced this profound transformation in global media flows first hand. Long gone are the days when I had to scour British media for news 'from home'. What I received was often superficial and tinged with a certain kind of superiority inherent in British coverage of what was then called the 'Third World'. I would visit London's mini-India in Southall to buy week-old newspapers and back issues of news magazines from India. Although London offered a range of entertainment, for someone who grew up with the vast canvas of Indian films, I had to settle for watching poor quality videos of my favourite films. This was late 1980s: pre-globalisation, pre-satellite television and pre-Internet.

Fast forward to 2006 and my media consumption pattern has been revolutionised. I now have access to three 24/7 television news networks – two in English and one in Hindi – as well as two dedicated channels showing Indian films round-the-clock and two music channels playing non-stop film music. I read web editions of at least two Indian daily newspapers and two news magazines. Enhanced multimedia capacity and falling costs of telecommunication have broadened and accelerated access to media and information on most aspects of life in India. Apart from improving the quality of life at a personal level, these changes are also extremely significant professionally for someone who studies media and communication in a global context.

My experience has been replicated by millions of individuals who live, according to Homi Bhaba, 'between cultures'. The movement of people across national or cultural boundaries has been followed by new flows of media, which have grown both in quality and quantity. The proliferation of satellite and cable television and online networks, enabled by increasingly sophisticated digital technologies and the growing availability of affordable communication satellites, has transformed the global media landscape. The deregulation and liberalisation of the broadcasting and telecommunications sector and its rapid privatisation in the 1990s – partly as a result of trade liberalisation regimes set up under the auspices of the General Agreement on Trade in Services and partly dictated by the new communication technologies – have helped to create a global marketplace for media products and new ways of communicating in real time across continents.

Emerging ethno-mediascape

'Globalization', says the 2004 UN *Human Development Report*, 'is quantitatively and qualitatively reshaping international movements of people' (UNDP, 2004: 87), triggering a different kind of mobility: the number of highly educated emigrants from developing to developed countries has doubled in the decade from 1990–2000 (World Bank, 2006: 66). These professionals maintain ties with the countries of their origins, supporting professional networks, promoting public diplomacy and private commerce, funding educational, cultural and linguistic policy. Internet-based expatriate networks of skilled professionals and students facilitate the transfer of knowledge and ideas. Television has reflected these demographic changes: in 1990, there were no 'ethnic' channels in Europe; by mid-2005, 51 channels were operating. Movements within Europe – from East to West, for example, Polish professionals to Ireland, have necessitated regular publication of Polish-language inserts in Irish mainstream newspapers.

The globalisation of the digital revolution has ensured that media content is instantaneously delivered and widely accessible in a uniform format – in the form of text, sound, still-and-moving pictures and databases. These data can be stored, copied, shared, manipulated. Corporations are already speaking about a 'pervasive media' environment. As an IBM report envisioned: 'Between now and 2010, the increasing affordability, saturation, transmission speed and massive data storage capacity of emerging digital technologies will enable new formats and functionalities, multiplying and deepening the connectivity of users around the globe' (IBM, 2004).

The use of the Internet has grown exponentially: from just 3 per cent of the world's population in 1995 to more than 15 per cent of the global population by 2005 – nearly a billion people, though 90 per cent of those were resident in industrialised countries (North America, 30 per cent; Europe, 30 per cent; and Asia-Pacific, 30 per cent). At the end of 2004, most Internet users lived in Asia (nearly 330 million), followed by Europe (243 million) and the US (185 million). In 2000, developing countries accounted for only 25 per cent of Internet users in the world; by 2005, this figure had reached nearly 40 per cent. By 2004, an estimated 77 per cent of the world's population was able to access mobile networks (UNCTAD, 2005).

Such technological changes have created a surge in transnational traffic in media products. This process has primarily benefited the major media corporations – Disney, AOL-Time Warner, News Corporation – which dominate media content and delivery mechanisms by their ownership of multiple networks and production facilities. This corporate hegemony of world media has raised profound concerns about cultural homogenisation; however, there is also a perceptible trend towards regionalisation and localisation of media content to suit the cultural priorities of audiences, given the heterogeneity of the global market. Though the Northern conglomerates continue to shape the global media landscape, the flow of global media products is not just one way from the media-rich North (and within it the Anglo-American axis) to the media-poor South. There is evidence that in an increasingly global communication environment, new transnational networks have emerged, including from the periphery to the metropolitan centres of global media.

Partly spurred on by the dynamics of market-oriented media, creative and cultural industries in the non-Western world have experienced an unprecedented growth in most genres of media: Korean and Indian films, Latin American soap operas and Arabic news. Some of the most potentially far-reaching changes are taking place in the Asian mediasphere. Chinese films, such as *Crouching Tiger, Hidden Dragon* (2000), *Hero* (2003) and *The House of Flying Daggers* (2004), have put China on the global entertainment map while popular martial art 'action cinema' has global fans. The Chinese presence in the global media world has been accelerated via Hong Kong – home to such trans-Asian networks as STAR TV and Channel V (both part of Rupert Murdoch's media empire). The success of the 2005 Chinese film *Perhaps Love* – the first musical since the 1950s (*People's Daily*, 2005) and made with expertise from Bollywood – is indicative of the potential of media collaborations among major non-Western cultures, involving the world's two largest populations and its two biggest diasporas: 35 million Chinese, 20 million Indian (UN, 2005).

The global (which in essence means Western, or more accurately American) offering interacts with the national and the local in ways that produce often hybridised, 'glocal' media products, hallmark of a postmodern cultural sensitivity. The interaction has not always been smooth – the adoption, adaptation and rejection of the global are legion. The dynamic of the international flow of images and ideas needs to be reconfigured at a time when the political, economic and technological contexts in which media are produced and consumed are becoming increasingly global. A commercially driven, consumer-oriented media environment encourages multiple flows: Brazilian television being watched in China; Indian films having a following in the Arab world. The implications – political, economic and cultural – of such media flows from the emerging nodal points of media production need fuller exploration to grasp the monumental change in speed, volume and quality of media flows across continents. In the emerging multivocal, global mediasphere, media power may not just be concentrated in one centre but distributed among many mini-centres or satraps located in regional hubs. The global dissemination of non-Western media can reduce inequalities in media access, contribute to a more cosmopolitan culture, and in the long run perhaps affect national, regional and even international political dynamics. The media and communication contra-flows can shape cultural identities, energise disempowered groups, and help create political coalitions and new transnational private and public spheres.

Does the growing reverse traffic in transnational media flows show that Western media domination has diminished? Do such multi-directional flows have a potential to develop counter-hegemonic channels at a global level to check US domination of the global media bazaar? How effective are these contra-flows since their output is relatively small and their global impact largely restricted to the diasporic communities or geo-linguistic constituencies, their primary target market? Will contra-flow of media lead to greater empowerment of cultures and mediated symbols often in the margins of globalisation discourse and will this be achieved at the loss of influence and authority among the cultures that have dominated media flows?

Most of the academic discourse on media globalisation has been about how the Western or the global impacts, interacts and reacts with the national (non-Western). What this book aims to do is to map out how the non-Western, non-mainstream media flows are impacting on the global communication environment. The hope is that the interventions in this volume will stimulate a discourse about the growing visibility, importance and impact of non-Western media flows on media cultures internationally.

The book in outline

The book is divided into four thematically linked sections. The first part aims to contextualise the phenomena of global media flows and contra-flows. The second part maps out the emergence and growth of non-Western media. Chapters in this part survey the key non-Western players in four different genres of media – animation, film, television soaps and news. Regional perspectives on global flows and contra-flows are discussed in Part III of the book, with contributions covering China, Russia, South Korea and South Africa. The three chapters in the final part of the book examine emerging trends in the global mediascape. A common thread running through the chapters in this part is the role of new communications technologies, especially the Internet, in creating transnational solidarities and cultural identities. Among the themes explored is the growth of web-based alternative community and news networks.

The book begins with an overview of global media flows and contra-flows where I propose a typology of media flows – global, transnational and geo-cultural. I then map out what are termed the 'dominant flows', largely emanating from the United States; followed by contra-flows, originating from the erstwhile peripheries of global media industries, designated 'sub-altern flows'. While celebrating the global circulation of media products from a wider range of hubs of creative and cultural industries, my chapter points out the disparities in the volume and economic value of such flows in comparison to the dominant flows and cautions against the tendency to valorise the rise of non-Western media, arguing that they may reflect a refiguring of hegemony in more complex ways. In their contribution, Myria Georgiou and Roger Silverstone (whose untimely death has deprived the field of an outstanding scholar) consider the diasporic dispersal of popula-tions as the impetus for the transnational dispersal of communications. They argue that, just as migration itself transgresses national boundaries of state and culture, so too do the communications that migration generates; thus, how these communications are mediated by diasporic groups provides us with a basis for enquiry into the operation of contra-flows in global media.

Anandam Kavoori critiques the whole notion of contra-flow, arguing that it is predicated on a set of referents – nation-state, West and the East, North and South – that are primarily concerned with 'spatial location', which tends to ignore the way distribution and consumption of media reflect a pro-cess of 'deterritorialisation'. The assumption that the cultural products are equally a function of national origin is also contested in his chapter. Drawing on the works of Arjun Appadurai and relating it to postcolonial theory and transnational cultural studies, Kavoori offers a fresh insight into the theoreti-cal terrain of media globalisation, suggesting ways in which the debate could progress.

After having set the context – both theoretical and empirical – of global contra-flows, the second part of the book examines the phenomenon of the rise of the non-Western media, increasingly visible in the global symbolic space. Koichi Iwabuchi, author of a book on decentred globalisation, argues that in many parts of the globe there is evidence pointing to the rise of non-Western regional media circulation as well as the rise of non-Western media exports. Global media flows are significantly de-Americanised and there is evidence of the ascent of non-Western exports and intra-regional non-Western flows, necessitating a corrective to a US-centric analysis of media and cultural globalisation. Focusing on the global popularity of Japanese media products and prevalence of glocalism and the activation of non-Western regional connections, Iwabuchi argues that these trends are actually constitutive of the restructuring process of uneven cultural globalisation.

Nitin Govil's chapter looks at the globalisation of the Indian film industry – so-called 'Bollywood'. Govil examines how the world's largest film factory is positioning itself economically and politically to operate in a global marketplace. He argues that Bollywood embodies the multiple histories and directions of cultural flow in the way that it has incorporated and indigenised a range of global and local forms to provide an experience that has become part of the mass popular culture way outside its geo-linguistic domain. Another Southern media flow that is clearly a transnational phenomenon is the Latin American telenovela, viewed across the world from Africa to Europe and from Asia to the US. Cacilda Rêgo and Antonio La Pastina, both specialists on Brazilian popular culture, explore the global popularisation of telenovelas, particularly those from Brazil, the world's largest producer. Tracing the history of the genre in Brazil, Rêgo and La Pastina maintain that the flow of telenovelas from Latin America can be seen as a challenge to Hollywood's hegemony of media exports and that their worldwide success suggests that they are no longer a uniquely Latin American but a global television phenomenon.

The fourth major non-Western media organisation to emerge and change the pattern of global media flows is the pan-Arabic news network, Al-Jazeera. Naomi Sakr, who has written extensively on the impact of satellite television on the Arab media, argues in her chapter that the 24/7 news network evokes conflicting interpretations among its supporters and detractors. She discusses this within three main lines of argument: Al-Jazeera as a counter-hegemonic source of contra-flow; as a source of news and information created to reinforce a US-designed order in the politically sensitive Middle East; and finally as a new force shaping Arab politics and widening the public sphere.

Part III of the book focuses on the growing trend towards regional media flows. Youna Kim's chapter charts the extraordinary growth of media exports ($800 million in 2004) from South Korea. Drawing on government and other sources, she demonstrates the validity of the use of the term so-called 'Korean Wave' or '*Hallyu*' sweeping the East Asian media sphere. Kim's focus is on the transnational circulation and consumption of Korean television drama and sees it as an example of the 'de-centralising multiplicity' of global media flows. Another regional dimension to the discourse is provided by the contribution from South Africa, the regional hub of media and cultural industries in Africa. In their contribution, two veteran observers of the African media scene, Ruth Teer-Tomaselli and Arnold de Beer, along with colleague Herman Wasserman, examine how South Africa has used its position of strength to distribute its own media content as well as content from global networks to African audiences across the continent through such platforms as MultiChoice and M-Net.

Terhi Rantanen extends the terms of the debate on media flows by bringing in what she calls 'media in transition', focusing on media systems in two major non-Western socialist or post-socialist powers: Russia and China. Both countries, she notes, were insulated from outside media flows, a situation that changed with the opening up of the state-controlled media systems which have now to tread a delicate balance between the national imperative and the global competition. The challenge of global competition is also at the heart of the chapter on China's news media by Steven Guanpeng Dong and Anbin Shi, both based at the Tsinghua University in Beijing. They discuss this in the context of the launch of a 24-hour news channel CCTV-News. That media flows are not just about content but may also encompass professional practice is reflected in the chapter, which also shows how Chinese journalists and media analysts are endeavouring to develop a Chinese version of civic journalism that can operate with credibility in a global news arena.

The final part of the book aims to explore the impact of new communication technologies on media flows. Oliver Boyd-Barrett draws from an investigation of six US alternative news websites, one of whose distinguishing features is that they provide links to stories available on the online sites of mainstream and alternative US and foreign news media. The chapter argues that this practice of linking should be construed as an anti-hegemonic process of 'reframing', which involves the construction of alternative ideological universes as well as distinctive portfolios of news stories. In her contribution, Lisa McLaughlin focuses on the power dynamic associated with a Southern-based activist group and its engagement with the dominant Western narratives of 'difference' and 'otherness', in order to become visible and to be heard on the 'global stage'. The discussion is contextualised through a case study of the Revolutionary Association of the Women of Afghanistan (RAWA). The final chapter by Musa Maguire discusses the emergence of the Islamic Internet, which he argues represents a 'counter-flow in ideology and information'. Maguire, who is researching Islamic websites for his PhD, laments the fact that the mainstream discourses in the West have excluded Islam from any serious academic analysis.

The idea of pooling intellectual resources to produce a book that explores the idea of contra-flow was triggered by a paper I presented at the London School of Economics and Political Science and I am indebted to the late Roger Silverstone for inviting me. James Curran, editor of Routledge's prestigious Communication and Society series, has been extremely generous in his support for this project from its very inception, for which I am indebted to him. Colleagues at the University of Westminster have been consistently helpful, not least by granting me a sabbatical to complete work on this book.

Given its subject matter, the book is international both in intellectual scope and in participation, drawing on expertise from a skilled and talented group of individuals who have contributed to cover different dimensions of global media mobility. I owe them all a deep sense of gratitude. My editors at Routledge – Natalie Foster and Aileen Irwin – have been a pleasure to work with and I am very appreciative of their admirable professionalism. Last but by no means least, as ever, thanks are due to my wife Liz for all her help and patience during the editing process.

References

IBM (2004) *Media and Entertainment 2010: Open on the Inside, Open on the Outside: The Open Media Company of the Future.* IBM Institute for Business Value Future Series report available on http://www.ibm.com/bcs.
People's Daily (2005) Musical movie 'Perhaps Love' hits box office record, 7 December. *The People's Daily* (English web edition). Available at: http://english.people.com.cn/ 200512/07/eng20051207.226188.html.
UNCTAD (2005) *Information Economy Report 2005.* Geneva: United Nations Conference on Trade and Development.
UNDP (2004) *Cultural Liberty in Today's Diverse World: Human Development Report 2004*, United Nations Development Programme. Oxford: Oxford University Press.
United Nations (2005) *Migration in an Interconnected World: New Directions for Action.* Report of the Global Commission on International Migration. Geneva: United Nations Publications.
World Bank (2006) *Global Economic Prospects 2006: Economic Implications of Remittances and Migration.* Washington: World Bank Publication.

Part I
Contextualising contra-flow

Chapter 1

Mapping global media flow and contra-flow

Daya Kishan Thussu

In his magisterial work *The Information Age*, Manuel Castells has argued that flows dominate contemporary life: 'our society is constructed around flows', he writes, 'flows of capital, flows of information, flows of technology, flows of organisational interactions, flows of images, sounds, and symbols' (Castells, 2000: 442). In an increasingly networked global society such flows have shown extraordinary growth in direction, volume and velocity. My aim in this chapter is to attempt a mapping of media flows, both as mainstream commercial commodities to be consumed by heterogeneous global audiences, and as alternative messages and images – emanating from a wide range of actors – from anti- and alter-globalisation activists to revisionist radicals circulating on an emerging 'alternative Internet' (Atton, 2004).

My focus is on the global flows and contra-flows of visual media, mainly television and film, as, despite the exponential growth of the Internet in the last decade, it was being used only by about 15 per cent of the world's population in 2006, while television and film had a much larger audience base. The chapter proposes a typology to divide the main media flows into three broad categories: global, transnational and geo-cultural. It then goes on to examine what it terms as the 'dominant flows', largely emanating from the global North, with the United States at its core; followed by contra-flows, originating from the erstwhile peripheries of global media industries – designated 'subaltern flows'. While celebrating the global circulation of media products from a wider range of hubs of creative and cultural industries, the chapter emphasises the disparities in the volume and economic value of such flows in comparison to the dominant ones and cautions against the tendency to valorise the rise of non-Western media, arguing that they may reflect a refiguring of hegemony in more complex ways.

Multi-vocal, multi-directional, multimedia

In the late 1990s, the UNESCO *World Culture Report* argued that media globalisation had increased Western cultural influence but noted that it also triggered possibilities of other models based on 'different cultural, institutional and historical backgrounds . . . such alternatives are likely to multiply in the era of globalisation, in spite of appearances, which may paradoxically witness greater diversity than uniformity' (UNESCO, 1998: 23).

The global media landscape in the first decade of the twenty-first century represents a complex terrain of multi-vocal, multimedia and multi-directional flows. The proliferation of satellite and cable television, made possible by digital technology, and the growing use of online communication, partly as a result of the deregulation and privatisation of broadcasting and telecommunication networks, have enabled media companies to operate in increasingly transnational rather than national arenas, seeking and creating new consumers worldwide. With the exception of a few powers such as the United States, Britain and France, whose media (particularly broadcasting, both state-run and privately operated) already had an international dimension, most countries have followed a largely domestic media agenda within the borders of a nation-state.

Gradual commercialisation of media systems around the world has created new private networks that are primarily interested in markets and advertising revenues. Nationality scarcely matters in this market-oriented media ecology, as producers view the audience principally as consumers and not as citizens. This shift from a state-centric and national view of media to one defined by consumer interest and transnational markets has been a key factor in the expansion and acceleration of media flows: from North to South, from East to West, and from South to South, though their volume varies according to the size and value of the market.

The US-led Western media, both online and offline, and in various forms – information, infotainment and entertainment – are global in their reach and influence (Bagdikian, 2004; Boyd-Barrett, 2006; Thussu, 2006). Given the political and economic power of the United States, its media are available across the globe, if not in English then in dubbed or indigenised versions. As its closest ally, Britain – itself a major presence in global media, particularly in the field of news and current affairs – benefits from the globalisation of Americana. The only non-Western genre with a global presence is Japanese animation (and this would not have been possible without the economic underpinnings of the world's second largest economic power). These represent what might be termed as 'dominant media flows'. Though some peripheral countries have emerged as exporters of television programmes and films (Sinclair *et al.*, 1996), the USA continues to lead the field in the export of audio-visual products. From news and current affairs (CNN, Discovery) through youth programming (MTV), children's television (Disney), feature films (Hollywood), sport (ESPN) to the Internet (Google), the United States is the global behemoth. One result of the privatisation and proliferation of television outlets and the growing glocalisation of US media products is that American film and television exports witnessed nearly a five-fold increase between 1992 and 2004 (see Figure 1.1).

The convergence of television and broadband has opened up new opportunities for the flow of media content. As US-led Western media conglomerates have regionalised and localised their content to extend their reach beyond the elites in the world and to create the 'global popular', many Southern media organisations have benefited from synergies emerging from this glocalisation process. Some have skilfully used their position within a media conglomerate, drawing on technological and professional expertise to grow into global operators. In addition, the globalisation of Western or Western-inspired media has contributed to the creation of professional careers in media and cultural industries. The localisation of media content and the outsourcing of digital media for transnational corporations – from Hollywood post-production to animation and digital data management – have provided the impetus for the formation of important global hubs for creative industries: by 2006, for example, India had emerged as a key destination for outsourcing media content (UNESCO, 2005a).

A second layer of international media players may include both private as well as state-sponsored flows. The Indian film industry (popularly referred to as Bollywood) and the Latin American telenovelas are the two major examples of transnational global flows that operate in a commercial environment. The South Africa-based, pan-African network M-Net is another example of such transnational and regional communications. Among the state-supported flows we can include Euronews, the 24/7 multilingual news consortium of Europe's public service broadcasters, TV5 and Radio France Internationale, aiming at the francophone market. Other transnational actors may include the Arab news network Al-Jazeera, the pan-Latin American TV channel Televisora del Sur ('Television of the South', Telesur) based in Venezuela, and the round-the-clock English-language global television channel, Russia Today (RTTV), intended to provide news 'from a Russian perspective', launched in 2005. The expansion of CCTV-9, the English language network of China Central Television, reflects the recognition by the Beijing authorities of the importance of the English language as the key to success for global commerce and communication and their strategy to bring Chinese public diplomacy to a global audience. These originators of transnational media flows have a strong regional presence but are also aimed at audiences outside their primary constituency. These can be categorised as representing 'subaltern flows' (see Table 1.1 over page). As one recent study of Al-Jazeera concluded: 'The information age is upon us and in the decades ahead we can expect only more Al-Jazeeras, adding to an ever greater torrent of information, as regional ideas spread around the world and become global' (Miles, 2005: 426).

A third category of geo-cultural media caters to specific cultural-linguistic audiences, which may be scattered around the world. The Chinese television channel Phoenix and the pan-Arabic entertainment network MBC are examples of media representing what may be labelled as 'geo-cultural flows',

Table 1.1 A typology of media flows

Dominant flows	Contra-(subaltern) flows	
Global	Transnational	Geo-cultural
Hollywood	'Bollywood'	Phoenix
MTV	Al-Jazeera	Zee TV
Disney	Telenovelas	TRT-International
CNN	TV5	Al-Hayat
Discovery	Telesur	Baidu.com
BBC	Radio France Internationale	MBC
ESPN	CCTV-9	NHK World TV
Google	RTTV	islamonline.net
CNBC	Euronews	Roj TV
Wall Street Journal	M-Net	
Japanese animation	Korean films	

aimed largely at diasporic populations, which may not necessarily be defined solely by language – for example, a network such as India's Zee TV is watched by second-generation British Asians who may not have competency in Hindi. The emerging transnational and geo-cultural networks both represent contra-flows and may operate in both dimensions.

The extension of satellite footprints and the growth of Direct-to-Home (DTH) broadcasting have enabled Southern media networks to operate across the globe, feeding into and developing the emergent 'diasporic public spheres' (Appadurai, 1996). With the acceleration of movements of populations around the world, primarily as a result of economic globalisation, major geo-cultural markets based on languages such as Spanish, Mandarin, Hindi, Arabic, Turkish and French are becoming increasingly prominent in transnational communication. Here again a combination of state-supported and privatised media flows is discernible. The state-run Turkish Radio and Television (TRT) has been operating an international channel TRT-INT as well as TRT-AVRASYA TV (later renamed as TRT-TÜRK) specifically for Central Asia. The Chinese portal Baidu.com and the Islamic website islamonline.net are two prominent cases of online networks based on geo-cultural and/or linguistic affinities. For some geo-cultural groups, such flows may be crucial for identity affirmation: the Kurdish satellite channel Roj TV, for example, is an important constituent in the diasporic lives of the world's largest 'stateless' population.

State-supported initiatives have also been an important contributing factor for the globalisation of cultural products. In South Korea, for example, state policies of a quota system for local films and support for such events as the Pusan International Film Festival, have put Korean cinema on the world map. In India, one example of this public–private convergence is the Frames, an annual 'global convention' showcasing the Indian film and entertainment industry. Organised by the Federation of Indian Chambers of Commerce and Industry (FICCI) every year since 2001, it attracts delegates from across the world. The creation of such bodies as the India Brand Equity Foundation – a public–private partnership between the Ministries of Commerce and Industry and the Confederation of Indian Industry with the primary objective, 'to build positive economic perceptions of India globally' – is another example of this public–private synergy (IBEF, 2005). When in 2005, TV18, an Indian television channel, joined hands with Zee Network to launch an English-language news channel, South Asia World, aimed at the UK and USA, the Indian Prime Minister Manmohan Singh welcomed this development in an advertisement aired on the channel.

Global media flows as 'dominant flows' of Americana

The global trade in cultural goods (films, television, printed matter, music, computers) almost tripled between 1980 and 1991, from $67 billion to $200 billion (UNESCO, 1998; UNESCO, 2000) and has grown at a rapid pace with the liberalisation of these sectors across the world. The United States is the leading exporter of cultural products and the entertainment industry is one of its largest export earners. UNESCO's 2005 report on *International Flows of Selected Goods and Services* estimates that the global market value of the cultural and creative industries was $1.3 trillion and was rapidly expanding. According to the report, between 1994 and 2002 international trade in cultural goods increased from $38 billion to $60 billion (UNESCO, 2005a) and, as Table 1.2 demonstrates, the trade, as with other sectors of global commerce, is heavily weighted in favour of the industrialised world, with Europe having more than 60 per cent of the share of global exports of books, newspapers, periodicals and recorded media, as against Africa's almost negligible share.

Table 1.2 Exports of selected media products, 2002

Region	Books		Newspapers and periodicals		Recorded media	
	Value $ million	Global share %	Value $ million	Global share %	Value $ million	Global share %
Europe	6,599	61	3,096	70	11,344	61
North America	2,317	21	1,041	24	3,426	19
Asia	1,489	14	144	3	3,364	18
Latin America & Caribbean	310	3	78	2	246	1
Africa	35	0.3	6	0.1	20	0.1

Source: UNESCO, 2005a, figures rounded up, for 2002.

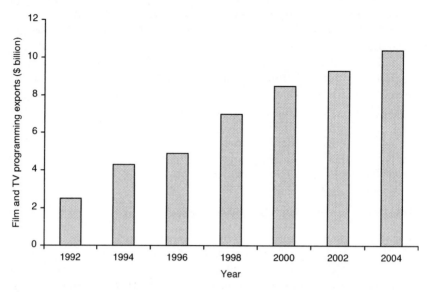

Figure 1.1 Growing global flow of Americana: US film and TV exports
Source: US Government, 2005.

The United States leads the global export market in media products: according to the US government's Bureau of Economic Analysis, receipts for film and television tape rentals, covering 'the right to display, reproduce and distribute US motion pictures and television programming abroad', have shown a steady increase from $2.5 billion in 1992 to $10.4 billion in 2004 (US Government, 2005) (see Figure 1.1).

In terms of regional distribution, Europe continues to be the largest market for American film and television content: in 2004, the value of exports was $6.7 billion, more than 60 per cent of all US exports in the sector, while the Middle East accounted for a mere $114 million. American television programmes are broadcast in over 125 countries and yet the disparity between American exports of television programming and films and imports of these products is striking. As Table 1.4 demonstrates, in 2004 the US imported TV programmes and films worth $341 million, while exports were worth more than 30 times that at $10,480 million. With its largest trading partner – Europe – US exports ($6,787 million) were worth 120 times its imports from the continent ($56 million). This disparity is consistent with recent trends in the trade in television. The balance of trade in television programmes between the EU and the USA more than tripled between 1989 and 1993 and the EU sustained a trade deficit 15 times the total value of their exports for 1995 to 2000 in this sector to North America (UNESCO, 2005a: 47).

Table 1.3 US exports of film and TV programmes, 2004, by region

Region	Value of film and TV exports ($ million)
Europe	6,787
Asia and Pacific	1,835
Latin America	757
Africa	124
Middle East	114
All countries	**10,480**

Source: US Government, 2005.

The opening up of the audio-visual market both to pan-European and international operators has changed the television landscape in Europe, with a twenty-fold increase in the number of channels available to European audiences in the past decade and a half – from 93 in 1990 to more than 1,700 in 2005, with entertainment channels showing the most robust growth. This has substantially increased the US presence on European television, especially in film-based programming, which is often dubbed into local languages. One reason for this, it has been argued, is that no 'lingua franca' unites European television viewers in front of their screens, and if there is a media 'cultura franca', it is based on American-style popular entertainment forms – soaps, game shows, talk shows, hospital and detective series – but preferably with nationally specific themes and settings (Richardson and Meinhof, 1999: 174–5). Empirical research conducted in the late 1990s examining the origin of films and TV series broadcast on 36 public and commercial channels in six European countries confirmed that, despite support

Table 1.4 US exports/imports of film and TV programmes to selected countries, 2004

	Export ($ million)	Import ($ million)
Britain	1,820	34
Germany	970	2
France	914	14
Japan	894	27
Canada	861	29
Netherlands	725	2
Spain	645	1
Italy	560	1
Mexico	284	9
Brazil	197	6
All countries	**10,480**	**341**

Source: US Government, 2005.

from the European Union to develop a pan-European television industry, US programming dominated the airwaves across Europe (de Bens and de Smaele, 2001).

While US-based companies remain undisputed leaders in selling TV programmes around the world (accounting for more than 70 per cent of all sales), Britain leads the world in the export of television formats. In 2003 Britain sold formats to the value of nearly $1 billion, accounting for 45 per cent of international format sales by hours and 49 per cent by titles (Clarke, 2005). Britain holds a prominent position within the global creative industries and is Europe's largest media exporter: in 2004, it sold TV programmes worth $1,513 million. According to the UK Government Department of Culture, Media and Sport, the creative industries grew in Britain by an average of 6 per cent annually between 1997 and 2003 and their exports totalled $20.3 billion in 2003 (DCMS, 2005).

One key reason for US domination of the global entertainment market is its film industry: Hollywood films are shown in more than 150 countries worldwide and dominate market share in most countries (Miller *et al.*, 2005) (see Table 1.5). In the 1970s Hollywood earned one-third of its revenue from overseas: by 2005 more than half of its revenues came from foreign markets. According to the Motion Picture Association, in 2004 the worldwide box office was worth $25.24 billion, with the world's top ten grossing films being produced by Hollywood.

Table 1.5 Film market share, selected countries, 2004

	Domestic films %	Foreign films %	
		Hollywood	Other
India	93	7*	—
USA	83	10†	7
China	55	45*	—
South Korea	54	41	5
France	39	47	14
Japan	38	62*	—
Germany	24	76*	—
Italy	20	62	18
Spain	14	78	8
Britain	12	84	4
Russia	12	81	7
Canada	4	90	6
Australia	1	89	10

Source: European Audiovisual Observatory, 2005, figures for 2004, rounded up.

Notes:
* Not specified.
† European co-production.

A study by the European Audiovisual Observatory on cinema admissions in 34 European countries for 1996–2004 found that the top ten films in this period were all Hollywood films. In the same period, the top five European films by admission were all English-language films, four of which had been financed by Hollywood companies. Within the EU overall, nearly 72 per cent of films shown in 2004 were from Hollywood, over 25 per cent were European, and just over 2 per cent of market share belonged to the rest of the world (European Audiovisual Observatory, 2005). For countries with a limited or non-existent audio-visual domestic industry, the dependence on Hollywood is even more striking. According to UNESCO, more than one-third of the countries in the world do not produce any films at all, while Africa as a whole (constituting 53 countries) has only produced just over 600 films in its history – fewer than India produces every year (UNESCO, 2005a: 47). Even in countries with developed local film production networks and markets, US films represent a majority of imports, as Table 1.6 shows, and, given the global increase in TV channels dedicated to film, it is unlikely that the dependence on Hollywood will decrease.

The extensive reach of US-based media, advertising and telecommunications networks contributes to the global flow of consumerist messages, helping the US to use its 'soft power' to promote its national economic and political interests (Nye, 2004). With its ability to transcend linguistic and geographical boundaries, transnational television is particularly important in relation to media flows. Television is central to a 'global mass culture', one dominated 'by the image, imagery, and styles of mass advertising' (Hall, 1991: 27). The flow of international television programmes from the West (mainly the US) to other parts of the world, documented by two UNESCO-sponsored studies (Nordenstreng and Varis, 1974; Varis, 1985) has become more pronounced in the era of multi-channel television, though there is a

Table 1.6 US film imports in major film-producing countries

Country	Latest data year	Total film imports	US imports (%)
Israel	2003	173	87
India	2003	198	80
Australia	2003	245	73
Mexico	2003	267	64
Spain	2004	461	55
Russia	2004	446	54
Germany	2004	363	37
Italy	2004	349	36
Japan	2004	470	28
France	2004	556	24
Egypt	2003	300	22

Source: European Audiovisual Observatory/national statistics and Screen Digest, 2005.

small but significant contra-flow from the non-Western world, as discussed below. The UNESCO studies conducted amid heated debates about the New World Information and Communication Order during the 1970s and 1980s suggested that there was generally a one-way traffic, mainly in entertainment-oriented programming, from the major Western-exporting nations to the rest of the world.

In the era of globalisation, the one-way vertical flow has given way to multiple and horizontal flows, as subaltern media content providers have emerged to service an ever growing geo-cultural market. However, as trade figures demonstrate, the circulation of US media products continues to define the 'global'. But how these products are consumed in a cross-cultural context poses a contested range of responses, made more difficult due to the paucity of well-grounded empirical studies. Some have argued that the global–national–local interaction is producing 'heterogeneous disjunctures' rather than a globally homogenised culture (Appadurai, 1990). Others have championed the cause of cultural hybridity, a fusion formed out of adaptation of Western media genres to suit local languages, styles and conventions (Robertson, 1992; Martin-Barbero,1993; Kraidy, 2005).

On the other hand, critical theorists have argued that the transnational corporations, with the support of their respective governments, exert indirect control over the developing countries, dominating markets, resources, production and labour. In the process they undermine the cultural autonomy of the countries of the South and create a dependency on both the hardware and software of communication and media: 'transnational corporate cultural domination' is how one prominent scholar defined the phenomenon (Schiller, 1992: 39). Galtung also argued that information flows maintain and reinforce a dependency syndrome: the interests, values and attitudes of the dominant elite in the 'peripheries' of the South coincide with those of the elite in the 'core' – the North. The core–periphery relations create institutional links that serve the interests of the dominant groups, both in the centre and within the periphery (Galtung, 1971). In this analysis of global flows, the audience and media content was largely ignored: that the content can be interpreted differently by different audiences and that the so-called periphery may be able to innovate and improvise on the core was discounted. Theoretical debates have largely been confined to how the rest of the world relates to, adopts, adapts or appropriates Western media genres. There is relatively little work being done on how the 'subaltern flows' create new transnational configurations and how they connect with gradually localising global 'dominant flows'.

Localisation of global Americana

Glocalisation is central to the acceleration of Western or Westernised media flows across the globe. What seems to be emerging is a glocal media product, conforming to what Sony once characterised as 'global localisation': media content and services being tailored to specific cultural consumers, not so much because of any particular regard for national cultures but as a commercial imperative. Glocalisation strategies exemplify how the global can encompass both the transnational and geo-cultural by co-opting the local in order to maintain the dominant flow. This localisation trend is discernible in the growth of regional or local editions of Western or more specifically American newspapers or magazines; the transmission of television channels in local languages and even producing local programming, as well as having local language websites.

Major US studios are increasingly using local production facilities in Europe, Asia and Latin America. Columbia TriStar, Warner Brothers and Disney have set up international TV subsidiaries to produce English-language co-productions, to be followed by country-specific programming. Sony has contributed to local-language film production in Germany, Hong Kong, France and Britain, and television programming in eight languages. Global media companies are particularly keen to consolidate their position in the world's two largest markets: China and India. Cartoon Network has indigenised operations in India, producing series based on the Hindu religious epics, the *Ramayana* and the *Mahabharat*, while Disney Consumer Products has established more than 1,800 'Disney Corners' in Chinese department stores. Disney Publishing grew ten-fold in the 11 years after the launch of *Mickey Mouse Magazine* in China (Disney, 2005). In 2005 CNN started a round-the-clock English-language news operation in collaboration with the Indian television software company TV18, reaching a global south Asian audience.

STAR TV, part of media mogul Rupert Murdoch's News Corporation, has aggressively adopted the policy of indigenisation in offering localised channels, including: STAR Chinese Channel (for Taiwan), STAR Japan, STAR Plus and STAR News (the latter two for India) and VIVA Cinema for the Philippines. ESPN-STAR Sports, the result of STAR's agreement with ESPN to provide coverage of pan-Asian and international sport events, is Asia's most widely watched channel. Among the business television channels, too, Asia is a priority area. By 2006, CNBC Asia, CNBC-TV18 (India) and Nikkei-CNBC (Japan) were available in more than 34 countries across the Asia-Pacific region. CNBC also had an alliance with China Business Network, a subsidiary of the Shanghai Media Group. In the Middle East, Western or Westernised TV platforms such as Orbit, Viacom's pay-TV joint venture Showtime and Murdoch's Star Select are increasingly localising their content to go beyond the expatriate constituency in the Gulf region. This 'Arabisation' includes using subtitles for American programming and moderating language and depictions of nudity and sex.

In Latin America localised Americana is well represented by such American brands as MTV Latin America, Canal Fox, CNN En Español, Fox Kids Network and Fox Sports Americas. In America's own 44 million strong Hispanic market a key player, Telemundo, is owned by NBC. In Africa, South-Africa-based pay TV networks M-Net and MultiChoice, both having a pan-African audience, broadcast American content, including that from Discovery, Hallmark, CNN and Cartoon Network.

In print media the localisation process is well established. *Newsweek* has a network of local-language publications in Japanese, Korean, Spanish, Arabic and Polish. The regional editions of major US business publications such as the *Asian Wall Street Journal*, *Far Eastern Economic Review*, *Fortune Asian* and *Fortune China* have a small but influential pan-Asian readership. In India, *Time* and *Fortune* magazines have distribution agreements with *India Today*, the country's most widely read publication, with a weekly circulation in 2006 of 1.4 million. In Latin America, US players are present in significant numbers, with *The Wall Street Journal Americas* published as a supplement in leading newspapers in nine Spanish-speaking countries, and weekly in eight countries, including three Portuguese-language newspapers in Brazil. *Time* also produces a pan-regional newspaper supplement in Latin America in Portuguese and Spanish. *América Economía*, a Dow Jones publication, is Latin America's leading pan-regional business magazine, published bi-weekly in Spanish and Portuguese. *Fortune* also has a Latin American edition, *Fortune Americas*, with a readership of 1.5 million.

Apart from the news publications mentioned above, many international media brands publish multiple international editions of magazines like *Reader's Digest*, *Esquire* and *Good Housekeeping*. *National Geographic*, which specialises in wildlife, the environment and travel adventure, had 27 local-language editions in 2006 and a combined circulation worldwide of more than 9 million. This localised Americana is supported by regionalised advertising, increasingly using regional and national languages and cultural values to sell consumer and other products through the different media.

In many traditional societies, interactions with mediated Western culture can produce complex results. Martin-Barbero has argued that people 'first filter and reorganise what comes from the hegemonic culture and then integrate and fuse this with what comes from their own historical memory' (1993: 74). This plurality of interpretation of media messages exists within a broader new-liberal ideological framework. It could be argued that localised Americana is promoting a globalised, 'Westernised' elite that believes in the supremacy of the market and liberal democracy, as defined by the West. The global business channel CNBC notes candidly that 'strong affinity with high net worth individuals and CEOs means our viewers exert both tremendous consumer and commercial influence' (NBC, 2005).

'Subaltern' contra-flows: anti-hegemonic or pro-Americana?

In parallel with the globalisation of Americana – whether in its original or hybridised version – new transnational networks have emerged, contributing to what one commentator has called 'Easternisation and South–South flows' (Nederveen Pieterse, 2004: 122). There is evidence that global media traffic is not just one way – from the West (with the USA at its core) to the rest of the world, even though it is disproportionately weighted in favour of the former. These new networks, emanating from such Southern urban creative hubs as Cairo, Hong Kong and Mumbai, and trading in cultural goods (Curtin, 2003), represent what could be called 'subaltern flows'. Over the last ten years the media world has witnessed a proliferation of multilingual growth of content emanating from these regional creative centres (Banerjee, 2002). The availability of digital technology, privatised and deregulated broadcasting and satellite networks has enabled the increasing flow of content from the global South to the North, for example, the growing international visibility of telenovelas or Korean and Indian films, as well as regional broadcasting, such as the pan-Arabic Middle East Broadcasting Centre (MBC), the pioneering 24/7 news network Al-Jazeera, or the Mandarin language Phoenix channel, which caters to a Chinese diaspora.

Non-Western countries such as China, Japan, South Korea, Brazil and India have become increasingly important in the circulation of cultural products, as indicated by Table 1.7. Japanese animation, film, publishing and music business was worth $140 billion in 2003, with animation, including *manga* (comics), *anime* (animation), films, videos and merchandising products bringing in $26 billion, according to the Digital Content Association of Japan (JETRO, 2005). South Korea has emerged as a major exporter of entertainment – film, television soap operas, popular music and online games – with television dramas such as *Jewel in the Palace* being extremely popular in China, prompting commentators to speak of a Korean wave (the

Table 1.7 Export of cultural goods by selected non-Western countries, 2002 ($ million)

Countries	Books	Newspapers and periodicals	Recorded media
China*	668	40	510
Japan	108	34	371
Russia	240	15	59
Mexico	120	33	146
South Korea	72	4	175
India	43	13	191
Brazil	12	11	11
Turkey	8	2	13
South Africa	19	2	8
Egypt	6	1	0.3

Note
* Includes Hong Kong and Macao.

Source: UNESCO, 2005a, figures for 2002, rounded to nearest million.

'*Hallyu*') sweeping across east and southeast Asia (Shim, 2006; Kim in this volume).

One reason for the growing visibility of such products is the physical movement of people from one geographical location to another, brought about by a process of 'deterritorialisation', which García Canclini described as 'the loss of the "natural" relation of culture to geographical and social territories' (1995: 229). According to a report of the UN Global Commission on International Migration, the world had nearly 200 million migrants in 2005, partly as a result of globalisation of commerce and communication. Though migration is generally associated with the working classes, increasing internationalisation of a professional workforce, employed by the transnational corporations, international non-governmental organisations and multilateral bureaucracies, as well as a growing number of foreign students, has ensured greater mobility of middle-class populations around the world (UN, 2005).

Transnational satellite broadcasters and online media companies have tapped into these emergent geo-cultural and linguistic groups (Karim, 2003; Chalaby, 2005). In Britain, South Asian channels including Zee, Sony, Star and B4U, are available on Sky's digital network, while in the USA, such platforms as Echostar DISH system and DirecTV provide a range of programmes for various diasporic groups. MBC is one of the most widely viewed channels in the Arab world, claiming an audience of 130 million viewers and helping to shape a new kind of Arab identity, based on language and culture rather than nationality.

The Qatar-based Al-Jazeera, which, since its launch in 1996 has redefined journalism in the Arab world, is a prominent example of contra-flow in global media products. By 2006, this pan-Arabic 24/7 news network was claiming to reach 50 million viewers across the world, undermining the Anglo-American domination of news and current affairs in one of the world's most geo-politically sensitive areas. If the live broadcast of the 1991 US military action against Iraq contributed to making CNN a global presence, the 'war on terrorism' catapulted Al-Jazeera into an international broadcaster whose logo can be seen on television screens around the world. In the region, satellite networks have led to what one commentator has called 'the structural transformation of the Arab public sphere' (Lynch, 2006). That public sphere also has an Islamist agenda; Al-Jazeera has been labelled by its critics as 'the voice of Bin Laden', having aired his taped messages. For the wider world, it has provided an alternative source of information emanating from a news-rich arena and as its services are available in English, its presence is likely to become more important in global news discourse.

Private media corporations have been more successful in accelerating the contra-flow in media products. Since they do not necessarily represent a particular country, they have contributed to creating geo-linguistic or geo-cultural identities, for example the Hong Kong-based Mandarin-language,

Phoenix Chinese Channel, which is part of News Corporation. In the decade since it hit the airwaves in 1996, Phoenix has emerged as a key example of a geo-cultural television news and entertainment network which has made its presence felt among Chinese-speaking communities around the world (more than 35 million Chinese people live outside China). Phoenix sees itself as 'the window to the world for the Chinese global community' and says it 'seeks to promote a free flow of information and entertainment within the Greater China region' (Phoenix website).

Transnational telenovelas

Another key example of transnational 'subaltern flow' is the Latin American soap opera, the telenovela, which is increasingly becoming global in its reach (Large and Kenny, 2004; Martínez, 2005; Rosser, 2005). The transnationalisation of telenovelas has been made possible through Televisa in Mexico, Venevisión in Venezuela, and Globo TV in Brazil – the leading producers of the genre. The Brazilian media giant TV Globo (exporting 26,000 hours of programmes annually to 130 countries) and Mexico's Televisa (the world's largest producer of Spanish-language programming, which in 2004 earned $175m from programming exports, largely from telenovelas), are also the two primary exporters of this popular genre of television across the globe (Rosser, 2005).

By 2005 the telenovela had developed into a $2 billion industry, of which $1.6 billion was earned within the region and $341 million outside, being broadcast in 50 languages and dialects and reaching 100 countries from Latin America to southern and eastern Europe, to Asia, Africa and the Arab world (Martínez, 2005). Apart from being a commercial success, telenovelas can also help in the construction of a transnational 'hispanic' identity, as the Venezuelan scholar Daniel Mato has suggested (Mato, 2005). The appeal of the genre lies in the melodramatic and often simplistic narrative which can be understood and enjoyed by audiences in a wide variety of cultural contexts (Sinclair, 1999). Bielby and Harrington have argued that this reverse flow has influenced soap operas back in the US, leading to 'genre transformation' especially in day-time soaps (Bielby and Harrington, 2005).

The success of telenovelas outside the 'geo-linguistic market' of Spanish and Portuguese consumers, shows the complexity of media consumption patterns. Such telenovelas as *The Rich Also Cry* were very successful in Russia in the 1990s, while Sony developed its first telenovela in 2003 – *Poor Anastasia* for the Russian network, CTC (Martínez, 2005). The genre has become popular even in Western Europe: a German company has produced their own telenovela, *Bianca: Road to Happiness*, shown in 2004 on the public channel ZDF. In India, Sony has successfully adapted the popular Colombian telenovela, *Betty la Fea* into Hindi as *Jassi Jaissi Koi Nahin*, which became one of the most popular programmes on Indian television (Large and Kenny,

2004). The transnationalisation of telenovelas is an indication of contra-flow in television content. As one commentator has noted:

> In all, about two billion people around the world watch *telenovelas*. For better or worse, these programmes have attained a prominent place in the global marketplace of culture, and their success illuminates one of the back channels of globalization. For those who despair that Hollywood or the American television industry dominates and defines globalization, the *telenovela* phenomenon suggests that there is still room for the unexpected.
>
> (Martínez, 2005)

'Bollyworld'

Given its size and diverse social and cultural antecedents, India is among the few non-Western countries to have made their presence felt in the global cultural market. Particularly significant is India's $3.5 billion Hindi film industry which, in terms of production and viewership, is the world's largest: every year a billion more people buy tickets for Indian movies than for Hollywood films. More films are made in India each year than in Hollywood, but their influence is largely confined to the Indian subcontinent and among the South Asian diaspora, though in recent years many 'cross-over' films have changed this situation (Kaur and Sinha, 2005). The unprecedented expansion of television in the 1990s and early 2000s was a boost for the movie industry, with the emergence of many dedicated film-based pay-channels. In addition, advancements in digital technology and the growth of broadband have ensured that Indian films are regularly shown outside India, dominating the cinema of South Asia and the South Asian diaspora as well as constructing a popular culture based on 'Bollywood'.

The globalisation of Bollywood has ensured that Indian films are increasingly being watched by an international audience as well as a wider diasporic one: Hindi films are shown in more than 70 countries and are popular in the Arab world, in central and southeast Asia and among many African countries. This has made it imperative for producers to invest in subtitling to widen the reach of films, as well as privileging scripts which interest the overseas audience. Indian film exports witnessed a twenty-fold increase in the period 1989–99 – by 2004 exports accounted for nearly 30 per cent of the industry earnings (FICCI, 2004; UNESCO, 2005a). Plans for joint ventures between Indian film producers and Hollywood giants received a boost with the decision of the Indian government, announced in 2000, to allow foreign companies to invest in the film industry. One result of such interest is that diasporic film makers such as Mira Nair (director of *Monsoon Wedding*) and the British-based Gurvinder Chaddha (director of such internationally successful 'British-Asian' films as *Bend It Like Beckham* and *Bride and Prejudice*) have acted as a bridge between Western and Indian popular cinema.

In 2004 PricewaterhouseCoopers valued the entertainment and media sector in India at $7 billion and it was expected to grow at about 14 per cent over the next five years to reach over $10 billion by 2009 (FICCI, 2004). By 2005, such neologisms as 'Bollyworld' were being used – referring to an Indian cinema 'at once located in the nation, but also out of the nation in its provenance, orientation and outreach' (Kaur and Sinha, 2005: 16).

Hybridity as hegemony

These prominent examples of 'subaltern' and 'geo-cultural' media flows may give a false impression that the world communication has become more diverse and democratic. A careful analysis of the reality of global media flows and contra-flows demonstrates a more complex process, however. The imbalance between the 'dominant' and the 'subaltern' and 'geo-cultural' global media flows reflects the 'asymmetries in flows of ideas and goods' (UNDP, 2004: 90). Despite the growing trend towards contra-flow as analysed in this book, the revenues of non-Western media organisations, with the exception of Japanese animation, are relatively small and their global impact is restricted to geo-cultural markets or at best to small pockets of regional transnational consumers. None of the Latin telenovelas has had the international impact comparable with US soaps such as *Dallas* or the cult following of *Friends* or *Sex and the City*, and, despite the growing presence of Indian films outside India, its share in the global film industry valued in 2004 at $200 billion was still less than 0.2 per cent.

At the same time, 'dominant flows' are becoming stronger. It is no coincidence that the world's biggest television network MTV (reaching 418 million households in 2005) is American, as are CNN International (260 million households worldwide) and Discovery Channel (180 million households worldwide). In 2004, out of the world's top five entertainment corporations, according to *Fortune* magazine, four were US-based: Time Warner (2004 revenue: $42.8 billion); Walt Disney (2004 revenue: $30.7 billion); Viacom (2004 revenue: $27.05 billion); and News Corporation (2004 revenue: $20.8 billion). Wal-Mart was for the fourth year running the world's largest corporation, with a revenue in 2004 of nearly $288 billion and profit of $10.2 billion. Not surprisingly, US-based companies – 181 in total – dominated the list (*Fortune*, 2005). Voice of America claims to have 100 million weekly listeners for its 44 languages; AP reaches 8,500 international subscribers in 121 countries, while APTN is a major television news agency. The world's top three largest business newspapers and magazines are American: *The Wall Street Journal* (2005 global circulation 2.3 million), *Business Week* (1.4 million) and *Fortune* (1.1 million). The world's top three magazines too are American: *Reader's Digest* (2005 global circulation, 23 million), *Cosmopolitan* (9.5 million) and *National Geographic* (8.6 million), as are the two major international news magazines: *Time* (2005 global circulation: 5.2 million) and *Newsweek* (4.2 million). The world's top three advertising agencies in 2005 were all based in the US: Young & Rubican (gross worldwide income $9.25 billion), The Ogilvy Group ($6.48 billion) and J. W. Thompson ($5.05 billion) (Thussu, 2006).

The question of how contra is contra and against whom also acquires salience. With its slogan 'News from the South', the pan-Latin American 'anti-hegemonic' news network Telesur promises to be an alternative to CNN. 'It's a question of focus, of where we look at our continent from', Jorge Botero, Telesur's news director told the BBC. 'They look at it from the United States. So they give a rose-tinted, flavour-free version of Latin America. We want to look at it from right here' (quoted in Bruce, 2005). It has been dubbed as *al-Bolivar* – a combination of Al-Jazeera and the Latin American hero. The French government has announced a 24-hour international TV news network, the French International News Channel (CFII) that aims to be the French-language CNN – 'CNN à la Française'. 'France must . . . be on the front line in the global battle of TV pictures' was how President Jacques Chirac justified the network, a joint venture between state-owned broadcaster France Télévisions and commercial television company TF1 (AFP, 2005). These examples, however, are exceptions rather than the rule – both are state-sponsored flows and their impact on global communication is yet to be felt.

In ideological terms, commercial contra-flows champion free-market capitalism, supporting a privatised and commodified media system. One should therefore avoid the temptation to valorise them as counter-hegemonic to the dominant Americana. Subaltern flows are unlikely to have a significant impact on the American hegemony of global media cultures, which, arguably, has strengthened not weakened given the localisation of media content, despite the supposed decentring of global media. This can also bode ill for local cultural sovereignty, as one UN report noted: 'the unequal economic and political powers of countries, industries and corporations cause some cultures to spread, others to wither' (UNDP, 2004: 90). Moreover, as Americana expands and deepens its hegemony, a hybridised and localised media product can provide the more acceptable face of globalisation and therefore effectively legitimise the ideological imperatives of a free-market capitalism.

Towards a new cartography of global communication

Media flows have a close relationship with economic power: traditionally, trade has followed television. According to a 2003 Goldman Sachs report, over the next few decades Brazil, Russia, India and China, the so-called

BRIC economies, could become much larger forces in the world economy. A 'new geography of trade', with East Asia, and China in particular taking the lead, is already having 'a significant impact on international trade flows' (UNCTAD, 2005: 153).

By 2005, South Korea was leading the world in broadband penetration, with nearly a quarter of its population having access to broadband, while China had emerged as the world's largest television market, overtaking the United States. China also had the world's largest number of mobile phone users and had become the largest exporter of IT products (OECD, 2005). In communication hardware too China had made impressive progress: the China Great Wall Industry Corporation, a major satellite company, had launched 30 satellites since 1990.

The global expansion of India's informational technology industry has created the phenomenon of 'offshore outsourcing'. According to the National Association of Software Service Companies (NASSCOM), the apex body of India's IT industry, the sector has witnessed an annual growth rate of more than 25 per cent, earning $17.2 billion in export revenue for 2005 (NASSCOM, 2006). As a UNESCO report noted:

> Today the value of Indian cultural and creative industries is estimated at $4.3 billion. This sector is growing at an annual rate close to 30 per cent and analysts forecast that exports may continue to grow by 50 per cent in the coming years. An important factor in this impressive performance is that Indian companies are succeeding in bringing international audiences to the cinemas, in addition to the traditional diaspora communities of the USA, the United Kingdom and the Middle East. This strategy includes expansion to non-traditional countries, both industrialised and emerging, such as Japan and China.
>
> (UNESCO, 2005a: 44)

Though large population countries such as China and India are yet to fully integrate into the global market, changes in the media and communication industries in these two countries have been remarkable, making them the second and the fourth largest users of the Internet in absolute terms. Such demographic shifts may lead to the decline of English dominance on the Internet, as other languages, including non-European ones, proliferate. In 2006, Chinese was the second largest language of online communication (UNESCO, 2005b). India and China, a British Council report notes, 'probably now hold the key to the long-term future of English as a global language' (Graddol, 2006). In the long run, what John Hobson in his important book has called 'oriental globalisation' is likely to become more important, given the rapid economic rise of the world's two largest populated countries with old histories and new geo-political ambitions (Hobson, 2004).

Media flows and contra-flows form part of the wider struggle over information flows which define power relations in the global information economy. In the era of 'full-spectrum dominance' and the 'global information grid', a hybridised, glocal Americana is likely to circulate with faster velocity, greater volume and higher economic value. It is no coincidence that on the logo of the Pentagon's Information Awareness Office, the motto is *Scientia est potentia* – knowledge is power'. Despite the massive movement of media across continents, cultures and communities, one should not lose sight of the fact that 'soft' media power is firmly underpinned by 'hard' political and economic power.

References

AFP (2005) 'France enters "battle of the images" with "French CNN"', Agence France Presse. Paris, November 30.

Appadurai, Arjun (1990) 'Disjuncture and difference in the global cultural economy', *Public Culture*, 2 (2): 1–24.

Appadurai, Arjun (1996) *Modernity at Large: Cultural Dimensions of Globalisation*. Minneapolis: University of Minnesota Press.

Atton, Chris (2004) *An Alternative Internet: Radical Media, Politics and Creativity*. Edinburgh: Edinburgh University Press.

Bagdikian, Ben (2004) *The New Media Monopoly* (7th edn). Boston: Beacon Press.

Banerjee, Indrajit (2002) 'The locals strike back? Media globalization and localization in the new Asian television landscape', *Gazette*, 64 (6): 517–35.

Bielby, Denise and C. Lee Harrington (2005) 'Opening America? The telenovelaization of US soap operas', *Television & New Media*, 6 (4): 383–99.

Boyd-Barrett, Oliver (2006) 'Cyberspace, globalization and empire', *Global Media and Communication*, 2 (1): 21–41.

Bruce, Iain (2005) 'Venezuela sets up "CNN rival"'. BBC News, 28 June.

Castells, Manuel (2000) *The Rise of the Network Society: The Information Age: Economy, Society and Culture*, vol. 1 (2nd edn). Oxford: Blackwell.

Chalaby, Jean (ed.) (2005) *Transnational Television Worldwide – Towards a New Media Order*. London: I. B. Tauris.

Clarke, Stewart (2005) 'UK leader in global format sales', *Television Business International*, April.

Curtin, Michael (2003) 'Media capital: towards the study of spatial flows', *International Journal of Cultural Studies*, 6 (2): 202–28.

DCMS (2005) *Creative Industries Economic Estimates: Statistical Bulletin*, October. London: Department of Culture, Media and Sport.

De Bens, Els and Hedwig de Smaele (2001) 'The inflow of American television fictions on European broadcasting channels revisited', *European Journal of Communication*, 16 (1): 51–76.

Disney (2005) *Annual Report, 2005*. New York: Disney Corporation.

European Audiovisual Observatory (2005) *Focus 2005: World Film Market Trends*. Strasbourg: European Audiovisual Observatory.

FICCI (2004) *The Indian Entertainment Industry: Emerging Trends and Opportunities*. Mumbai: Federation of Indian Chambers of Commerce and Industry in association with Ernst & Young.

Fortune (2005) Fortune Global 500, August.

Galtung, Johan (1971) 'A structural theory of imperialism', *Journal of Peace Research*, 8 (2): 81—117.

García Canclini, Nestor (1995) *Hybrid Cultures: Strategies for Entering and Leaving Modernity*. Minneapolis: University of Minnesota Press.

Graddol, David (2006) *English Next: Why Global English May Mean the End of 'English as a Foreign Language'*. London: British Council.

Hall, Stuart (1991) 'The local and the global: globalization and ethnicity', in A. King (ed.), *Culture, Globalization and the World-System — Contemporary Conditions for the Representation of Identity*. London: Macmillan.

Hobson, John M. (2004) *The Eastern Origins of Western Civilisation*. Cambridge: Cambridge University Press.

IBEF (2005) *Entertainment and Media*. New Delhi: India Brand Equity Foundation. Available at http://www.ibef.org.

JETRO (2005) 'Japan animation industry trends', *Japan Economic Monthly*, June.

Karim, H. Karim (ed.) (2003) *The Media of Diaspora: Mapping the Global*. London: Routledge.

Kaur, Raminder and Ajay Sinha (eds) (2005) *Bollyworld: Popular Indian Cinema Through a Transnational Lens*. New Delhi: Sage.

Kraidy, Marwan (2005) *Hybridity, or, the Cultural Logic of Globalisation*. Philadelphia: Temple University Press.

Large, Kate and Jo Anne Kenny (2004) 'Latino soaps go global', *Television Business International*. January.

Lynch, Marc (2006) *Voices of the New Arab Public: Iraq, Al-Jazeera, and Middle East Politics Today*. New York: Columbia University Press.

Martin-Barbero, Jesus (1993) *Communication, Culture and Hegemony: From Media to Mediations*, trans. E. Fox. London: Sage.

Martínez, Ibsen (2005) 'Romancing the globe', *Foreign Policy*, November.

Mato, Daniel (2005) 'The transnationalization of the telenovela industry, territorial references, and the production of markets and representations of transnational identities', *Television & New Media*, 6 (4): 423–44.

Miles, Hugh (2005) *Al-Jazeera: How Arab TV News Challenged the World*. London: Abacus.

Miller, Toby, Nitin Govil, Richard Maxwell and John McMurria (2005) *Global Hollywood* (2nd edn). London: British Film Institute.

NASSCOM (2006) *NASSCOM Strategic Review 2006*. Mumbai: National Association of Software Service Companies.

NBC (2005) *Annual Report, 2004*. New York: National Broadcasting Corporation.

Nederveen Pieterse, Jan (2004) *Globalization or Empire?* London: Routledge.

Nordenstreng, Kaarle and Tapio Varis (1974) *Television Traffic — A One-Way Street? A Survey and Analysis of the International Flow of Television Programme Material*, Reports and Papers on Mass Communication, no. 70. Paris: UNESCO.

Nye, Joseph (2004) *Power in the Global Information Age: From Realism to Globalization*. London: Routledge.

OECD (2005) *Science, Technology and Industry Scoreboard*. Paris: OECD.

Phoenix website: http://www.phoenixtv.com.

Richardson, Kay and Ulrike Meinhof (1999) *Worlds in Common? Television Discourse and a Changing Europe*. London: Routledge.

Robertson, Roland (1992) *Globalization: Social Theory and Global Culture*. London: Sage.

Rosser, Michael (2005) 'Telenovelas, the next instalment', *Television Business International*, December.

Schiller, Herbert (1992) *Mass Communications and American Empire* (2nd edn). New York: Westview Press.

Shim, Doobo (2006) 'Hybridity and the rise of Korean popular culture in Asia', *Media, Culture & Society*, 28 (1): 25–44.

Sinclair, John (1999) *Latin American Television: A Global View*. Oxford: Oxford University Press.

Sinclair, John, Elizabeth Jacka and Stuart Cunningham (eds) (1996) *New Patterns in Global Television – Peripheral Vision*. Oxford: Oxford University Press.

Thussu, Daya Kishan (2006) *International Communication: Continuity and Change* (2nd edn). London: Arnold.

UN (2005) *Migration in an Interconnected World: New Directions for Action*. Report of the Global Commission on International Migration. Geneva: United Nations Publications.

UNCTAD (2005) *Trade and Development Report 2005*. Geneva: United Nations Conference on Trade and Development.

UNDP (2004) *Cultural Liberty in Today's Diverse World: Human Development Report 2004*, United Nations Development Programme. Oxford: Oxford University Press.

UNESCO (1998) *World Culture Report 1998: Culture, Creativity and Markets*. Paris: United Nations Educational, Scientific and Cultural Organization.

UNESCO (2000) *International Flows of Selected Cultural Goods 1980–1998*, UNESCO Institute for Statistics. Paris: United Nations Educational, Scientific and Cultural Organization.

UNESCO (2005a) *International Flows of Selected Cultural Goods and Services 1994–2003*, UNESCO Institute for Statistics. Paris: United Nations Educational, Scientific and Cultural Organization.

UNESCO (2005b) *Measuring Linguistic Diversity on the Internet*. Paris: United Nations Educational, Scientific and Cultural Organization.

US Government (2005) *US International Services: Cross-border Trade in 2004*. Washington: US Bureau of Economic Analysis, October.

Varis, Tapio (1985) *International Flow of Television Programmes*, Reports and Papers on Mass Communication, no. 100. Paris: UNESCO.

Chapter 2

Diasporas and contra-flows beyond nation-centrism

Myria Georgiou and Roger Silverstone

The debates on the direction of communication flows have long moved away from the original cultural imperialism thesis, which implies linearity and one-way relationships of causality between producer (West) and receiver (and the rest). More recent debates on multiple flows, asymmetrical inter-dependence and transnational corporate networks have studied the global and regional complexities, shaking off the stigma of linearity and causality.

Studies of national and regional adaptation of production forms and the emergence of hybrid media genres, as well as analyses of the role of national elites and audiences have brought forward the importance of consumption, cultural proximity and regional dynamics. What has not been shaken off (and there has not been a real desire to do so) is the central role of *the national* in inter-national communications. For all the debates on the local and the global, the transnational corporations and the regional players, the study of communication flows and contra-flows is still preoccupied with national corporations (which turn transnational or regional players), governments and national audiences. It is obvious that we cannot, and should not, erase the nation as a site of both political and cultural activity and regulation completely. There remain the recalcitrance of the transnational and the instabilities and movements of communication and cultural forms, whose understanding is not reducible to the singularity of the national.

In this chapter we address the diaspora as a locus of the transnational, and use the dispersal of populations as the basis for an enquiry into the dispersal of communications. Our argument is that the mediated communications generated around and by such groups provide a key route into the under-standing of the contra-flows of global media. Just as migration itself disturbs the boundaries of the state and the culture of a nation, so too do the communications that migration generates. Statehood remains, but its boundaries are ignored and the dominance of the existing media players, themselves of course equally unconstrained by such boundaries, is challenged by the presence of alternative threads of global communication that observe different rules and move in different directions.

The case of diaspora is, therefore, the most visible challenge to ideologies of the boundedness of people, cultures, identities and the media. Diasporas are transnational cultural communities.[1] They are communities of people origi-nating in a geographical location (often a nation-state) and settling in another. Their travels and (re-)settlement are usually plural and include multiple mobilities of people and diverse cultural practices. Diasporas are ultimately transnational as they are forced in some way or another to flee an original homeland and to seek (a better) life somewhere else. Diasporic iden-tity is about the roots as much as it is about the routes of the diasporic journey (Clifford, 1994; Gilroy, 1995). As diasporas find themselves spread across at least two – and usually many more – nation-states, their political and cultural identity and practices are far from reproductions or extensions of the nation. Questions of multiple or parallel loyalties, connections to more than one public sphere, and association with political causes that surpass boundaries are some of the key ways in which the *nation-ness* of political identities is cancelled.

The diasporic everyday has to do as much with the family and the life left behind (or imagined to have been left behind), as it is about the neighbour in the country of settlement and the relatives and friends in a number of coun-tries where diasporic networks expand. As a reflection of this complexity, communication flows in diasporic space – which is a transnational space – go in all different directions. They include primary forms of communication, such as telephone, travel, interpersonal encounters, and advanced communi-cation technologies, such as radio, television and the Internet.

Diasporic communication flows are variously flows against the dominant (what this volume is identifying as contra-flows), but they complement others and co-exist with many more. If we argue that *contra* implies some form of opposition, either intentional or not, to hegemonic ideologies, then in the case of the diaspora these oppositional contra-flows should be seen in relation to the dominant forms of the political and of the production and con-sumption of culture, both national and transnational. As such, the complex-ity and plurality of their relationship to these other, perhaps more dominant or insistent flows of communication needs to be asserted (Silverstone, 2006).

Indeed diasporic media and communication practices are sites where national and transnational political ideologies and cultural expressions, or counter-expressions, of identity are often seen and heard. Diasporic media are involved in the development of ideologies and representations outside the major global and national media and the mainstream national and inter-national political arenas, which often exclude voices from the periphery and from non-mainstream political organisations. Very often the *raison d'être* of diasporic media is the development of such contra-flows, or at least the creation of the ideology of their development.

Media as sites of politics, or politics as sites of mediation

Mediation is a political process in so far as control over mediated narratives and representations is denied or restricted to individuals, groups and regions by virtue of their status or their capacity to mobilise material and symbolic resources in their own interests. Mediation is also a political process in so far as dominant forms of imaging and storytelling can be resisted, appropriated or countered by others. This can take place both inside media space, and through the development of contra-flows of information and communication (through diasporic or other alternative and minority media), or on the edge of it, through the everyday tactics of symbolic engagement. The latter create another informal and mundane form of contra-flow (as expressed in the stubborn refusal to embrace dominant and hierarchical forms of mediated communication, in gossip and communication outside the media, in participation in multiple and conflicting mediascapes).

The media, seen through the lens of these contested processes, provide frameworks for identity and community, equally contested of course, but significantly available as components of the collective imaginary and as resources for collective agency. In this context, diasporic media can be seen as threats to the globalisation of media forms and firms, as destabilising elements in international affairs and in relation to (inter-)national politics, as often proud (even if sometimes fundamentalist) voices against global and regional hierarchies in communication and in politics. Diasporas appear, or more often do not appear, in mainstream media; and when they do appear it is often through stereotypical and alienating images. But diasporas also represent themselves (and others) in their own media, those that they produce and consume in and across the societies in which they are minorities, as well as those that they consume in such (dis)locations, but which are produced in societies where they might be, or once might have been, majorities.

Diasporic media range from the exchange of letters, videos and mobile phone texts and images, to the printed press, domestic and satellite television, and the Internet (Gillespie, 1995; Dayan, 1999). They are produced by the displaced to express and reflect their daily lives as minorities, but also by mainstream cultures elsewhere, which offer a link for the displaced to a world of home, both real and imagined (or to a world once left but not conceptualised as home). As such, diasporas and their media have a key role to play in the development of contra-flows and in the diversification of mediascapes outside the (full) control of nation-states and corporate transnationalism.

Media provide frameworks for inclusion, and by the same token, frameworks for exclusion. Those frameworks are at once transnational, national, ethnically specific, regional and local. The cultures that sustain and that are sustained by them are differentially placed with respect to each other and to their mainstreams. They are never homogeneous; and the media which are both produced and consumed reflect differences of gender and generation, as well as differences of politics and religion within cultures and communities.

As already indicated, diasporic mediascapes consist of online media and more conventional media, such as television, radio and press. All of those, especially the electronic ones, have also diversified and now include public, state-run, commercial and community broadcasts and products that integrate technologies and content, connecting people in local and transnational spaces. The presence of such media threads and flows raises a number of questions. The first is that of the integrity or the fragmentation of the emerging public sphere, its singularity or its plurality. As Arjun Appadurai notes: 'The challenge for this emergent order will be whether such heterogeneity is consistent with some minimal conventions of norm and value, which do not require a strict adherence to the liberal social contract of the modern West' (1996: 23). It follows that the next question would need to address the capacity of such flows to provide genuine political and cultural alternatives, and maybe even conflicting ones, to the mainstream. The emerging situation is much more complex than simply a negative or positive reply to these questions would reflect. Nationalistic and cosmopolitan ideologies are in constant tension in the diaspora and they often take place around the media.

Diaspora in media culture

Pluralism appears as central to any understanding of the representation of diasporic populations in media culture, and this too at a number of different levels. Media representation involves both participation and recognition. And participation is a matter of the capacity to contribute to the mainstream (that being national and/or transnational), to enable the minority voice or visibility on (trans-)national channels or the national press, but it is also a matter of the capacity to gain a presence on one's own terms on the nationally owned spectrum or on the global commons of the Internet. Participation ultimately involves the equal sharing of a common cultural space. There are different issues that can be addressed here, and different politics, but all raise the questions of whether or how to enable smaller groups (or groups with less access to media and political centres of power) to speak, but also, and this is crucial, to enable them to be heard. Who is speaking and on behalf of whom? But we must ask too, who is listening and with what consequences?

Diasporic minorities are producers; they are audiences and they are addressees. As audiences they have the distinct advantage, it might be suggested, of being able to choose, often quite radically, between different representational spaces, different programmes, different languages and different accounts of global or national conflicts. Greek Cypriots in the diaspora for example, have access to media from Cyprus, from Greece, from their country of settlement, from other countries where Greek diasporas live. Additionally, they access and use various national and global media, which are broadcast in languages they understand (Georgiou, 2006). Mixing and choosing between a huge variety of locally and globally produced media and media produced by members of the diaspora, the *homeland* media industry, but also media produced by major or minor media players in transnational cultural spaces, is a part of the banal everyday living of diaspora. Such choices are material with consequences for both their own sense of themselves and their position in national cultures, but inevitably they are also material for those national cultures themselves and the degree to which states can meaningfully include all of its residents and citizens.

The politics of the national mediascapes are often politics of struggle and conflict. Many European governments are hesitant to accept Kurdish satellite Med TV in their territory, as the station has been accused of being attached to a militant Kurdish party (Hassanpour, 2003). The American government forced the only Somali Internet service provider connecting the Somali diaspora to shut down because of suspected links with terrorists (Karim, 2003). Diasporic communications increasingly find themselves caught in national and global politics and important decisions. As satellite television and the Internet in particular are being increasingly used to bring diasporic politics into the public sphere, governments and transnational political institutions pay a closer attention to them. The case of Al-Jazeera, of course, has become the most noticeable example, attracting attention and attacks from some of the most significant players in national and global politics.

As addressees, diasporas emerge as problematic perhaps most significantly in diasporic websites, such as those designed to support asylum seekers or refugees. Here choices are made between a general mode of address, one that seeks to engage both the subjects of the site but also looks to a wider public for both financial and political support. This is a both/and rather than an either/or mode of address, which could be as self-defeating as it is productive. The refugee and migrant network of support and communication, seen in the UK in sites such as that of the Refugees, Asylum Seekers and the Mass Media Project (www.ramproject.org.uk) and Refugees Online (www.refugeesonline. org.uk) brings activists and refugees closer together into a community of interest and political action. These sites, at the same time, raise awareness around issues of diversity, when they address the general public and potentially advance dialogue between minorities and the mainstream. However, in attempting to reach the broader public and in their attempt to condemn racism and xenophobia, these websites often adopt an instrumental discourse (e.g. focusing on presenting directories and statistical information; selling items for support of network). The complexity of diasporic identity and diasporic transnationalism is often overlooked in the development of 'popular' and 'accessible' models of diversity (Siapera, 2005).

There is a tension expressed in all that follows, both within, and surrounding, diasporic media and the symbolic and material presence of diasporic minorities within national and transnational mainstream media, which is articulated at the interface between plurality and power. Questions of identity are central but intensely difficult to resolve both theoretically and in the experienced realities of everyday life. In this respect, the media context is no different from the wider cultural and social context in which the dilemmas of difference and visibility are endemic in diverse societies which are, once again, becoming increasingly ambivalent with regard to the manifestations of otherness within national borders.

What, however, is not at issue is the nature of the change in media culture and the challenges to national politics and to national broadcasting systems in particular. The significance and strength of these challenges vary hugely, of course, from one country to another, but taken together they promise a sea-change in the way in which global communication, both public and private, is conducted. The metaphors used to describe these changes are familiar enough: *networks*, *rhizomes* and *mediascapes* variously capture both the fluidity and freedoms now apparent in personal and collective communication. At stake is the continuing capacity of the nation to insist on its cultural specificity, with possibly significant consequences for its inhabitants' participation in, and identification with, national community. At stake too is the capacity of diasporic groups to form their own transnational or global media cultures, which, for better or worse, could offer frameworks for participation and agency no longer grounded in singular residence and no longer oriented exclusively to the project of national or singular citizenship. At the same time, the struggle for power takes place around defining the global as a space for communication and for belonging outside its corporate transnationalising interpretations.

Transnational public spheres against top-down international affairs?

The politics of popular culture is, arguably, gaining ground against mainstream politics (cf. Street, 1997), but the established national political sphere is still of major importance and has implications for the diasporic communities and for the nation-states of both their origin and settlement. Looking into the possibilities for liberating and participatory diasporic politics, Appadurai argues that there is a growing potential for the development of diverse and inclusive diasporic public spheres (1996) and he suggests that, as electronic media become predominant in mediated communication, the formal literacy in a common language becomes less of an obstacle to participation in transnational public spheres. The potential for decentralised, transnational diasporic spheres emerges, therefore, as the nation-state begins to lose its monopoly of social, political and cultural exchanges and as images, sounds and people are less bounded and grounded within singular political and cultural territories.

The challenges against nation-centric political ideologies which emerge with the presence of diasporic populations are the product of communication practices in all three dimensions of their living space: the transnational, the national and the local, but especially in the transnational and the local. The transnational is largely mediated by two technologies: satellite and the Internet. The local – and we will be talking about the urban local in particular here – is challenged in communication practices which are not necessarily framed within a narrow media setting. Mediation and media cultures are not all about television and the Internet. Music, interpersonal communication, mobility in and out of communication spaces, such as Internet cafés, local libraries, community centres and clubs are as much part of the diasporic media cultures as are the Internet and satellite television. The national is the site for a more assimilative move in the direction of providing spaces for minorities to appear, as individuals (for example presenters), characters (in soap operas) or in the 'colouring' of existing genres (in ethnically or culturally distinct sit-coms). But the national is also the site for the location of both the production and consumption of diasporic media, the location of the lived everyday and the focus of any longing for a displaced homeland amongst diasporic populations. It is the latter characteristic of the national that we will focus on rather than the former.

The transnational: the contra-flow of the imaginary

Projects of diasporic politics, those referring to the country of origin, political participation (or refusal to participate) in the country of settlement, and to minority politics which oppose dominant ideologies within diasporic groups, have all found a space of expression on the Internet as in no other medium. As Manuel Castells has put it:

> the internet is not simply a technology: it is a communication medium (as the pubs were), and it is the material infrastructure of a given organisational form: the network (as the factory was). On both counts the internet became the indispensable component of the kind of social movements emerging in the network society.
>
> (Castells, 2002: 139)

Diasporic politics, as opposing, antagonising and competing with national politics, is part of the growing culture of cyberpolitics, which in turn is largely transnational and which adopts tactics of connecting offline locations (and politics) with online transnational networking activities. Campaigners for a Kurdish or for a Palestinian state can reach sections of their diasporic groups (and seek support among them) as never before. So can fundamentalist groups. The reasons Internet users turn to such sites cannot be predicted and only in-depth research can try to answer the extent to which their visible presence translates into practical action.[2] This is not our task here. No matter what individual Internet users are looking for, the point is that diasporic political movements can reach audiences in geographical and numerical scale in unprecedented ways. The Internet has become a tangible setting where alternative, fragmented, or transnational public spheres emerge. In some of these cases at least (for example, among the Tamil where even the state, Eelam, in Sri Lanka, to which they are attached does not formally exist (Jeganathan, 1998), we see a form of imagined community emerging or finding a space of expression. It may be possible to suggest therefore that transnational political communities become realisable – to extend Anderson's original thesis (1983) – albeit in the mind of each Internet user as she seeks, finds and connects to like-minded diasporic fellows sharing the same communication space.

But beyond the Internet, there is another communication technology which is increasingly appropriated by diasporic populations; this is satellite broadcasting. Al-Jazeera has shaken the world with its stubborn success against Western global media. Chapter 7 in this book discusses the case of Al-Jazeera in more detail, but this example being widely known outside specific diasporic audiences, is no more than one of the very successful diasporic media claiming a voice and a role in the provision of political information and agenda-setting in international affairs. The powerful global media have been trying to regain influence among audiences, which would rather watch the news on a diasporic news bulletin (or watch the diasporic as well as the mainstream news and thus become more critical and demanding viewers). Research on Arabic audiences, for example, has shown how the diversity of news consumption – in mainstream Western and diasporic satellite media – becomes an everyday mechanism for audiences to critically engage with all media (El-Nawawy and Iskander, 2002; After September 11 Research Project, 2002). Satellite diasporic television is booming and it is definitely here to stay and play a role in international political information and communications.

The local: the contra-flow of the city

In the city, the taken-for-granted domination of the nation-state on cultural and political ideologies is challenged. The city is the location where nationhood is questioned from within. The particular dynamics of the city and of urban life allow different populations to live together, different cultures to co-exist and intermix in new urban, multicultural and hybrid settings while not necessarily embracing the national project. Studying diasporic cultures in the urban context where they are experienced – and where many of the media develop and are consumed – involves contextualising diasporic (media) cultures in the space where they become possible. As James Donald (quoted in Robins, 2001: 89) notes, the city poses 'the internal impossible question of how we strangers can live together'. As we live together, hybrid cultures, identities and alternative scenarios for inclusion and participation emerge, next to others of exclusion, discrimination and racism.

Diasporic populations are an integral part of contemporary urban economic and cultural life, even if their contribution in national and mainstream transnational ideologies is not acknowledged as such. The city – where diasporic populations usually live – is the space where the private and the public and the experience of mediation take their meanings in relation to urban cultural practices and in co-existence with other city dwellers. The *mobile foreign subjects*, who are not foreign anymore, challenge the purity of the nation and suburban privatised closure and instead participate in the construction of diverse, creative and sometimes anarchic urban cultures. Diasporic populations' participation in the formation of a working-class cosmopolitanism (Werbner, 1999) brings dialogue and new encounters between strangers, between people of different backgrounds, in the city.

In urban meetings and mixings, in the public performance of diverse cultures and in the anarchy of co-existence and competition for ownership and participation, distinct kinds of publicness and exposure emerge in public life and in cultural representation. The different kinds of music heard and imposed around town, the large satellite dishes insulting middle-class/white aesthetics, the loud, colourful and supposedly tasteless hybrid spaces hosting Internet cafés, combined with hair-salons and/or grocers, create aural and visual cultural fusions and spatial amalgams, in cacophony as much as in harmony. The city expresses the movement of the Other from the periphery of the empire to its core (the metropolis – the city) (Eade, 2001). As migrants and diasporas move to the centre, they occupy a symbolic and physical space that is powerful in its presence and in the active alteration of what it used to be through participation in economic, cultural and social life. The emergence of horizontal cultural formations challenges the vertical divisions of the nation-state and of consumerist transnationalism.

The national: the contra-flow of the political

Diasporic audiences are capable of shifting their attention and their commitments from their own media (local and transnational) to the national mainstream media, and in so doing finding opportunities for comparison but also possibilities for choice. Research has shown that even those with minimum knowledge of the dominant language of the country of settlement flick between mainstream national channels for a favourite soap opera or for catching up with (fractions and/or images of) the local and national news (Aksoy and Robins, 2000; Ogan, 2001; Georgiou, 2006). As diasporic media co-exist and compete with others, the appropriation of both is filtered by the diverse experience of their audiences. Diasporic media audiences have a media literacy that surpasses particularistic consumption. This diversity of consumption is important not just in terms of diasporas' capacity to sustain their own culture and identity but also for the character of the mainstream national media culture, indeed the culture of the nation-state itself, as the latter can no longer easily control and contain the images, voices and narratives which have for so long laid exclusive claims on the attention of its citizens.

Awareness of the significance of diasporic media for the political mobilisation of the diaspora is evident in both top-down initiatives – by the governments of the original homeland and by community leaders – and bottom-up everyday practice – as people turn to the media to keep up to date with political developments. The diasporic and national hegemonic ideologies of transporting nationalism in transnational spaces however faces some significant obstacles. Diasporisation and transnational connections imply the emergence of networks. The settlement of diasporic populations in different social and cultural contexts, as well as the increased possibility for mobility and interactivity between different nodes within diasporic networks, comes with increased cultural and political autonomy and inevitable ruptures in the umbilical cord – and the ideologies of the umbilical cord – that link the homeland and the diaspora. Hanafi (2005) describes the case of PALESTA (Palestinian Scientists and Technologists Abroad) network, which started as an initiative of the Palestinian Authority in order to strengthen links with the Palestinian diaspora. The Internet network was formed as a centralised effort where all communication was taking place around one centre – the homeland. As PALESTA grew successfully, the taken-for-granted centrality of the homeland became challenged. Its users developed their activities beyond the control of the centre and mostly in inter-diasporic communication. The rupture of the umbilical cord caused tensions between the diaspora and the centre. Nonetheless, in most cases, these ruptures are conditional. The diversity of cultural references in diasporic spaces, competing nationalisms, and global, individualistic capitalism, create constant tensions between centrifugal and centripetal ideologies of (national) belonging.

On one hand, mediation and networking advance the sense of proximity to other dispersed populations and to the country of origin. On the other, they amplify the level of critical reflection and selective engagement with the imagined community as increased information and interaction remind the members of diasporic groups that the original homeland is not sacred and pure and that the dispersed populations who share a common origin are not characterised by cultural sameness. The increased exchange of images and sounds from the country of origin and other sections of the diaspora becomes a constant reminder of diversity and of the real and present face of the country of origin and the fellow members of the imagined community.

The complexity of identity or the contra-flows within

The plausibility of these structural changes should not obscure the material realities of diasporic everyday life in the production and consumption of media. These realities are grounded in the struggles of connection and communication, in the conflicts around identity and identification, in the shared but fraught project of finding a voice. These empirical realities inevitably muddy the waters of grand theories and the perception of global trends. Indeed they focus, and quite properly, on the dilemmas of the everyday as individuals, families and communities seek to manage their lives on the borderland between inclusion and exclusion. Media are sometimes crucial to this management; sometimes not. They offer security in the familiarity of sounds and images. But they also threaten that security in their many representational failures. And for those members of minorities at work within media (as well as those denied such work), the media are crucial both at an individual as well as at a collective level in constructing identities and transnational communities. Identity construction is a complex process. This complexity is often revealed in the contra-flows to hegemonic discourses within diasporic groups.

First, they are expressed in subversive everyday communication practices and the diasporic diversity of engagement with media – both in terms of which media are consumed – but also in the way diasporas engage with media in various ways, as already discussed. In terms of audiencehood (or citizenship), such contra-flows might create a distance from political projects promoting national and consumerist homogeneity, but they often lead to a distancing from equally essentialist and hierarchical projects from within. Diasporic nationalism, as well as the promotion of authoritarian and repressive discourses, is not rare in diasporic media (e.g. fundamentalist religious sites; satellite television promoting uncritical devotion to the country of origin). In such cases, in terms of production, the contra-flows to the national and commercial mainstream are more about antagonising other national and commercial interests. Such projects are usually tested and contested on the level of consumption.

These contra-flows within also refer to the relationship between minorities within minorities, i.e. the diasporic media that are peripheral, extremist, marginalised within their own diasporic mediascapes. We are thinking here in particular of fundamentalist projects. These flourish, when they do at all, especially on the Internet. With al-Qaeda developing its own website, the moral panics about the Islamic diasporic public sphere being taken over by Osama bin Laden and his comrades have reached a record high, but are not confined to the national mainstream. They are significantly the object of dismay within their own minority cultures. Less visible projects of this kind include diasporic political voices that are excluded from the mainstream diasporic politics even when they do not entice violence – e.g. the Palestinian left finds a space of expression denied in national and diasporic public domains. Cypriot gay and lesbian organisations are practically banned from the main diasporic media stages. They find their expression in local activities and transnational online fora. Often political expression and identity politics – especially when represented in the mainstream politics of communities – find an entry to the public sphere through the Internet.

In this context, questions about diverse and competing mediascapes and ideoscapes become crucial. And even if they cannot be resolved here, yet in a sense the debates that define them, above all those that centre on competing rights and (sadly less often) competing obligations, both of minorities and majorities, are central. These debates involve questions of uncompromising difference and processes of hybridisation; those that privilege the particular over the universal; those that insist on a continuing role for the nation and those that stress transnationalism; those that desire a single public sphere and those that wish for, or fear for, its rupture; those that challenge innocent, or naïve, claims for participation; and those that refuse the dominance of cultural difference over the inequities of political and economic position. All of these debates are vivid and vividly unresolved.

An examination of the production and consumption of diasporic media cultures, both in terms of the production of particularistic media and associated consumption practices critically involves a refusal of the various kinds of essentialism that bedevils many of the discussions on identity and community within and across national boundaries. In the present context, the media are seen not to be determining of (the other) (*contra*) identities, but contributing to the creation of symbolic community spaces in which identities can be constructed. Diasporic identities are not others to the mainstream. They are not *contra*. These identities are essentially plural (Silverstone, 2006; Georgiou, 2006). And this is the case at the level of the individual, where one's status as a Somali or as a Vietnamese depends on cultural context (as well as on gender, generation and class), the mode of the media's address as well as one's position in relation to it, either as consumer or producer. It is also the case at the level of the community, where media practices provide links between the group and multiple others, both within and beyond the nation. Within and across nation-states, where the discussion of contra-flows has emerged, the broadcasting culture of the twentieth century has advanced claims for national coherence and national, singular, mediated public spheres (which can extend to transnational spaces, as they are reflected in many nation-states' policies to expand their broadcasting services to *their* diasporas). Such ambitions for national and transnational coherence are increasingly vulnerable to the presence of both alternative media and alternative media voices that dig deeper into the local and, often excluding ethnically specific, spill into the multiple global discordances of satellite and Internet communication.

Participation, inclusion but also exclusion from the community is not in this case (or any more) framed within singular geographical boundaries or within inescapable dualities of dependence: diaspora/homeland or migrants/host country. Geographical boundedness and dualities are being constantly challenged in the actual diasporic experience, which builds upon a number of complex, and even competing, links and relations. The links and flows cut across many different places and follow many different directions. Thus, members of diasporic groups sustain relations with friends in the country of origin, but also relations with friends in the local non-ethnic community. Diasporic belonging is non-exclusive and, in times of increased transnationalism, high mobility and intense mediation, it can only be conditional and parallel to other forms of belonging. People use diasporic as well as non-diasporic media; they appropriate technologies in order to renew repertoires of diasporic identity, but also in order to fulfil age group interests, professional or other political interests, hobbies and friendships in and across places.

The emphasis on the diversity of spatial contexts, of cultural content and communication flows, is a reminder of the growing significance of network structures and the transnational mechanisms of sharing images, sounds and information and their consequences for imagining a multipositioned and inevitably diverse community. In this context, boundaries have not faded away and this is not the time for romantically celebrating liberating cosmopolitanisms. Boundaries are still there, though now they are often more symbolic than physical; they are more diverse, and they are defined as much by exclusionary mechanisms within global capitalism as they are by national and diasporic exclusionary discourses.

Conclusions

Diasporas are cosmopolitans of a different kind to the high-flying, jet-setting cosmopolitans in control of global capitalism. The discussion about diasporic communication flows is not restricted or controlled by national or corporate transnational interests. Diasporic populations are usually the invisible cosmopolitans and the unnoticed participants in the formation of transnational (media) cultures; they are initiators of urban and trans-urban networks, which are sometimes, though not necessarily, antagonistic towards the nation-state, which diversify urban spaces in creative and communication practices, and which develop parallel, competing and complementing elements of mediated consumer cultures. Diasporas build transnational networks, develop particularistic cultural formations and construct distinct identities in mediation – in the mixing denied by the ideology of boundedness and separation of the nation-state and the modernist separated spheres of economic, cultural and political life.

Diasporas are postmodern – and, in a way, pre-modern – formations, as they constitute messy, anarchic and uneven networks, emerging in equally messy flows of communication and connection. Networks of family and kin, of economic and political interests and of cultural activities, become merged, fused and confused. In their (con)fusion, they reflect a range of ideologies: from the most conservative traditionalist and nationalistic, to the cosmopolitan celebration of capitalism and the cosmopolitan resistance to nationalism and profit. The contradictions, oxymora and struggles of diaspora are expressed in public transnational dialogues and debates, which tend to be highly mediated.

The contradictory dynamics of diaspora reflect the lack of clear-cut order or singular direction for ideologies and communication within cosmopolitanism. As Ulrich Beck suggests:

> I doubt that cosmopolitan societies are any less ethical and historical than national societies. But cosmopolitanism lacks orientation, perhaps because it is so much bigger and includes so many different kinds of people with conflicting customs, assorted hopes and shames, so many sheer technological and scientific possibilities and risks, posing issues people never faced before. There is, in any case, a greater felt need for an evident ethical dimension in the decisions, both private and public, that intervene in all aspects of life and add up to the texture of cosmopolitan societies.
>
> (Beck, 2002: 20)

The diasporic condition unravels some of the key characteristics of cosmopolitanism, but it does so from a distinct position which might be *beyond* nation-centrism but not *outside* the national. Diasporas do not exist outside the authority of nation-states. National media and politics can even increase their influence outside national boundaries, partly because diasporas appropriate them in transnational consumption and public spheres. Diasporas however live *beyond* nation-states, if we refer to the nation-state as defined in Western modernity to frame identity, culture and politics. The complexity of the diasporic condition is often reflected in communication practices that are diverse, contradictory and unstable.

Contemporary transnational connections and the persistence of diaspora as a relevant cultural category can only be understood in the context of transnationalism, competing cosmopolitanisms and intense mediation.

> It becomes possible to think of identities which are multiple . . . An Egyptian immigrant in Britain might think of herself as a Glaswegian when she watches her local Scottish channel, a British resident when she switches over to the BBC, an Islamic Arab expatriate in Europe when

she tunes into the satellite service from the Middle East, and a world citizen when she channel-surfs on to CNN.

(Sinclair *et al.*, 1996: 25)

The diversity characterising diasporic media consumption and appropriation illustrates some of the major existing limitations in the analyses of communication and cultural flows. The argument that the major challenges to one-way flows emerge in the production and consumption of commercial projects (either global or regional) is still rooted in the assumption of consumption within singular national frameworks. This assumption is significantly limiting. Audiences and cultural communities more often participate in co-existing media culture(s) – particularistic, diverse, mainstream – than in singular framed communities.

The direction and quality of flows and contra-flows we need to understand are not only those of mainstream media production, nor are they exclusively about privileged players within a newly emergent cosmopolitanism. They are also about the growing variety of audiences' media outlook. They are about the emergence of transnational players in media culture which are not only corporate but based within the community. And they are about the diversification of communication activities which are not constrained within the media of television, radio, press and the Internet, but which also involve various appropriations of communication technologies in localities, cities and transnational networks that stimulate new ways of communicating, informing and belonging.

Notes

1 Diasporic communities are, of course, imagined. The use of the concept of *community* here relates to processes of imagination and identification. There is no assumption that community exists as a real structure.
2 On this issue, and with arguments based on just such empirical research albeit on transnational social movements rather than specifically diasporic groups, see Cammaerts (2005).

References

After September 11 Research Project. Research Report (2002). Available at: http://www.afterseptember11.tv/
Aksoy, Asu and Kevin Robins (2000) 'Thinking across spaces: transnational television from Turkey', *European Journal of Cultural Studies*, 3 (3): 343–65.
Anderson, Benedict [1983] (1991) *Imagined Communities: Reflections on the Origins and Spread of Nationalism*. London: Verso.
Appadurai, Arjun (1996) *Modernity at Large: Cultural Dimensions of Globalization*. Minneapolis and London: University of Minnesota Press.

Beck, Ulrich (2002) 'The cosmopolitan society and its enemies', *Theory, Culture & Society*, 19 (1–2): 17–44.

Cammaerts, Bart (2005) 'ICT-usage among transnational social movements in the networked society: to organise, to mobilise and to debate', in Roger Silverstone (ed.), *Media, Technology and Everyday Life in Europe*. Basingstoke: Ashgate, pp. 53–72.

Castells, Manuel (2002) *The Internet Galaxy: Reflections on the Internet, Business and Society*. Oxford and New York: Oxford University Press.

Clifford, James (1994) 'Diasporas', *Cultural Anthropology*, 9 (3): 302–37.

Dayan, Daniel (1999) 'Media and diasporas', in J. Gripsrud (ed.), *Television and Common Knowledge*. London and New York: Routledge.

Eade, John (2001) *Placing London: From Imperial Capital to Global City*. London: Berghahn.

El-Nawawy, M. and A. Iskander (2002) *Al-Jazeera: How the Free Arab News Network Scooped the World and Changed the Middle East*. Cambridge, MA: Westview.

Georgiou, Myria (2006) *Diaspora, Identity and the Media: Diasporic Transnationalism and Mediated Spatialities*. Cresskill, NJ: Hampton Press.

Gillespie, Marie (1995) *Television, Ethnicity and Cultural Change*. London: Routledge.

Gilroy, Paul (1995) 'Roots and routes: black identity as an outernational project', in H. W. Harris, Howard C. Blue and Ezra E. H. Griffith (eds), *Racial and Ethnic Identity: Psychological Development and Creative Expression*. London and New York: Routledge.

Hanafi, Sari (2005) 'Reshaping geography: Palestinian community network in Europe and the new media', *Journal of Ethnic and Migration Studies*, 31 (3): 581–9.

Hassanpour, Amir (2003) 'Diaspora, homeland and communication technologies', in Karim H. Karim (ed.), *The Media of Diaspora*. London and New York: Routledge.

Jeganathan, Pradeep (1998) 'Eelam.com: Place, nation and imagi-nation in cyber-space', *Public Culture*, 26 (3): 515–29.

Karim, H. Karim (2003) *The Media of Diaspora*. London and New York: Routledge.

Ogan, Christine (2001) *Communication and Identity in the Diaspora: Turkish Migrants in Amsterdam and their Use of Media*. Lanha, MD: Lexington.

Robins, Kevin (2001) 'Becoming anybody: thinking against the nation and through the city', *City*, 5 (1): 77–90.

Siapera, Eugenia (2005) 'Minority activism on the web: between deliberative democracy and multiculturalism, *Journal of Ethnic and Migration Studies*, 31 (3): 499–519.

Silverstone, Roger (2006) *Media and Morality: On the Rise of the Mediapolis*. Cambridge: Polity Press.

Sinclair, John, Elizabeth Jacka and Stuart Cunningham (eds) (1996) 'Peripheral vision', in J. Sinclair, E. Jacka and S. Cunningham (eds), *New Patterns in Global Television: Peripheral Vision*. Oxford: Oxford University Press, pp. 1–32.

Street, John (1997) *Politics and Popular Culture*. Cambridge: Polity Press.

Werbner, Pnina (1999) 'Global pathways: working class cosmopolitans and the creation of transnational ethnic worlds', *Social Anthropology*, 7 (1): 17–35.

Chapter 3

Thinking through contra-flows: perspectives from post-colonial and transnational cultural studies

Anandam P. Kavoori

Let me state my position at the outset: The notion of contra-flows is problematic for a number of reasons: it is predicated on a stable set of empirical referents – those of *spatial location* (the West and the East; North and South); a fixity in the expectations of such categories – primarily those of the nation-state, and in an assumption that contemporary cultural flows are regulated by a narrowly controlled global marketplace. It is equally problematic in its assumption of *spatial exclusivity* of cultural products, once again based on their national origin – such as, say, Bollywood cinema or Japanese animation. Finally, the assumption (and metaphor) of spatial flow (as in the word, contra-flow) does disservice to the deterritorialization of cultural products in the contemporary world.

Drawing on postcolonial theory and transnational cultural studies, I offer the following definition of contra-flows:

> Media contra-flows are the semantic and imaginative referents for the institutional, cultural and political matrix of a world framed by processes of global cultural power and local negotiation: a world experienced through the identity politics of nations, individuals and cultures and negotiated through contestations of locality, nationality and global citizenship.

I shall spend the rest of this chapter unpacking this definition by focusing on three interrelated contexts to analyze the term 'contra-flow' – the theoretical language it is predicated on; the media texts it is usually restricted to and, finally, the sets of audience orientations it presupposes. In each case, I will suggest that the word 'contra-flow' is problematic and may obscure rather than clarify the direction, intent and assembling of cultural production in the world today. My comments in each section will be framed in relation to (and developing on) key quotations from the well-known theorist of global culture, Arjun Appadurai and relating to my definition of contra-flows. These quotes need to be seen as context-setting rather than directly relating to the concept of contra-flows – a task that I address *relationally* in my deliberation. These quotes will be followed by a discussion section that calls into question how contra-flows have been addressed and how they might be more profitably interrogated.

Let me begin by opening the stage as to what constitutes the world of 'contra-flows'. In its most immediate referent, the term 'contra-flows' is used to refer to that mass media programming that reverses the dominant (Western, First World) direction. But there are other equally important elements that are not usually focused on. These include the development of alternate technologies (the Internet, the cell phone, gaming), divergent institutional arrangements (cross-pollination between media and education industries, for example) and capitalist strategies (emergence of regional and national corporations with transnational affiliations); emergence of hybrid texts and the development of cultural formations that draw little sustenance from older social/national orders.

Theoretical predicates and their limitations

> Globalization is a source of debate almost everywhere. It is the name of a new industrial revolution (driven by powerful new information and communication technologies), which has barely begun. Because of its newness, it taxes our linguistic and political resources for understanding and managing it. In the United States and in the ten or so most wealthy countries of the world, globalization is certainly a positive buzzword for corporate elites and their political allies. But for migrants, people of color and other marginals (the so-called 'South' in the 'North'), it is a source of worry about inclusion, jobs and deeper marginalization. And the worry of the marginals, as always in human history, disturbs the elites. In the remaining countries of the world, the under-developed and the truly destitute ones, there is a double anxiety: fear of inclusion on draconian terms, and fear of exclusion, for that seems like exclusion from History itself.
>
> Three interrelated factors which make globalization difficult to understand in terms of earlier histories of state and market. The first is the role of finance capital (especially in its speculative forms) in the world economy today: it is faster, more multiplicative, more abstract and more invasive of national economies than ever in its previous history. And because of its loosened links to manufacture and other forms of productive wealth, it is a horse with no apparent structural rider.
>
> (Appadurai, 2001: 3)

The term 'contra-flows' draws sustenance from the dominant frames for international communication research over the postwar period, those of the three worlds model, which underpin models of governance, policy formation and regulation across disciplines and cultures. Two theoretical streams emerged from this engagement – developmentalist and dependency theories. Both theories focus on issues of media programming as a subset or derivative of economic forces; developmentalist approaches framed contra programming as nativistic and inert; while Western, 'developed' models stood at the apex of the paradigm (usually drawn as a pyramid) from which was calibrated the relative openness or ideological fixity of other media systems. These media systems were framed with terms like eastern, socialist, orientalist, totalitarian, communist, etc. In other instances, regions/continents framed the context of such a difference, such as in the use of 'African media systems', 'Asian values', 'Oriental ethos' and so forth.

Dependency approaches, on the other hand, framed the same set of relationships using the vocabulary of a historically predicated and consistently static relationship between the First and Third Worlds. As Hardt (1992: 136) puts it, 'the aspect of dependence, as an aspect of a more comprehensive theory of imperialism, has been used to account primarily for the economic structures and relationships among developed and underdeveloped countries'. In addition, the developmentalist and dependency approaches continued the ethnocentric use of the characteristics of West European and North American society as goal-states from which calibrated indices of underdevelopment could be constructed (Golding, 1977: 39). Developmentalist approaches linked issues of the world to those of modernity and dependency approaches to a critique of modernity as a basis for categorization and modernism as a synonym for Western culture and practices.

Postmodernism, the other dominant framework through which global cultural issues were framed, worked both against developmentalist and dependency approaches in its rejection of the Enlightenment project, universalist rationality and progressivism. Ironically, however, postmodernist interpretations of globality focused on the emergence of a common culture of consumption and style (Ferguson, 1992: 71) and saw global social fragmentation along lines of neo-tribalism, as evidence that social coercion and state powers were being replaced by individualized acts of collectivizing will. Contra-flows appeared here too at the margins, as niche programming, a convenient shorthand for identity politics.

All these approaches are a legacy to a transcendent vision of globality: specifically, a perspective at its core driven by notions of unreflexive Western dominance and its natural result: global cultural homogenization. Contra-flows in the end are placed in the specific diacritical space of localism with only one of two options available to it: assimilation or defiance. Little attention is given to the range, diversity and complexity of such programming and to the world they are shaping. As Pandurang puts it:

> Current analytical models are not adequate for exploring new forms of multi-culturality that are in the process of emerging. What is needed is a theoretical framework that goes beyond formulations of cultural

imperialism and simplified binaries and speaks from the affective experience of social marginality and from the perspective of the edge – they
offer alternative views of seeing and thinking, and thereby allow for
narratives of plurality, fluidity, and always emergent becoming.

(Pandurang, 2001: 2)

As the above quote indicates, postcolonial and transnational cultural studies
perspectives focus less on the institutional and political arrangements of the
contemporary world but rather on the cultural and symbolic world of lived
experience. They see the contemporary world as having multiple nodes of
power both economic and cultural. As a counterpoint to theories of cultural
imperialism, they see the world as made up of multiple axes and points of
departure. Drawing extensively on the poststructuralist vision of the world,
they see

discourses as tactical elements or blocks operating in the field of force
relations; there can exist different or even contradictory discourses
within the same strategy . . . [Power is] a multiple and mobile field of
force relations wherein far-reaching, but never completely stable, effects
of domination are produced.

(Foucault, 1980: 100)

Let me begin to outline the vocabulary that needs to emerge to engage with
the complexities of the contemporary media moment. To repeat, the first
line of my definition, 'Media contra-flows are the semantic and *imaginative*
referents . . .'

Contra-flows in the global imagination

The crucial point, however, is that the United States is no longer the
puppeteer of a world system of images that is only one node of a complex
transnational construction of imaginary landscapes. The world we live
in today is characterized by a new role for the imagination in social life.
To grasp this new role, we need to bring together the old ideas of
images, especially mechanically produced images (in the Frankfurt
school sense) the idea of the imagined community (in Anderson's sense)
and the French idea of the imaginary (imaginaire) as a constructed landscape of collective aspirations, which is more and no less real than the
collective representations of Émile Durkheim, now mediated through
the complex prism of modern media.

(Appadurai, 1996: 31)

What is *the* global imaginaire? Simply put, there isn't one. They are multiple
and they are mediated through the complex prism of modern media.

Modern media in turn are part of 'the institutional, cultural and political matrix of a world framed by processes of global cultural power and local negotiation' (my definition). The global *imaginations* then are fostered by agents that cannot be enumerated through the artificialities of textual closure – through those of genre (film and telenovelas – to use the two most common referents for contra-flows) nor through the expectations of individual actors as agents of the imagination or the collective representation of such expectations through a marketplace. It is not enough to say that the marketplace is where the imagination is fostered, even created in the mirror images of the individual actors. In fact, there is a double prism at work: people see themselves as actors in a play in roles predetermined by their singular imagination, which is paradoxically global. Let me illustrate with an absurd example: one traveler sits in a tourist *gaon* (village) hut in Delhi, a village created for her consumption. She drinks bottled water served by a waiter in a tight white suit. Celine Dione sings overhead.

Across the globe, another traveler sits in tourist hacienda, say in Mexico, say Guatemala. She too drinks bottled water served by a waiter in a tight white suit. Michael Jackson sings overhead. There are the obvious commonalities here: the disappearing rural landscape simultaneously adjacent and disappearing; the easy fit between the fictive and the real; even the absurdity of the tourist moment. But there is something else at work as well: the development of *simultaneous* imaginations that structure concurrent globalities-in-localities. These can be easily inferred as forms of media imperialism or even as forms of glocalizations – their very presence (the tourist, the song, the setting) assumes a singular reproducibility of genre (corporate popular music in this case).

This is the space of contra-flows – not seen in its traditional vocabulary of Third World forms flowing to the First, but in the semantic and imaginative space of local mediation of global forms. I am reversing the equation, the very theoretical language that has allowed us to see this question purely as one of 'flow' – unequal or otherwise. This leads directly to the issue at the end of my definition – 'of global cultural power and *local* negotiation'. I now turn to the dilemma of locality as I repeat my definition: 'Media flows are the semantic and imaginative referents for the institutional, cultural and political matrix of a world framed by processes of global cultural power and local negotiation.'

The problem of locality

I view locality as primarily relational and contextual rather than as scalar or spatial. I see it as a complex phenomenological quality, constituted by a series of links between the sense of social immediacy, the technologies of interactivity and the relativity of contexts. This phenomenological quality, which expresses itself in certain kinds of agency,

sociality and reproducibility, is the main predicate of locality as a category or subject.

(Appadurai, 1996: 178)

Put simply, the task of producing locality (as a structure of feeling, a
property of social life, and an ideology of situated community) is increasingly a struggle. There are many dimensions to this struggle, and I shall
focus here on three. (1) The steady increase in the efforts of the modern
nation-state to define all neighborhoods under the sign of its forms of
allegiance and affiliation, (2) the growing disjuncture between territory,
subjectivity and collective social movement and (3) the steady erosion,
principally due to the force and form of electronic mediation, of the
relationship between spatial and virtual neighborhoods. To make this
more complex, these three dimensions are themselves interactive.

(Appadurai, 1996: 189)

The two quotes from Appadurai allow for two specific themes around locality
that need to be engaged with in the context of contra-flows. These are those
of (a) framing locality and (b) producing locality.

Framing locality

Contra-flows are usually seen through national frames such as Japanese
anime, India's Bollywood, Brazilian *bossa nova* and so forth. The work of such
frames is problematic because they draw on essentialist notions of nationalism and cultural notions of purity. These frames provide fuel for something
quite different from their traditional anchoring in concepts of development
and underdevelopment: they work as markers, diacritical signs in the negotiation for access to a single global stage, operating as both a shorthand for
local elites (usually dressed in national clothing) and as an emblem for a self-
satisfied cultural homogeneity that does little service to the very complex
processes by which such contra-flows are constituted.

Bollywood, for example, has always been a cultural tactic that has been
internally referential (in its articulation of a patriarchal nationalism and
Hindu reification) and externally voluble in its continuous reference to a
series of global anxieties: British colonialism, pan-Asianism, South Asian
regionalism, Americanization, cultural imperialism and so forth. They are
present (in different time periods) in every element of Bollywood performa-
tivity – in dance sequences, in dress styles, in models for personal behavior
and agency. But all this is lost in the summative force of the term 'contra-
flows', based as it is in the logic of cultural unity, national essentialism and a
static global public sphere.

Producing locality

The notion of contra-flows as it is usually used is also based on a narrowly defined set of local contingencies around concerns of cultural labor, institutional power arrangements and individual agency. In each case, the nation is seen as the primary agent for all three dimensions of Appadurai's idea of locality production (a structure of feeling, a property of social life, and an ideology of situated community). But it is, as he adds, a struggle. It is a struggle that takes new meaning in contemporary times with the use of what I shall refer to as 'subaltern cultural technologies'. These subaltern cultural technologies – whether audio tapes, low-end camcorders or high-end digital cameras and cell phones – assert that the production of locality is not narrowly constructed through the conduits of the nation-state (which are mainstream media, both state and corporate in origin). Rather, locality is being continuously produced through identity forms that work around those of the nation-state, of which the most visible are terrorists. However, we should include in any such production more innocuous categories: belly dancers linked through web communities across the First and Third Worlds, producing new localities of performance; or cricket aficionados playing in First World settings, recreating their localities of home (India, Pakistan) in a diasporic context.

Whether it is terrorist beheadings or Bollywood dance numbers or cricket square drives, what we are witnessing is the emergence of a new textuality that finds both its relevance in a new definition of what constitutes contra-flows. In other words, I have a different view of the inherent question in my definition: 'a world framed by processes of global cultural power and local negotiation'. I see a different kind of contra-flow: textualities in transition framed in and through a range of subaltern technologies that create, transmit and intersect with the traditional categories of the nation-state. I turn now to a consideration of what is at the heart of this question: the framing, content and structuration of media texts.

Media texts

Electronic information technologies are part and parcel of the new financial instruments, many of which have technical powers, which are clearly ahead of the protocols for their regulation. Thus, whether or not the nation state is fading out, no one can argue that the idea of a 'national economy' (in the sense first articulated by the German geographer Friedrich List) is any more an easily sustainable project. Thus, by extension, national sovereignty is now an unsettled project for specific technical reasons of a new sort and scale. Third, the new, mysterious and almost magical forms of wealth generated by electronic finance markets appear directly responsible for the growing gaps between rich and poor, even in the richest countries in the world.

> The structure of contexts cannot and should not be derived entirely
> from the logic and morphology of texts. Text production and context
> production have different logics and metapragmatic features. Contexts
> are produced in the complex imbrication of discursive and non discursive
> practices, and the sense in which contexts imply other contexts, so that
> each context implies a global network of contexts, is different from the
> sense in which texts imply other texts and eventually all texts.
>
> (Appadurai, 1996: 187)

I want to first assess contra-flows through the traditional lens of nationalist
origin (and begin negotiation with the second half of my definition: 'a world
experienced through the identity politics of nations, individuals and cultures').
Seen through the lens of postcolonial analysis, texts are continuously disappearing into the past, erasing and aligning their specific place of national
origin. Their beginning (if there is one) is when the 'colonizing power
inscribes itself onto the body and space of its others and which continues as an
often occluded tradition into the modern theater of neo-colonialist international relations' (Williams and Chrisman, 1994: 13). How do we then
locate the genesis, intent and progeny of key national media texts that make
up the stuff of contra-flows? Some of the confusion behind this lies with how
contra-flows have been constructed around traditional notions of 'culture'.

Once cultures could be prefigured visually – as objects, theaters, texts
(Clifford, 1986: 12). Postcolonial studies see culture as always relational, an
inscription of communicative processes that exist historically between subjects in relations of power (ibid.: 15). The late Edward Said has probably
done most both to identify the nature of this process in understanding the
dynamics of orientalism and then to argue that understanding 'culture'
cannot be divorced from processes of historical and contemporary colonialism. The two terms often thought of separately – culture as the process of
community beliefs and colonialism as a political and social framework for
appropriating others (economically, culturally) are brought together. As Said
argues:

> Essences such as Englishness and Orientalisms, modes of production such
> as Asiatic and Occidental, all of these in my opinion testify to an ideology
> whose cultural correlatives well precede the actual accumulation of
> imperial territories worldwide.
>
> (Said, quoted in Jewsiewicki and Mudimbe, 1994: 34–50)

Said, then, locates culture and colonialism as part of a single practice.
Culture is in a sense manufactured through colonial frameworks of categorization and appropriation. The importance of this idea is not limited to older
colonial discourses such as orientalism, but to contemporary discourses
about media texts (especially those that are exemplars of contra-flows) as

they surface in news reports, popular culture, policy papers, and academic settings, such as this book.

The issue of contra-flows in such a culture/colonization schema then draws on Foucauldian notions of discourse rather than on the traditional frameworks of cultural imperialism. They can be framed through what Shome calls 'discursive imperialism'. She states that:

> [T]he question that is perhaps most central to the post-colonial project is: how do Western discursive practices, in their representations of the world and of themselves, serve to legitimize the contemporary global power structures? To what extent do the cultural texts of nations such as the United States and Britain reinforce the neo-imperial political practices of these nations? These are very important questions to investigate for they illustrate how in the present times, discourses have become the prime means of imperialism. Whereas in the past, imperialism was about controlling the 'native' by colonizing her/him territorially, now imperialism is more about subjugating the 'native' by colonizing her/him discursively.
>
> (Shome, 1996: 505)

It is this idea of discourse that underlies Spivak's notion that postcolonial power is incorrectly based on the static binary opposition of colonizer/colonized, which does not allow for the heterogeneity of 'colonial power' nor does it disclose the complicity of the two poles of that opposition. Understanding processes of cultural and colonization then is not limited to the constitutive powers of colonizers over the colonized (by the articulation and re-articulation of culture), but by understanding that processes of contra-flows are multiply structured, variously localized and differentially articulated.

At the core of such an exercise is a re-fitting of our conceptual lenses around contra-flows; seeing such textualities as one part of the global cultural economy which is structured by a 'complex, overlapping, disjunctive order' (Appadurai, 1990: 296). This disjunctive order is constituted by the interaction of five 'scapes' of interaction: the ethnoscape, technoscape, the infoscape, the financescape and mediascape, which are interconnected and even overlapping. In an often quoted paragraph, Appadurai says, 'the conditions under which the current global flows take place are through the growing disjunctures between ethnoscapes, technoscapes, finanscapes, mediascapes and ideoscapes. People, machinery, money, images, and ideas now follow increasingly non-isomorphic paths' (1990: 301).

In the context of contra-flows, we can now add the notion of 'terrorscape', that is simultaneously an objective presence (that intersects with these others scapes) but also a discursive one. The emergence and intersection of such presences exist through the range of news media, from hyper-nationalist

American media, through al-Hurra and Al-Jazeera to the very niched manifestations of web casting, a rejuvenated traditional media (radio, video
cameras, cassette recorders) and the emergence of new hybridities (such as
blogging and cell phones) and those that create new analogies for violence
through recreation (such as gaming). These are used for recruitment in
equal measure by institutions established for regulated violence (the US
Army, for example uses video war games as a recruiting tool) and by cyber
watchers/terrorists/hackers as they close the gap between the material and
the discursive.

To summarize then, the two ends of this process – the national and the cultural – need to be aligned; which is something at odds with how contra-flows
have traditionally been seen. To reiterate the terms of this new definition:
'a world experienced through the identity politics of nations, individuals and
cultures'. In this new rendering of contra-flows, there exists a fundamental
shift in thinking about the implications of contra-flows, from narrowly
defined economic structuration to their placement in the realm of cultural
negotiation and identity politics, a concern to which I now turn, addressing
the last part of my definition, 'negotiated through contestations of locality,
nationality and global citizenship'.

Identity politics/audience

> More importantly, the mysterious roamings of finance capital are
> matched by new kinds of migration, both elite and proletarian, which
> create unprecedented tensions between identities of origin, identities of
> residence and identities of aspiration for many migrants in the world
> labor market. Leaky financial frontiers, mobile identities and fast-
> moving technologies of communication and transaction, together pro-
> duce a variety of debates, both within and across national boundaries.
>
> (Appadurai, 2001: 3)

The two key concepts from postcolonial and transnational cultural studies in
relation to identity are those of diaspora and hybridity, which are both of
central significance to the issue of contra-flows in the world today. Diaspora
refers to the process which Appadurai calls 'deterritorialization', where not
only money, commodities and persons unendingly chase each other around
the world, but also group imaginations of the modern world find their fractured and fragmented counterpart. Hybridity reveals that ideas of essentialism are of little service in understanding issues of identity; rather, identity in
the postcolonial world is marked by indeterminacy. As Bhaba puts it:

> Post-colonialism is about borderlands and hybridity. It is about cultural
> indeterminacy and spaces in-between. Resisting attempts at any
> totalizing forms of cultural understanding (whether imperialistic or

nationalistic), the post-colonial perspective argues for a recognition of
the hybrid location of cultural values.

(Bhaba, 1992: 439)

One of the implications of such a framework is that the reception of contra-
flows (seen in a heterogeneous fashion rather than in monolithic national
frames) is linked to a range of complex cultural identity formations which
can be described variously as cosmopolitans, ex-centric natives or mimics
(Bhaba, 1992). To take the next step, we can assert the idea that 'in the
increasingly integrated world system[,] there is no such thing as an independent cultural identity but that every identity must define and position itself
in relation to the cultural frames affirmed by the world system' (Ang, 1991:
253). The central task as seen by postcolonial critics is to extend this analytic
by a focus on issues of the 'politics of location', where notions of complex
identity articulation and interpellation by constituent power relations are
manifest, across traditional lines of identity affiliation (class, race, nation,
gender, sexuality) but equally in parallel realms of violence (terrorists, mili-
tants, hijackers, hackers), and entertainment (belly dancers, Bollywood
performances, karaoke singers, telenovela webzines).

Mohanty argues that developing such a politics of location (which we can
apply to a framing of the reception of contra-flows) requires exploration of
the 'historical, geographical, cultural, psychic and imaginative boundaries,
which provide ground for political definition and self-definition' (Mohanty,
1987: 3). Location is not seen as something rigid but as a 'temporality of
struggle' (ibid.: 40) characterized by multiple locations and non-synchronous
processes of movement between cultures, languages, and complex configurations of meaning and power (Mani, 1990: 26). In locating such a province for
understanding identity rather than the totalizing one of national identity, a
key assumption is that 'identity is neither continuous nor continually interrupted but constantly framed between the simultaneous vectors or similarity,
continuity and difference' (Frankenberg and Mani, 1993: 295).

Today, such a politics of location needs to be simultaneously placed within
the life-space of postmodern nation-states and their multiple identity formations; the co-option of post-nationalist identities by a global corporate
citizenship; the emergence of a range of hybridities (along the lines of
hyphenation); new identity modulations (aligned with emergent models for
consumption, for example, in food, clothing, entertainment, media use) and,
most crucially, in the lack of fixity that traditional categories (race, nation,
language) hold in the mobile landscape of contemporary culture.

This is not to say that such a structuration implies a post-national world, or
even a happier world framed by the narratives of corporate-sponsored entertainment, free of the demands of violence. Quite the opposite: it is a world
with new exigencies where the forces of globalization and violence com-
mingle with those of media and contra-flows. I turn to a discussion of these

an afterthought to consideration of identity politics but as its
itution, as seen in the key word in the last part of the definition
of locality, nationality and global citizenship'.

Identity politics/violence

There are many ways that we can approach the problems of globalization and violence. One could take the United States and ask whether
the growth in the prison industry (and what is sometimes called the
'Carceral State') is tied to the dynamics of regional economies, which
are being pushed out of other more humane forms of employment and
wealth creation. One could consider Indonesia and ask why there is a
deadly increase in intra-state violence in the name of indigenous populations against state-sponsored migrants. One could study Sri Lanka and
ask whether there are real links between the incessant civil war there
and the global diaspora of Tamils, with such results as Eelam.com, an
example of cyber-secession.

(Appadurai, 2001: 5)

Appadurai's quote problematizes two ends of the spectrum of contra-flows:
the utopian and dystopian. Going beyond popular ideas of 'Jihad vs.
McWorld' or 'terrorism is the dark side of globalization', it articulates the
idea of global violence with the life of nation-states both (simultaneously) in
their assertive and disintegrative mode. His work builds on at least a decade
of critical engagement with the dynamics of nationalism in the postcolonial
and transnational cultural studies literature. Let me first offer a thumbnail
sketch of the central arguments. The first is a relatively direct critique of the
mythos (and ideology) of nation-making itself. Such as:

The collective appropriation of antiquity, and especially of shared
memories of a golden age, contributes significantly to the formation of
nations. The greater, the more glorious that antiquity appears, the easier
it becomes to mobilize the people around a common culture, to unify the
various groups of which they are composed and to identify a shared
national identity.

(Smith, quoted in Mehta, 2002: 2)

Such an 'imagined community', conventional analysis suggests, leaves audiences with little room for negotiation. Postcolonial and transnational cultural studies, however, differ in the impact of such imaginings, drawing on a
range of theorists and examples to illustrate the complexity behind such a
totalization. The literary analyst Roger Bromley, for example, critically
applies theoretical concepts put forth by a range of cultural theorists such as
Bakhtin, Lyotard, Deleuze, Guattari, Hall, Bhaba and Gilroy to narratives

grouped together according to geo-locations of the receiving society (the United States, Canada and Britain). These concepts are used as take-off points. He widens Stuart Hall's concept of the third scenario (a non-binary space of reflection) into the working idea of the third space.

Characters with hyphenated identities pose problems in terms of classification and therefore raise questions about notions of essential difference. Hall also describes this dialectic of belonging and not belonging as somewhere in between. He discusses the fiction he has selected as constructed around figures 'who look in from outside while looking out from inside to the extent that both inside and outside lose their defining contours'. Thus a third space emerges that challenges fixed assumptions of identity and he reads this as a vital space for revaluation. Discussions of form and language are also crucial elements throughout. Bromley illustrates how multilingual, polyvocal, varifocal, intertextual and multi-accented texts work against the propensity of the dominant culture to homogenize. Transformation and textual negotiations are also examined as key features of the uses of language in border writing (Pandurang, 2001: 3).

The problem of hyphenated identities (belonging and not belonging) is central to how I see the problem of violence and contra-flows. Posed as a third space, the websites of both terrorists and nationalists, the recruitment videos of both state armies and terrorist groups, music videos extolling suicide bombers and country music stars singing of patriotism, are complicit in the key characteristic of violence as contra-flow: a global imaginaire (and the real act of violence) that echoes the markers of modernity and anti-modernity, nationalism and post-nationalism (seen in the use of individual bodies to articulate these tensions).

In this sense, the suicide bomber and the rock star become as much of a palliative of the problem of global violence as their originator; both often circuitously tied together in the same virtual spaces and chat rooms, acting together to create new communities of fans/terrorists. These *contra-flows* then become the misplaced term for a global animosity sharing common symbols (flags, videos), hardware (computers) and most crucially a self-reflexive sensibility about their own roles working through the last line of my definition 'contestations of locality, nationality and global citizenship'. Through such a lens, we can examine the concrete examples of mediated terrorism, state-sponsored violence to be concurrent with the paradoxes of global capitalism and the spread of new technologies. As Appadurai puts it:

> One way to unravel the horror of the worldwide growth in intimate bodily violence in the context of increased abstraction and circulation of images and technologies is to consider that their relationship is indeed not paradoxical at all. For the body, especially the minoritized body, can simultaneously be the mirror and the instrument of those abstractions we fear most. And minorities and their bodies are after all the

products of high degrees of abstraction in counting, classifying and sur-
veying populations. So the body of the historically produced minority
combines the seductions of the familiar and the reductions of the abstract
in social life. It therefore allows fears of the global to be embodied and,
when specific situations become overcharged with anxiety, for that body
to be annihilated.

(Appadurai, 2001: 5)

Directions

As a concluding thought to this chapter, I want to suggest two new avenues
for scholarship on contra-flows (as I have defined it). The first needs to be a
project that draws on my notion of 'subaltern technologies'. There are a
number of questions that require examination. I identify three:

1   What are the modalities of textual integration across the realms of con-
    text, text and reception that are reflected across the global sites of contra-
    flows (as described here)? It may seem obvious that the use of web cams
    by rain forest conservationists is different from the posting of beheadings
    on terrorist websites. But the question remains as to their *concurrence* and
    their locality as sites for the differential articulation of contra-flows.
2   What are the dynamics of audience intersection with such subaltern tech-
    nologies? How, again, are these manifest in the dynamic interplay between
    agency and effect; between corporate structured narratives (online video
    games, for example) and their rearticulation by local agents (online
    video game players, who are simultaneously global and local)?
3   What are the wider processes of technological transformation that
    impinge on the range, form and scope of these subaltern technologies?
    This could be usefully addressed first through a historical lens: examining
    the links, for example, between revolutionary movements and the emer-
    gence of a global middle class (a question rarely asked). A future-oriented
    analysis could examine the issue of biotechnology and its relation to how
    the human body is being currently reshaped through use of the cell
    phone but then extended to 'inserted' technologies (chips, stems, pros-
    thetics, etc.).

The second direction that the field of contra-flow research might examine is
in the realm of the global imaginaire with the use of a new concept that I
would like to call 'the fashion of fascism'. What does that mean? Minimally,
it is a concept that links the discursive and the structural, the worlds of political violence and aesthetic pleasure. But let me provide a thumbnail agenda
by identifying three research questions based on the qualities of the 'fashion
of fascism':

- The emergence of the fashion of fascism lies in the concrete examples of media policy directives that orient patriarchal forms of identity politics into the realm of popular political culture. This is seen most critically in the construct of George Bush, who uses mass media performance to simultaneously parody competitors (such as John Kerry) and create a parody of presidential performance. This double ambivalence is the only thing that allows us to make sense of why the American public voted the way it did. It is this relationship, this divide between consciousness and action, that has permeated public life and created this element of the fashion of fascism.

- The fashion of fascism lies equally in the production of popular culture in the home. This reorientation of thinking about contra-flows allows for a reversal in the institutional basis for media texts. The home and the PC keyboard is the location of such fashion. A language is emerging that is examining such texts – words like blogging or cellevision – but a lot more needs to be done. Projects examining the relationship of suburban living (alienation, spatial dislocation) with new technologies of relationality and new modes of agency/effect would be one important step in this direction.

- Finally, a re-examination of old-fashioned fascism (from above). The vocabulary that exists in the popular media is still centered around institution-centered sources (politicians, public relations, media commentators, etc.) but more needs to be done to track the specific processes by which these are articulated into policies of exclusion and inclusion across fields not related such as demography (who is counted; who counts), religion (as faith and as political tactic) and of course, media. Minimally, this calls for political scholars to examine demography, demographers to examine the role of religion, and for media scholars to do all of the above.

References

Ang, I. (1991) *Desperately Seeking the Audience*. London: Routledge.
Appadurai, A. (1990) 'Disjuncture and difference in the global cultural economy', *Theory, Culture and Society*, 7: 295–310.
Appadurai, A. (1996) *Modernity at Large*. Minneapolis: University of Minnesota Press.
Appadurai, A. (2001) 'New logics of violence', *Seminar*. Available at: http://www.india-seminar.com/2001/503; accessed 9 November 2005.
Bhaba, H. (1992) 'Post colonial criticism', in S. Greenblatt and G. Gunn (eds), *Redrawing the Boundaries: The Transformation of English and American Literary Studies*. New York: Modern Language Association of America.
Clifford, J. (1986) *Writing Culture*. Berkeley: University of California Press.

Ferguson, M. (1992) 'The mythology about globalization', *European Journal of Communication*, 7: 69–93.

Foucault, M. (1980) 'The eye of power', in M. Foucault, *Power/Knowledge*, ed. C. Gordon. New York: Pantheon.

Frankenberg, R. and L. Mani (1993) 'Crosscurrents, crosstalks', *Cultural Studies*, 7: 292–310.

Golding, P. (1977) 'Media professionalism in the Third World: The transfer of an ideology', in J. Curran, M. Gurevitch and J. Woollacott (eds), *Mass Communication and Society*. London: Edward Arnold for the Open University Press.

Hardt, H. (1992) *Critical Communication Studies: Essays on Communication, History and Theory in America*. New York: Routledge.

Jewsiewcki, B. and V. Mudimbe (1994) 'For Said', *Transition*, 63: 34–50.

Mani, L. (1990) 'Multiple mediations', *Inscriptions*, 5: 1–23.

Mehta, R. (2002) 'National mythology', *Jouvert*, 6.

Mohanty, C. (1987) 'Under Western eyes: feminist scholarship and colonial discourses', *Feminist Review*, 30: 61–88.

Pandurang, M. (2001) 'Cross cultural texts and diasporic identities', *Jouvert*, 6.

Said, E. (1979) *Orientalism*. New York: Vintage.

Shome, R. (1995) 'Postcolonial interventions in the rhetorical canon: An "other" view', *Communication Theory*, 6: 40–59.

Shome, R. (1996) 'Race and popular cinema: The rhetorical strategies of whiteness in City of Joy', *Communication Quarterly*, 44 (4): 502–18.

Williams, C. and P. Chrisman (1994) *Colonial Discourse and Postcolonial Theory: A Reader*. New York: Harvester.

Part II
Non-Western media in motion

Chapter 4

Contra-flows or the cultural logic of uneven globalization?

Japanese media in the global agora

Koichi Iwabuchi

In the study of media culture, the transcendence of contrapositions such as ideological domination–semiotic resistance, political economy–active audience reception, and global homogenization–local appropriation has been an unsettled key issue. While the necessity of overcoming binary thinking is recognized and emphasized, the second of each of the contrapositions gained more currency in the 1980s and 1990s. And since the turn of the century in particular, the pendulum seems to be swinging back to the first of the contrapositions, given the intensification in the global penetration of neo-liberal market fundamentalism and the widening gap between the haves and the have-nots. Political and economic structures attract more urgent critical attention in the analysis of cultural globalization than people's meaning-construction practices at the local level, while the relevance of the latter has never been exhausted.

In this context, media globalization is critically discussed in terms of the further penetration of American cultures and worldviews. Yet, such a view would be unproductively US-centric if it were to disregard the increase in non-Western exports and intraregional, non-Western flows. In the past decade, a 'West vs. the Rest' paradigm has been seriously contested in the studies of media and cultural globalization with the increase in the media flows from non-Western regions (Iwabuchi, 2002; Erni and Chua, 2004). In many parts of the world, media and cultural flows have been significantly de-Americanized or de-Westernized. This development can be positively regarded as evidence of the relative demise of the Western, especially American, cultural hegemony as well as a salutary corrective to a West-centric analysis of media and cultural globalization. However, this view would be incomplete and misleading if it failed to take account of the structure of asymmetrical media and cultural flows in the world. The question to be critically examined here is whether and how this development testifies to the deterioration of uneven global media structure and power relations. In what sense is it contra and against what?

This chapter will consider this question by examining the rise of Japanese media in the global markets. First, it will briefly look at the spread of

Japanese media culture in the light of three decentring trends of media globalization (Tomlinson, 1997): the rise of non-Western players, the prevalence of glocalism, and the activation of non-Western regional connections. This chapter posits that these developments are not seriously challenging but in fact constitutive of the restructuring process of uneven cultural globalization, in which apparently opposing forces are working simultaneously and interactively.

Cool Japan: the rise of non-Western players

In a widely cited book on the political economy of media globalization, Edward Herman and Robert McChesney (1997) state that Japan has money and technology but does not have a cultural influence on the world: 'Japan is supplying capital and markets to the global media system, but little else' (Herman and McChesney, 1997: 104). However, one of the conspicuous trends in media globalization is the rise of non-Western players, of which Japan is a notable example. Several commentators have attested to Japan's increasing cultural influence in the last several years: 'During the 1990's, Japan became associated with its economic stagnation. However, what many failed to realize is that Japan has transformed itself into a vibrant culture-exporting country during the 1990s' (*New York Times*, 23 November 2003); 'Japan's influence on pop culture and consumer trend runs deep' (*Business Week*, 26 July 2004); 'Japan is reinventing itself on earth – this time as the coolest nation culture' (*Washington Post*, 27 December 2003). Indeed Japan's media culture has become celebrated both domestically and internationally as a global cool culture and Japan as a cultural superpower.

While this seems to suggest that a dramatic change occurred vis-à-vis Japanese cultural exports in the late 1990s, the spread of Japanese media culture into the US and Europe has been a gradual and steady phenomenon. The prevalence of Japanese popular culture throughout the world came to the fore in the 1980s. At this period the focus was on the cultural influence of made-in-Japan communication technological products such as the Walkman, and subsequently on Japanese manufacturers' inroads into the content business, as exemplified by Sony and Matsushita's buyout of Hollywood studios in the late 1980s which sought to gain access to the huge archives of Hollywood movies and other content products. This new development was interpreted through a viewpoint that resonates with Herman and McChesney's, as exemplified by the lines a Japanese co-star delivers to the American protagonist, Michael Douglas, in the film *Black Rain*: 'Music and movies are all your culture is good for . . . We [Japanese] make the machines' (quoted in Morley and Robins, 1995: 159).

To adopt this perspective is to overlook the significant increase in Japanese exports of popular cultural products that was occurring in the same period. Following the success of Ôtomo Katsuhiro's hugely popular animation film,

Akira (1988), the quality and popularity of 'Japanimation' came to be recognized by the US market. In November 1995, the animated film, *The Ghost in the Shell*, was shown simultaneously in Japan, America and Britain. Its sales, according to *Billboard* (24 August 1996), propelled it to No. 1 in the US video charts. The export value of Japanese animation and comics to the US market amounted to $75 million in 1996 (*Sankei Shinbun*, 14 December 1996). Furthermore, the popularity of Japanese games software is demonstrated by the phenomenal success of Super Mario Brothers, Sonic and Pokémon. According to one survey, as a director of Nintendo pointed out, Mario was a better-known character among American children than Mickey Mouse (Akurosu Henshûshitsu, 1995).

The popularity of TV animation series *Sailor Moon* and the huge success of Pokémon in the global market of the late 1990s warrants further research into Japanese cultural exports (Tobin, 2004). Pokémon's penetration into global markets exceeds even that of Mario. As of June 2000, sales of Pokémon games software had reached about 65 million copies (22 million outside Japan); trading-cards about 4.2 billion (2.4 billion outside Japan); the animation series had been broadcast in 51 countries; the first feature film had been shown in 33 countries and its overseas box-office takings had amounted to $176 million; in addition, there had also been about 12,000 character merchandises (8,000 outside Japan) (Hatakeyama and Kubo, 2001). These statistics clearly show that Pokémon has become a 'made-in-Japan' global cultural phenomenon (see Tobin, 2004). Last but not least, Miyazaki Hayao's animation films are now widely respected and *Sen to Chihiro no Kamikakushi* won the best film award at the Berlin Film Festival in 2002.

According to Sugiura (2003), industry estimates Japanese exports of popular cultural products nearly tripled, from 500 billion yen in 1992 to 1.5 trillion yen in 2002. This rise is dramatic compared to a total export growth rate, which was 21 per cent for the same period. Animation consisted of 3.5 per cent of total exports from Japan to the US in 2002 and the cartoon Pokémon was shown in about 70 countries in more than 30 languages. Hello Kitty, a cat-like character produced by the Japanese company Sanrio earned $1 billion a year outside Japan (Sugiura, 2003).

I have argued elsewhere that most Japanese cultural exports to Western markets are culturally neutral, in that the positive image and association of a Japanese culture or way of life is not generally related to the consumption of the products (see Iwabuchi, 2002). Animation, computer games and characters may be recognized as originating in Japan and their consumption may well be associated with high technology or miniaturization; however, the appeal of such products is relatively autonomous from cultural images of the country of production. In contrast to American counterparts, these products do not attempt to sell the Japanese way of life. It is also well known that the characters of many Japanese animations or computer games tend to be consciously drawn as *mukokuseki*, which means that they are free from any association with particular national, racial or cultural characteristics.

Although the question of whether Japanese animations and characters invoke the image of Japanese culture and lifestyle is still a moot one, what is indisputable is that Japan has come to be regarded by a large number of young people in the US, Europe and Asia as an artistic country that produces cool animations, games and characters. Undoubtedly this shift in the perception of Japanese 'cultural odour' has much to do with the attraction of the texts and imagery in themselves. However, it also can be read symptomatically in relation to the development of decentring cultural globalization, whereby more non-Western media contents are circulating and being promoted in the global markets – a point I shall be returning to later.

Glocal me: TV format business

Another conspicuous trend of media globalization is the increasing centrality of localism based on cultural adaptation. While cultural globalization is often discussed in terms of the homogenization of world culture, cultural specificity and diversity are no less articulated in the process. As demonstrated by the term *glocalization*, the strategy of tailoring cultural products to local conditions has become a marketing strategy for transnational media corporations in order to achieve global market penetration (Robertson, 1995).

A prominent case in point is the rapid growth of the TV format business since the late 1990s. Thanks to the development of international television trade fairs and the maturation of television production techniques outside the US (particularly in Europe and Asia), the practice of localizing foreign TV formats has become more institutionalized and systematically managed. In the global reach of the format business, Japan also plays an important role. Around the turn of the millennium, Japanese television networks began buying new global television formats such as *Who Wants To Be a Millionaire?*, *The Weakest Link* and *Survivor*. Yet, the purchase of a few prominent European/American television formats tells only a partial story in the development of the contemporary Japanese television industry. While on the international stage, format television products have in the past been predicated on the maxim 'Western television format goes global', the paradigm is shifting. In fact, Japanese television industries, with their relatively sophisticated skills and experience in production, export a considerable number of programmes and formats to many parts of the world, far more than they import.

The Japanese television industry started selling Japanese formats to Western markets back in the late 1980s. This was recognized as an effective way to enter lucrative Western markets, where the trading price of television programmes was at least ten times higher than that in Asian markets. Initially though, Japanese programmes were not well received, apart from animation. TBS, the leading exporter of television programmes and formats in Japan, has so far sold programme formats to more than 40 countries. TBS started its format business when it sold the format of *Wakuwaku* [exciting] *Animal Land* – a quiz show dealing exclusively with animals – to the Netherlands in 1987 (still a popular show called *Waku Waku* in that country); the format has been sold to more than 20 other countries. Nippon Television Network (NTV), another commercial television station, has also sold several quiz show formats. For example, the format of *Show-by Show-by*, which is a quiz show about bizarre commerce and shops around the world ('shoubai' or 'show-by' means 'trade' in Japanese), was exported to Spain, Italy, Thailand and Hong Kong during the mid-1990s. Like *Wakuwaku Animal Land*, the advantage of this quiz show is its capacity to sell visual material of world scenes for quiz segments, as well as the actual concept of the programme.

The Japanese television industry has also pioneered the production of new kinds of audience participation programmes and reality television shows. It is a little known fact that the globally adapted format of *America's Funniest Home Videos* was originally produced by TBS. It was a segment of a variety show entitled *Katochan Kenchan Gokigen Terebi*, which was broadcast from 1986 to 1992. The American network ABC bought the rights to the format in 1989 and since then has exported the amateur video show format to more than 80 countries worldwide. The format of a video-game-like participation game-show, *Takeshi's Castle*, which was originally broadcast during the 1980s in Japan, has also been exported to several Western countries including the US, Germany and Spain.

Fuji TV's *Ryouri no Tetsujin* [Iron Chef] is an innovative cookery show in which professional chefs compete with each other. Each week two chefs, who in most cases represent different cuisines, are assigned to produce several dishes within one hour with one featured ingredient. Their struggles are dramatically reported and filmed in a live sports telecast style, with the stylishly decorated studio fitted out as the kitchen. Cooking skills, professional creativity, subtle presentation techniques, as well as the ultimate taste are all taken into consideration by four guest celebrities who adjudicate on proceedings. The programme was first exported to a US cable network but its popularity led the television producers of Paramount Network to make an American version by purchasing the format rights in 2001.

TBS has also been successful in selling reality television formats. One of the most widely distributed formats is *Shiawase Kazoku Keikaku* [Happy Family Plan]. It is a programme in which the father is assigned to master a task (such as juggling) within one week and to perform this successfully in the studio. If he succeeds, the family will receive the prize they nominated (such as an overseas trip) before the father was informed of the task. The highlight of the show is the father's final performance in the studio but this is foregrounded in the dedication with which he has tried to master the task with the encouragement of other family members. Documentary-style home-videoing of the father's exertions, frustrations, the pressures induced by repetitive failures, the subsequent strengthening of family ties, and the re-establishment or recovery of the father's authority in the family in the course of his mastering the skill constitute the key elements. The show won the 1998 Silver Rose Award in Montreux for Best Game Show and an International Emmy Award in the same year. Its format has been sold to more than 30 countries all over the world.

The idea of the glocal is said to have its origin in Japanese corporate marketing strategy (Robertson, 1995). Featherstone (1995: 9) has also argued, referring to the Japanese willingness and capacity to indigenize the foreign, that the strategy of glocalization has come to signify a new meaning of 'Japanization', which is 'a global strategy which does not seek to impose a standard product or image, but instead is tailored to the demands of the local market'. Yet it is untenable to mark the origin of practices that negate the idea of the origin itself. Such a view has become even shakier with the worldwide marketing and institutionalization of glocalism by media and cultural industries, in which those located in Japan are actively and collaboratively involved as one player among many.

Japan in East Asian media markets

It is East Asia that has provided Japanese media culture with its largest export market and most avid audience. The extensive reach of manga and anime is illustrated by the fact that an English version of the bestselling weekly manga magazine *Shonen Jump* is published in the United States. Yet the popularity of this cultural form is far more firmly entrenched in East Asia, where translated versions of Japanese weekly comics are available just a few days after the originals are published, and the number and variety of anime series broadcast by television stations is much greater than in the West. Television drama series with 11 or 12 episodes – a staple format of TV schedules in Japan – are fast becoming a genre in their own right. CDs by Japanese pop stars are released almost simultaneously in Japan and other East Asian countries. In Taiwan the many young people who love Japanese pop culture and follow it keenly have been named as the *harizu* (Japan tribe), which became something of a social phenomenon in the 1990s. A 2001 survey conducted by a Japanese advertising agency found that Japanese consumer culture and products were far more likely to be considered 'cool' by young people in the cities of East Asia than were their American equivalents. While the boom in popularity of Japanese media culture has now been stabilized, the penetration of Japanese media cultures in East Asian markets is still much more far-reaching, compared to their spread in the Euro-American markets.

Many observers refer to the cultural proximity of Japan and other Asian countries to explain the reception Japanese pop culture enjoys in East Asia. In short, they argue that Japanese cultural products are perceived as familiar by viewers and listeners in the region because Japan is felt to be culturally close to them. When I conducted a survey in Taipei in the late 1990s, I often heard the view expressed that Japanese TV series looked culturally closer, more familiar, more realistic, and therefore easier to empathize with than American series. One respondent said, 'Japanese series reflect the reality of our lives. American series portray neither our real experiences nor our yearnings.' Another commented, 'I had never seen programmes that express what we feel as accurately as Japanese dramas do. Lifestyles and culture in the West are so different from ours that it's hard to get emotionally involved in American TV series.' For these men and women, American shows may be unmatched in their production quality, but it is Japanese TV dramas they turn to for stories that they can relate to, and which they can discuss with their friends.

Japanese TV dramas then, with their cultural proximity, appear to be depicting the 'here and now' of East Asia in a way that US programmes fail to do. However, this development may also be subject to the process of cultural globalization and thus the perception of cultural proximity should not be considered as something given, static or natural. The comfortable sense of familiarity that Taiwanese and Hong Kong audiences feel when watching Japanese TV series is based on a sense of coevalness (Fabian, 1983) or contemporaneity stemming from shared socio-economic conditions. Experiences common to inhabitants of capitalist urban spaces – such as the simultaneous distribution of information and products and the spread of consumerist culture and lifestyles, the development of the media industry and market, the emergence of young middle-class people with considerable spending power, and the transformation of women's status and attitudes – have all given rise to a sense of contemporaneity in terms of socio-cultural life (which includes sexual relationships, friendship and working conditions). It is this that underpins the favourable reception of Japanese popular culture in the Asian region. In this sense, the experience of perceived cultural proximity must be viewed as something dynamic that describes what people, society and culture are *becoming*, not what they are. It is not so much a matter of being proximate as one of *becoming* proximate, and this means we must consider not only the space axis but also the time axis. The East Asian modernity that Japanese TV dramas represent has been articulated in the interaction between the global, the regional and the local (for a detailed discussion, see Iwabuchi, 2002).

Globalization has been experienced unequally around the world in the context of a modern history dominated by the West. The West's indisputable cultural, political, economic and military hegemony has forged what may be termed the modern 'world system', and the influence of the modernity configured in Western capitalist societies (especially the United States) pervades the world. But the modern experiences forced upon non-Western countries have at the same time produced disparate forms of indigenous modernity and have highlighted the fallacy of discussing modernity exclusively from the standpoint of Western experiences. As a corollary of ongoing asymmetrical cultural encounters in the course of the spread of Western modernity, people discovered that many of the world's cultures were becoming simultaneously (and paradoxically) similar to and different from their own (Ang and Stratton, 1996). 'Familiar differences' and 'bizarre similarities' interconnect on multiple levels within the dynamics of unequal global cultural encounters and are engendering a complex perception of cultural distance.

If Japanese popular culture is enjoyed in Asia with the same relish as local delicacies like *dim sum* or *kimchi* (*Newsweek*, Asian edition, 8 November 1999), this is because it represents, in an East Asian context, the cultural configuration, blending difference and similarity, that globalization encourages. In East Asia there are many young viewers who genuinely relate to the everyday (and more unusual) happenings in the lives of the young Tokyoites portrayed in Japanese TV dramas and who identify with the their dreams and aspirations. This shows, I would suggest, that Japanese media culture's being/becoming proximate also reflects the comfortable difference Taiwanese and Hong Kong audiences feel towards Japan. Asian viewers empathize with Japanese characters because Japan is perceived as similar but different; different but the same. The sense of realism in which sameness and difference, closeness and distance, and reality and dreams delicately mix, elicits sympathy from viewers – a kind of sympathy that perhaps cannot be gained from American media cultures.

Multi-directional regional media flows in East Asia

The further penetration of Japanese media culture in East Asia is closely related to the activation of regional media flows, which is the third decentring trend that has been facilitated by the cultural globalization process. In the 1990s, East Asian media markets rapidly expanded and close partnerships were formed in the media industry as companies pursued marketing strategies and joint production ventures spanning several different markets. Popular culture from places like Japan, Hong Kong, Taiwan and Korea is finding a broader transnational acceptance in the region, leading to the formation of new links among people in Asia, especially the youth. This trend has shown no sign of letting up. Asian markets have become even more synchronized, joint East Asian projects in film and music have become more common, and singers and actors from around the region are engaged in activities that transcend national borders.

In this context, Japanese popular culture is not the only form that represents Asia's here and now through the intermingling of similarities and differences among multiple modernities. Many other East Asian regions are also creating their own cultural forms within the social and cultural contexts specific to their countries, and media flows are becoming more and more multilateral. While it can be argued that the production of TV dramas in East Asia has been, to some extent, stimulated by Japanese series aimed at young audiences, the resulting series dexterously blend a variety of local elements, and are far more than mere imitations of Japanese shows. An especially interesting case is the Taiwanese drama *Meteor Garden*, which is based on a Japanese manga about the lives of high school students entitled *Hana yori dango* [Boys before Flowers]. This series skilfully transplants the comic's narrative to a Taiwanese context while retaining the original characters and their Japanese names. According to the *Asahi Shimbun* (12 July 2002), although this series is the subject of a broadcast ban in China because of fears that love affairs and violence depicted in the drama series might exert a bad influence on students, the series has become very popular among young Chinese, thanks to the circulation of pirated videos. This is a case in which a hybridization of Japanese and Taiwanese cultural imagination has created new East Asian cultural links that have circumvented political restrictions.[1]

The most conspicuous trend at the beginning of the twenty-first century is the rise of Korean 'Wave' or '*Hallyu*' (see also Chapter 8, this volume). It is often argued that Korean television drama production has been in no small way influenced by Japanese dramas (Lee, 2004). Ever since a South Korean series bearing many similarities to *Tokyo Love Story* was made in 1993, Japanese television series have given Korean drama production fresh direction. But rather than merely copying Japanese shows, the Koreans have produced drama series portraying Asia's here and now with their own appeal, which are being circulated in Asian markets. Korean television series and pop music are now receiving an even warmer welcome in places like Taiwan, Hong Kong and China than their Japanese equivalents.

One of the main reasons for the success of Korean television dramas is their depiction of family matters, which enables them to appeal to a wider range of viewers than do Japanese programmes. Many young viewers also prefer South Korean dramas to Japanese ones in terms of realism and their ability to relate to the characters and story-lines. According to interviews I conducted with Taiwanese university students in 2001, Japanese series tend to focus solely on young people's loves and jobs, and this restricts the scope of their stories. Korean dramas, on the other hand, while featuring young people's romances as a central theme, also portray the problems and bonds of parents and children, grandparents and other relatives. This resonates more deeply with the real-life experiences of young people in Taiwan. The restricted relationships and daily lives of young people featured in the world of Japanese TV dramas, which Ito (2004) describes as a 'microcosm', have attracted many followers in the Asian region, but Korean dramas have achieved a new level of realism by portraying a slightly different East Asian here and now.

Japan, too, is embracing the Korean Wave. Most notably, the Korean TV drama series, *Winter Sonata* proved a phenomenal success in 2003, so much so that many (mostly middle-aged women audiences) started to learn Korean, visit Korea and study the history of Japanese colonialism. In this process a significant number of audiences came to the realization that they harboured a prejudice against Korea as a backward country (see Mori, 2004). Belief in Japan's superiority over the rest of Asia – that it is separate from the rest, though belonging geographically and culturally to Asia – remains firmly rooted, but such attitudes are being shaken as countries in Asia become more and more interconnected through media flows. This may make Japanese people realize that they now inhabit the same temporality and spatiality as people in other Asian regions and that the peoples of Asia, while being subjected to common waves of modernization, urbanization and globalization, have experienced these phenomena in similar yet different ways in their own particular contexts. This may also prove to be an opportune moment for Japanese people to critically review the state of their own modernity by engaging with other East Asian media cultures.

How contra are they?

Undoubtedly, the cases discussed so far testify to the decentring trends against US-dominated media and cultural flows. However, is the development of Japanese media exports and regional flows in East Asia really contra to uneven globalization processes? And if so, to what extent? I would argue that this is not necessarily the case. The increase in Japanese cultural exports can be viewed as a sign that some changes are occurring in the structuring force of cross-border cultural flows and connections. Japan's cultural exports have boomed over the past decade, at a time when, paradoxically, it has become less relevant to assume absolute cultural and symbolic hegemony in specific countries or cultures. This has been a period when the globalization of culture has accelerated through astonishing advances in communications technology, thereby enabling people in all corners of the globe to link up instantaneously, through the integration of markets and capital by giant multinational corporations, and through the dynamics of local cultural indigenization that downplay the direct cultural power of any single country of origin. The interaction of these factors has made transnational flows of culture more complex and multi-directional, yet not in a way to radically transform the unevenness underlying the flows.

One way to comprehend this complexity is to re-examine the cases discussed above, to analyse how contradictory vectors are operating simultaneously and interactively. First is decentring and recentring. The decentralization of power configurations, as discussed earlier, can be seen in the emergence of (transnational) media corporations that are based in Japan and other non-Western countries as global players. While it is no longer convincing to automatically equate globalization with Americanization, there is no denying the enormity of the American global cultural influence and a new centre has not emerged to take the place of the United States. The point is that it is no longer possible or indeed desirable to view the uneven structure of global cultural connections as bipartite, with one-way transfers of culture from the centre to the periphery. Cultural power still does matter, but it is being dispersed through the web of corporate alliances taking place in various parts of the world. The power structure is being decentred at the same time as being recentred in this process.

Cross-border partnerships and cooperation among multinational corporations and capital involving Japan and other non-Western regions are being driven forward, with America as a pivotal presence. While the inroads Japanese companies have made into Hollywood and the global diffusion of anime and video games may look like signs that America is, comparatively speaking, losing its global cultural hegemony, in reality these phenomena simply illustrate that the pattern of global dominance by transnational media conglomerates centred on America and other developed countries is becoming more firmly entrenched. Sony Corporation's 1989 purchase of a major Hollywood studio was a dramatic demonstration of the breakthrough of Japanese corporations into the global entertainment software business, but this was always a matter of Japanese firms integrating themselves into American cultural power and distribution networks.

The spread of Japanese anime and video games throughout the world has also been underpinned by the stepping-up of mergers, partnerships and other forms of cooperation among multinational media corporations based in developed countries, principally the United States. It is US distribution networks that help Pokémon (distributed by Warner Brothers) and the anime films of *Hayao Miyazaki* (distributed by Disney) to be released world-wide. What is more, the Pokémon anime series and movies seen by audiences around the world – with the exception of those seen in some parts of Asia – have been 'Americanized' by Nintendo of America, a process that involves removing some of their Japaneseness to make them more acceptable to American and European audiences (Iwabuchi, 2004). In turn, Hollywood becomes more inclined to internationally oriented film production as it realizes the profitability of non-Western markets and the usefulness of collaborating with non-Western films, as shown by its remakes of Japanese and Korean films as well as by its employment of more directors and actors from Hong Kong and Taiwan. Transnational media flows are being reorganized in a highly dispersed and ubiquitous power structure through the intensifying collaboration of (multinational) media corporations and media creators that are based in various developed nations.

Regional flows are not free from this force either. As exemplified by STAR TV, owned by NEWS Corporation and MTV ASIA, global media giants are penetrating regional media flows by deploying localization strategies. It should also be noted that the activation of regional media flows is based on the rise of regional hubs such as Japan, Korea, Hong Kong and Taiwan and their corporate alliances. Major media corporations are forging trans-national partnerships and facilitating mutual promotion of media culture. Co-production and remakes of films are becoming more common, with the aim of targeting multiple markets in the region, which can be seen as the emergence of 'Asiawood' (*Newsweek Asia*, 21 May 2001). These trends in the region apparently indicate the activation of decentring multi-directional flows. However, in reality, the mode of media production is being recentred through the alliance of major media corporations in East Asian countries. This development engenders a new international hierarchy in terms of production capacity, with Japan, Korea, Hong Kong and Taiwan at the top tier.

Another key issue concerns the interplay of homogenization and hetero-genization: globalization does not mean simply the standardization of the world through the spread of the same products, values and images trans-mitted from the United States and other developed Western countries. Globalization is, in fact, constantly giving rise to new differences. Globally disseminated cultural products and images are consumed and received differ-ently within the specific cultural framework formed by the political, eco-nomic and social contexts of each locality and by people of differing statuses depending on their gender, ethnicity, class, age and other factors. At the same time, in each locality these products and images are reconfigured through a process of hybridization. American popular culture is exported to countries throughout the world, but the cultural products that perform best are those that mix in local elements while absorbing American cultural influences. Meanings are negotiated locally, resulting in the creation of new products that are more than mere copies.

Here again, this increase in cultural diversity is being governed by the logic of capital and organized within the context of globalization (Hannerz, 1996). As demonstrated by the prevalence of the television format business, globalization does not destroy cultural differences but rather brings about a 'peculiar form of homogenization' while fostering them (Hall, 1991). The global spread of American consumer culture has led to the creation of a series of cultural formats through which various differences can be adjusted. These formats could be described as the axis of the global cultural system. In this sense, one could say that 'America' has become a base format that regulates the process by which modern culture is configured around the world. As multinational media corporations press ahead with global tie-ups and partnerships, they are also trying to raise their profits by tailoring this axis to every corner of the world while promoting cultural diversity in every market. The world is becoming more diverse through standardization and more standardized through diversification. Symbolic power in the age of globalization is not concentrated in the place where the culture originated; it is exercised through the processes of active cultural negotiation that take place in each locality. In fact, it is now almost impossible to imagine local cultural creativity outside the context of globalization and the profits cannot be sufficiently produced without 'respecting' local specificity that is mostly equated with the national market in an essentialist manner. These moves are first and foremost organized and promoted by transnational corporations based in the developed countries, while cultural formats that are shared in many parts of the world originate almost exclusively from a handful of such countries.

Brand nationalism

The other key interplay of contradictory vectors is that of nationalism and transnationalism. It is argued that the efficacy of the nation-state's boundary policing in the modern constitution of politics, economy and culture is deeply problematized in the globalization process and that the term 'trans-national' more productively directs our attention to a new perspective of the flows, disregarding the boundaries set up and controlled by the nation-states. The most important of these flows are those of capital, people and media/images (Hannerz, 1996).

Nonetheless, transnational connections do not fully displace national boundaries, thoughts and feelings. Unlike the term 'global', the term 'trans-national' tends to 'draw attention to what it negates' (Hannerz, 1996: 6). As Michael Peter Smith (2001: 3) argues, while problematizing the assumed efficacy of the nation-state's boundary policing in the modern constitution of politics, economy and culture, the transnational perspective explicates 'the continuing significance of borders, state policies, and national identities even as these are often transgressed by transnational communication circuits and social practices'. Transnational media flows highlight the fact that it is no longer tenable for any country to contain its cultural orientation and agendas within clearly demarcated national boundaries. In spite of, or perhaps because of, the impossibility of controlling the globalization process within a national framework, the transgressive tendency of popular culture and its boundary-violating impulse of cultural hybridization are never free from the nation-alizing force of desperately seeking to re-demarcate and control cultural boundaries. As Roger Rouse (1995: 380) argues, '[t]he transnational has not so much displaced the national as resituated it and thus reworked its meanings'.

This point has become salient as states become more interested in the creation and promotion of 'cool' national brands. In the 1980s and 1990s, 'culture' extended its role to other spheres and became a useful vehicle for various social actors, including marginalized people and NGOs, to pursue their own political and economic interests (Yúdice, 2003). Today though, it is the alliance of the national governments and private (transnational) cor-porations that most powerfully use 'culture' in the establishment and export of national brand cultures such as media, tourism, fashion, foods and so forth. For states to maximize national interests and beat international competition, culture has come to be regarded as important politically to enhance 'soft power', and as important economically for attracting multinational capital and developing new industries in which creative industries play a significant role.

Perhaps 'Cool Britannia' might be the most famous state policy for this, but many national governments in East Asia are also eager to pursue this kind of policy. It is well known that the Korean government engaged with this policy in the 1990s, and that this contributed to the Korean Wave. Following this Korean success, the Japanese government has actively also sought to develop cultural policy. 'Cool Japan' is expected to become another Japanese core export commodity and the Japanese government has organized several committees to discuss what policies need to be implemented. Many Japanese universities have also established programmes to train professional creators by inviting the participation of prominent film directors and animation producers, including the internationally renowned film directors, Kitano Takeshi and Kurosawa Kiyoshi.

Politically, it is anticipated that media culture will improve the image of Japan in East Asia to such an extent that the historical memory of Japanese colonialism will be eradicated in the region. The need to export Japanese media culture is being even more eagerly discussed with the recent rise of anti-Japanese feeling in China and Korea vis-à-vis historical and territorial issues. Following a recent survey which revealed that Korean youth who consume Japanese popular culture tend to feel more empathy with Japan (*Asahi Shinbun*, 27 April 2005), the imperative to step up the export of media culture to Asian markets has become ever more pressing. This strategy is viewed as strengthening Japan's cultural diplomacy as it presents, from a Japanese perspective, an opportunity to enhance Asia's understanding of a postwar 'liberated' and 'humane' Japan.

While the nationalistic objectives of Japan's cultural policy may seem self-evident, discussion of Japanese cultural exports tends to be confined to a narrow context at the expense of wider public interests. Media culture's potential to stimulate transnational dialogue should certainly not be dismissed out of hand; it has promoted new kinds of mutual understanding and connections in East Asia. However, even though mediated cultural exchange may improve the image of the nation and enhance a sense of empathy and belonging in its audiences, yet history and the memory of colonialism cannot be easily erased. Historical issues necessitate sincere dialogue with the broad involvement of all citizens, which cultural policy should try to promote.

A preoccupation with market-oriented and international policy concerns will fail to give due attention to unprofitable and marginalized cultures and to the issues (re)generated by transnational cultural flows. There is an urgent need to discuss and develop policy agendas on various issues, such as the high concentration of media ownership in the hands of a few global companies; intellectual property rights; and the transnational, international and intranational division of cultural labour (Miller and Leger, 2001). It is also worth remembering that the new connections being forged through media culture are reinforcing practices of inclusion and exclusion of certain groups in the society. In East Asia, the transnational links have been developed between the dominant media industries and dominant media cultures of metropolises. They tend to exclude a tremendous number of people and their unprofitable cultural expressions and concerns in terms of gender, sexuality, race, ethnicity, class, age, region etc. East Asian connections forged through media culture are underpinned by the logic of capital and market, which benefit a fortunate few, while acting freely beyond the confines of national frameworks in accordance with the fundamental tenets of consumerism. These uneven transnational flows and connectivities are not just disregarded but eventually furthered by the collaboration between nation-states and the private media sector in the branding of the nation.

Concluding remarks

There is an optimistic view that the media are stimulating cosmopolitan awareness among the inhabitants of the 'global village'. However, a series of events at the beginning of the twenty-first century has again revealed how economic disparities around the world are growing to desperate levels and how such discourses as 'they' – savage rogues that threaten 'us' – are being replicated worldwide. With the borders dividing countries and cultures becoming porous and blurred, and the power structure fragmenting and dispersing, exclusion and imbalance are being violently institutionalized on a number of levels.

In this context, any attempt to interpret the increase in Japanese popular cultural exports in terms of a contra-trend to an 'Americanization' paradigm would be to misjudge the shifting nature of transnational cultural power. The decentring process of globalization makes it impossible to single out the absolute symbolic centre that belongs to a particular country or region. However, let me repeat that this does not mean that global cultural power has disappeared: it has been dispersed but at the same time made even more solid. The view that equates globalization with Americanization is no longer convincing when analysing the cultural context. This is not because many non-Western players are now producing contra-flows of media cultures in the global agora. A more crucial factor is that the unevenness in transnational cultural flows is intensified by the various kinds of alliances among transnational media industries in the developed countries.

As states intensify their alliance with (multinational) corporations, it is becoming imperative that public dialogue with all citizens be promoted to discuss how 'culture' can be used for the maximization of social interests. For this purpose, critically attending to how contra-flows seem to be collusive in (re)producing cultural asymmetry and unevenness on various levels (local, national, regional and global) – has become more pressing than ever before.

Note

1 Japanese TV stations also produced their own version of the drama series based on the comic in the autumn of 2005. This is clearly influenced by the popularity of the Taiwan drama series and in this sense it is an example of contra-flow within East Asia.

References

Akurosu Henshûshitsu (ed.) (1995) *Sekai shôhin no tsukurikata: Nihon media ga sekai wo seishita hi* [The Making of Global Commodities: The Day when Japanese Media Conquered the World). Tokyo: Parco Shuppan.

Ang, Ien and Jon Stratton (1996) 'Asianizing Australia: notes toward a critical transnationalism in cultural studies', *Cultural Studies* 10(1): 16–36.

Erni, John Nguyet and Siew Keng Chua (eds) (2004) *Asian Media Studies: Politics of Subjectivities*. Malden, MA: Blackwell.

Fabian, Johannes (1983) *Time and the Other: How Anthropology Makes its Object*. New York: Columbia University Press.

Featherstone, Mike (1995) *Undoing Culture: Globalization, Postmodernism and Identity*. London: Sage.

Hall, Stuart (1991) 'The local and the global: globalization and ethnicity', in A. King (ed.), *Culture, Globalization, and the World-System*. London: Macmillan, pp. 19–39.

Hannerz, Ulf (1996) *Transnational Connections: Culture, People, Places*. London: Routledge.

Hatakeyama, Kenji and Masakazu Kubo (2000) *Pokémon Story*. Tokyo: Nikkei BP.

Herman, Edward and Robert McChesney (1997) *The Global Media: The New Missionaries of Corporate Capitalism*. London: Cassell.

Ito, Mamoru (2004) 'The representation of femininity in Japanese television drama of the 1990s', in K. Iwabuchi (ed.), *Feeling Asian Modernities: Transnational Consumption of Japanese TV Drama*. Hong Kong: University of Hong Kong Press.

Iwabuchi, Koichi (2002) *Recentering Globalization: Popular Culture and Japanese Transnationalism*. Durham, NC: Duke University Press.

Iwabuchi, Koichi (2004) 'How "Japanese" is Pokémon?', in J. Tobin (ed.), *Pikachu's Global Adventure: The Rise and Fall of Pokémon*. Durham, NC: Duke University Press, pp. 53–79.

Lee, Dong-Hoo (2004) 'Cultural contact with Japanese TV dramas: modes of reception and narrative transparency', in K. Iwabuchi (ed.), *Feeling Asian Modernities: Transnational Consumption of Japanese TV Drama*. Hong Kong: University of Hong Kong Press.

Miller, Toby and Marie Claire Leger (2001) 'Runaway production, runaway consumption, runaway citizenship: the new international division of cultural labor', *Emergences* 11(1): 89–115.

Mori, Yoshitaka (ed.) (2004) *Nisshiki Kantyu* [Japanese style, Korean Wave]. Tokyo: Serika Shobo.

Morley, David and Kevin Robins (1995) *Spaces of Identities: Global Media, Electronic Landscapes and Cultural Boundaries*. London: Routledge.

Robertson, Roland (1995) 'Glocalization: time–space and homogeneity–heterogeneity', in M. Featherstone, S. Lash and R. Robertson (eds), *Global Modernities*. London: Sage, pp. 25–44.

Rouse, Roger (1995) 'Thinking through transnationalism: notes on the cultural politics of class relations in the contemporary United States', *Public Culture*, 7: 353–402.

Smith, Michael Peter (2001) *Transnational Urbanism: Locating Globalization*, Malden. MA: Blackwell.

Sugiura, Tsutomu (2003) *Hi wa mata noboru: Pokémon kokokuron* [On Pokémon Prospering the Nation], *Bungei Shunju*, October: 186–93.

Tobin, Joseph (ed.) (2004) *Pikachu's Global Adventure: The Rise and Fall of Pokémon*. Durham, NC: Duke University Press.

Tomlinson, John (1997) 'Cultural globalization and cultural imperialism', in A. Mohammadi (ed.), *International Communication and Globalization: A Critical Introduction*. London: Sage, pp. 170–90.

Yúdice, George (2003) *The Expedience of Culture: Uses of Culture in the Global Era*. Durham, NC: Duke University Press.

Chapter 5

Bollywood and the frictions of global mobility

Nitin Govil

Look at *Titanic* – it's a Hindi film. *Gladiator* is a Hindi film.
Woody Allen's *Everybody Says I Love You* is beautiful, just like a
Hindi film. James Bond always does well in India – that's a Hindi
film. Man, I want to be James Bond. Please make me the first
Indian James Bond

(Shah Rukh Khan, Bollywood superstar, quoted in Dalton, 2002)

Towards global convertibility

'Bollywood dancing,' Honey Kalaria explains in her 2003 home fitness video
Bollywood Workout, 'can transform you into quite a versatile dancer.' Promising the first program to employ 'ancient-modernized dancing techniques,'
Kalaria expresses a cheery conviction in Bollywood's capacity for dynamic
recombination. This juxtaposition of histories, places and vernacular forms
is one of the many reasons that Bollywood has functioned as a general principle of syncretism – or at least a 'byword for cool' – in the field of cultural
production (Aftab, 2002). Yet in the frenetic pace of contemporary global
information exchange, where the old economies of scale are outflanked by
the new 'economies of variety' (Moulier Boutang, 2000), Bollywood seems to
be dancing to a beat that is louder than ever.

As the founder of the first dance academy in Britain to offer classes in 'film-
inspired' modern Indian dance, Kalaria has a material stake in advertising
Bollywood's transformative powers. Her enthusiasm is also part of a broader
international interest in Bollywood that took off in the mid-1990s with the
release of Hindi films like *Dilwale Dulhaniya Le Jayenge* (1995), *Pardes* (1997),
Dil to Pagal Hai (1997), and *Kuch Kuch Hota Hai* (1998). Targeting South
Asian expatriate audiences with fantasies of middle-class mobility driven by
the loss and recovery of 'traditional Indian values,' the international success
of these films helped launch *Dil Se* to the box-office top ten in Britain in 1998
and *Taal* into the US top twenty a few years later. In 2000, six screens of a 30
screen multiplex built just outside Birmingham were dedicated to Hindi
films, part of a growing trend throughout the UK. For decades, Hindi

cinema had traveled to Britain, Fiji, Trinidad, Dubai, Tanzania, South Africa, Mauritius – in fact, any country home to a significant South Asian diaspora – across legal distribution networks, non- and quasi-legal, large-scale, pirate reproduction industries, and more mobile forms of tactical media exchange such as smuggled prints, dubbed videocassettes and multi-generation audiotapes. This interoperability of legal and non-legal distribution networks has long enabled the distribution of Hindi cinema among broader audiences in the Soviet Union, Nigeria, Malaysia, Afghanistan, Egypt, Singapore, Japan and the US. However, when Hindi film icon Amitabh Bachchan's Madame Tussaud's wax effigy was unveiled in 2000, the year after he had been voted 'Star of the Millennium' in a BBC News Online poll and the same year that the Film Federation of India announced that Indian film exports had topped $100 million for the first time (with Hindi films making up 95 per cent of the haul), it was taken as a sign that Bollywood had officially arrived as a global cultural force.

Bollywood fêted a celebration of its own at the first International Indian Film Awards ceremony in 2000 at London's Millennium Dome, with the show broadcast live to over 120 countries. The same year, Sony acquired overseas rights for *Mission Kashmir*, which became the first Hindi film to open in New York's Times Square after Sony had bought the overseas rights for 120 million rupees, covering 60 per cent of the film's production costs (Joseph, 2000: 44). It turns out that all this was just a preview of coming Bollywood attractions. The international success of *Kabhi Kushi Kabhi Gham* in 2001 was part of a public confirmation of Bollywood's 'ascent' to the mainstream Western media consciousness (Iordanova, 2002). Launched at the Venice Film Festival, *Lagaan* was nominated in the Best Non-English Language category for the 2002 Academy Awards in the United States; the same year Andrew Lloyd Webber premiered *Bombay Dreams* on stage.

Alongside these spectacular forms of global visibility, a more mundane but nonetheless crucial tribute came in the shape of Bollywood's inclusion in the hallowed lexicon of the English language. On 13 June 2001, the *Oxford English Dictionary* (OED) online edition listed an entry for 'Bollywood' for the first time. When the new OED illustrated print edition was published two years later, Bollywood joined 'Botox' and 'Viagra' as new terms of English language general circulation, with a list of 112 citations testifying to the proliferation of Bollywood as a shorthand for the 'Indian film industry, based in Bombay.' While it had served popular wisdom to suggest that Bollywood had been coined by a *Cineblitz* journalist in the 1980s, the *OED* claimed the origins of the term in H. R. F. Keating's 1976 novel, *Filmi, Filmi, Inspector Ghote*. In the novel, detective Ganesh Ghote investigates a murder on the Bombay set of *Khoon ka Gaddi* and muses:

> It must have been the title of the film they were making. But the Production Manager had spoken the words with such awe, as if they were

bound to be rich with meaning for whoever heard them, that he felt abruptly lost again. *Khoon ka Gaddi*. It meant *Cushion of Blood*. No, surely not. Ah yes, *gaddi* in the sense of a rajah's seat of honor. A throne. Yes, *Throne of Blood*, that sounded more likely.

(Keating, 1985: 14)

Even at the original scene of the crime, *Filmi Filmi* suggests a re-enactment: the novel that purportedly mentions Bollywood for the first time concerns a Hindi film production of *Macbeth* that references another cinematic trans-position of the Shakespeare play, Akira Kurosawa's 1957 film *Kumonosu-jô* ['Spider Web Castle'], released in the US as *Throne of Blood*. The *OED*'s refer-ence to Bollywood's 'origin' in Keating's novel therefore suggests a term implicated in a palimpsest of translations, copies and remakes. Bollywood's messy, originary mimeticism is borne out by Prasad's (2003) etymology of the term. In 1932, Wilford Deming, an American engineer who briefly worked with Ardeshir M. Irani on the production of the first Indian sound film, sent greetings to *American Cinematographer* magazine from 'Tollywood' – a reference to Tollygunge, the Calcutta suburb that housed a number of film studios. Thus, notes Prasad, 'it was Hollywood itself, in a manner of speak-ing, that, with the confidence that comes from global supremacy, renamed a concentration of production facilities' in its own image (Prasad, 2003: 17). From Tollywood, it was just a matter of time before the portmanteau 'Bolly-wood' struck the Hindi film industry centered in Bombay. Many critics, for example Virdi, have inveighed against the term, suggesting that Bollywood is 'weighed with misnomers about Hindi film as a mere Hollywood mimic' (Virdi, 2003: 21).

Bollywood's primary claim towards the multiple histories and directions of cultural flow, however, is contained within 'Bollywood' itself, a heteroglossic term that connotes a complex set of material and discursive links between Bombay and Hollywood. At the same time, in its equivocation to a global yet distinctively Indian – if not alternative – modernity, Bollywood is a *frictional* term that testifies to what Tsing calls the 'awkward, unequal, unstable, and creative qualities of interconnection across difference' (Tsing, 2005: 4). To follow Larkin's investigation of Hausa video re-significations of Hindi cinema iconography in Nigeria, Bollywood resonates globally precisely because of this 'interwoven process where Western media, Indian media, and local cultural production interact, at times coalescing and at other moments diverging' (Larkin, 2003: 178). Here Bollywood is aligned with the broader social impact of Indian popular cinema. Through the heterogeneous deploy-ment of folk forms, Indian cinema offered a way to indigenize global mass cul-ture through the matrix of the popular; at the same time, cinema repackaged the vernacular into mass cultural forms that allowed entry into the global modern (Nandy, 1998).

Yet it is a mistake to conflate Bollywood with Indian popular cinema, even though there are partial alignments. As Rajadhyaksha (2003) notes, Bollywood can be understood as a relatively new culture industry designed to integrate the packaging of big-budget Hindi films across an array of international promotional sites from shopping malls and multiplexes, TV game shows, fashion runways and dance extravaganzas, to soft-drink and fast-food advertising, sports marketing, music videos and cell phone ring tones. Bollywood is now part of an apparatus that facilitates the transnational mobility of Indian media more generally. In this chapter I would like to retain Rajadhyaksha's (2003: 30) idea of the *recent* emergence of Bollywood, not 'to drive a wedge' between Bollywood and the Hindi and other regional cinemas (the point that Bollywood tries but cannot speak for the diversity of Indian cinema is beyond question) but to understand how Bollywood cuts across flow and contra-flow in the globalization of the culture industries. Through a set of commodity logics that inscribe Indian popular cinema within a broader set of global medias, Bollywood articulates certain contemporary processes shaping transformation and interconnectivity in the field of cultural production. This chapter touches on four overlapping commodity logics: the formalization of informality; the portability of the national; the production of singularity; and the permanency of crisis. These four overlapping logics help explain how Bollywood practices – across texts, institutions, industries and spaces – intersect and diverge with the global networks of exchange in media culture today.

The formalization of informality

Beginning in the mid-1980s, a series of fiscal and political crisis forced the Indian government to reexamine, and in some cases overturn, the assumptions that had structured the national economy after Independence. The ensuing push towards 'market liberalization' in the late 1980s and 1990s was designed to 'reform' the infamously complex state regulatory apparatus, lift import and export restrictions, smooth the flow of commodity products for the Indian consumer, and bolster international confidence in India through the solicitation of non-resident Indian investment. Urged on by the powerful international lending agencies like the World Bank, India began to shift from postcolonial developmentalism towards market-oriented neoliberalism.

After Independence in 1947, the Indian state's commitment to rapid modernization focused on the nationalization of capitalist production in the communications areas of banking, transportation, postal, telecommunication and electronic systems (McDowell, 1997). Deprived of state infrastructural support granted to these 'legitimate' communication industries, cinema was not considered among these iconic projects of Indian developmental modernity. However, cinema did serve as the vehicle for social reformers and other groups that understood it more as 'a vice, like gambling and prostitution, that must be curbed through taxation and strict censorship' (Prasad, 1998: 126). This alignment between the regulation of screen consumption and the management of civic virtue underscored the proliferation of a quasi-national network of import/export councils, development corporations, and enquiry committees that cleared a space for the state to function as both 'patron and disciplinarian' for the Indian film industries beginning in the 1950s (Pendakur, 2003: 59). However, in the wake of 'economic liberalization' in the late 1980s and 1990s, the Indian film industry became more central to the re-imagination of the Indian state.

In 1998, the Indian government finally granted 'industry status' to its domestic film trade. Easing restrictions on foreign collaboration under the new regime, the Indian government encouraged the Indian film industry to look outward and recruit international capital via foreign media investment. Film and television industries were relieved of export-related income tax – an exemption which was extended to individuals and partnerships in the media trade in 2000. In early 1999, the Indian government allowed foreign equity of up to 100 per cent in film production and distribution, legislating automatic approval to foreign investment in film companies, provided that local partners contributed 25 per cent of the equity capital. Wholly owned subsidiaries of the foreign majors were given preference based on an established track record in the Indian market, consolidating the existing interrelationship of Indian producers and Hollywood distribution networks (Lall, 1999).

The state's 'official' interest in the capitalization of film production through the enabling of foreign investment seems incongruous given the usual practices of the Indian film sector. Since the collapse of the studio system in the 1950s, the Indian film industry has functioned as a speculative economy that subsists by articulating the interests of short-term entrepreneurial investors with longstanding patronage networks, using 'black' market and cash economies designed to avoid taxation regimes, and verbal contracts for above- and below-the-line labor. While Indian banks were trusted with creating new corporate funding for cinema production, for all the post-liberalization rhetoric of 'legitimate' institutional financing, the Industrial Development Bank of India sanctioned just over $13 million for film financing in 2001; this for a film industry with an annual turnover of over $800 million (Indo-Italian Chamber of Commerce and Industry, 2003).

As Naregal (2001: 39) notes, commercial Indian cinema has 'survived mainly through exploiting surplus merchant capital available through parallel money markets'. Furthermore, the Indian film industries depend on historical interrelationships between networks of informal/occasional labor and craft/trade unions that form intricate itineraries of work linked through custom, patronage, and transitory affiliation. How are these material informalities of the Indian film industry compatible with the new corporate language of organization, transparency, and accountability that has marked the entry of Indian cinema into international capital markets even as it has suffered spectacular failures domestically?

Contemporary Bollywood provides a language with which to think through the incongruity between informality and corporatization, and a site for a partial redress. This redress is partial because as the high-profile scandals of underworld influence on Bombay film production have destabilized the terrain of film financing, they have also popularized the gangster film and catapulted the figure of the cinematic don to a new level of popularity. In fact, the underworld don serves as a kind of mirror to the new cult of the Indian management guru, who prioritizes the acquisition of those knowledge forms designed to network Indian entrepreneurial cultures into the global mainstream. Like the underworld don and his 'Company,' the business school graduate and the management consultancy engender a certain reflexivity within capitalism (Thrift, 1998). This reflexivity is one price of entry into global capital markets, particularly as exchanges like the US Nasdaq require more stringent transparency from non-American firms than they do from domestic ones. At the same time, the rationalization of reflexive knowledge has assumed a growing priority within the industry to reform the Bollywood mode of production, 'which has essentially come to mean high cost and waste' (Pendakur, 2003: 34).

The porosity (Liang, 2005) of formal and informal practices is further illustrated by the features of Bombay film production, which, despite its high-profile support of copyright and anti-piracy reform, actually operates in a field where *illegality is not exterior to the proper domain of the film industry but constitutive of it.* In a moribund domestic exhibition space where the heterogeneous audiences of the single-screen theater are neglected in favor of the middle-class patrons of the multiplex, Bollywood's cultures of anticipation are still mobilized through pirated media, neighborhood cablewallahs and bootleg DVD parlors. In addition, through the everyday practice of scripting 'unauthorized' remakes not only of itself, but also of Hollywood, 'world,' and regional Indian films, Bollywood's improvisational mode of production assembles idioms, genres, and translations that dynamize a form vacillating between innovation and cliché (see Ganti, 2002). In order to support this rapacious capacity for re-signification, Bollywood engages the practical politics of cultural production in India, where 'nonlegality was never a performative or political stance, but a functional one' (Sundaram, 2002: 128).

While Rajadhyaksha (2003) is right to note that corporatization has not been fully implemented in the Indian film industry's drive for transparency and foreign investment, the impossibility of its realization of full legal compliance was acknowledged at the very conference that announced industry status for Indian cinema, where Amit Khanna, current chairman of Reliance Entertainment, noted that 'corporatization is an attitude' (Khanna, 1998). Here 'attitude' functions through a performance of deferral, locating Indian film corporatization within the 'not-yet' of capital, a rhetoric familiar to the well-worn narratives of underdevelopment (Chakrabarty, 2000). At the same time, the presence of deferral in the enunciation of corporatization means that Bollywood can speak the language of formalization – primarily through the forms of reflexivity enumerable to the global market – even as its practices engage histories of informal cultural production and the possibilities of quick response to changing media ecologies. In other words, even as it has moved towards corporatization, Bollywood operates only within the recognition of it as a kind of *limit*.

The portability of the national

On a visit to the US in 1964, Dilip Kumar remarked that Indian cinema could achieve greater international success by focusing on 'universal' themes while becoming 'more specifically Indian' (quoted in Canby, 1964). Here one of Hindi cinema's icons captures the contradiction of national cinema, where 'internalism is necessarily tempered by an awareness of exteriority as a shaping force' (Schlesinger, 2000: 24). Of course, the umbrella category 'Indian cinema' covers diverse local and regional practices that are far too heterogeneous in language, theme, and narrative to be collected under the sign of the national. However, Bollywood's enactment of India as a kind of 'multimedia spectacle' might give us some sense of the ways in which 'ethnic, regional and national identities are being reconstructed in relation to globalized processes of intercultural segmentation and hybridization' (García Canclini, 2001: 136; see also Govil, 2005).

'National cinema' first emerged as a concept within the field of cultural policy as Hollywood consolidated its European exports after the World War I decimation of local screen infrastructure (Thompson, 1996). Since this initial formulation, national cinema has been defined through two antinomies. First, national cinema refers to a set of representational practices produced under a centripetal logic of 'local' coherence – in terms of authorship, location, audience, narrative, genre and style – and a set of institutional practices through which the state exercises a mandate of preservation against the tide of the foreign – in terms of subsidies for film production, quotas, and other import restrictions. Second, national cinema refers to a set of relationships produced through a centrifugal logic that prioritizes dispersion over cohesion, whereby movements like Mexican national cinema and New German Cinema are validated as national expressions not because of their exclusivity but through their international circulation and relations with other industries (O'Regan, 1996). The longevity and global reach of national cinemas rests on their address of these centripetal and centrifugal dynamics.

The claim that all Third World texts are condemned to speak in the register of national allegory (Jameson, 1986) is supposed to have been relegated to an unfortunate stumble in an early engagement with postcolonial theory from the outside. Yet we are forced to re-confront the question of the national in the common mischaracterization of Bollywood as Indian national cinema. This misconception reveals a deeply entrenched majoritarianism at a time when the violent epistemology of cohesion in the national project has been so effectively coordinated by Indian right-wing movements like the Shiv Sena. Evoking national cinema in the Indian context creates a monstrous alignment between the cultural politics of nationalist primordialism and Bollywood's export-oriented narratives. Here the politics of authenticity are reproduced through the expatriate Indian's attempted reintegration into a culture s/he left behind to pursue material wealth in the West.

The conflation of the particularity of Bollywood and the generality of 'the' Indian film industry is ironic given that Bollywood's primary language (Hindi) is implicated in the colonial rationalization of Indian language diversity, the fomentation of divisions amongst stakeholders in Hindustani literary culture, and the dissemination of an elite Indian nationalism (see Orsini, 2002). Hindi's complex role in both colonial and counter-colonial governmentality demonstrates the complexity of its emergence as the Indian collective voice. This complexity is flattened out by Das Gupta's (1968) infamous vilification of the Hindi film industry as a producer of *All-India* films that presents to its 'family audience' the technologized spectacles of modernity only to resort to the comforts of traditional life, thereby generalizing the postcolonial everyday to the extent that it is emptied of meaning. As Mazumdar (2001) demonstrates, the location of the Hindi cinema industry in non-Hindi-speaking Bombay, its early adoption of Parsi theatrical culture, and its employment of film practitioners displaced by the India–Pakistan partition actually helped to preserve the cultural presence of Urdu even in the national climate of Hindi's gradual Sanskritization.

As sound technology was developed in the 1930s, Indian geo-linguistic diversity forced the early regional film industries 'to fashion products that could move among a series of markets through dubbing, multiple versions,' and the exchange of cultural labor (Vasudevan, 2000: 120). Bollywood's strength as a global cultural form is indebted to this history of the Indian film industries' obligation toward flexibility in addressing the politics of cultural difference. Nevertheless, the misconceived idea of Bollywood as Indian national cinema produces identity narratives that articulate both the *exclusive* condition of an everyday lived within a particular bounded realm and an *inclusive* category that can support the portability of national identity (Sassen, 1998). If, as Hardt and Negri put it (2000: 105), 'national particularity is a potent universality,' then the resolution of what appears to be a fundamental antinomy is realized in the project of modern Hindu nationalism. As Blom Hansen notes in his discussion of the globalization of *Hindutva* in the late twentieth century, the Hindu nationalist claim of an alternative universalism is no longer a critique of the West, but rather a strategy to invigorate and stabilize a modernizing national project through a disciplined and corporatist cultural nationalism that can earn India recognition and equality (with the West and other nations) through the assertion of difference.

(Blom Hansen, 1999: 231)

In this way, the fatal misrecognition of Bollywood as Indian national cinema recasts Dilip Kumar's fantasy of Hindi cinema's global relevance as the nightmare that lies just below the surface of a dream.

The production of singularity

Global cities function as command and control centers for the circulation and distribution of transnational economic, financial and technological flows. As sites for the concretization of the global economy, these cities internalize the inequalities associated with the classic modern duality of center and periphery (Sassen, 1994). Implicated in the space-based logics of acceleration, decentralization, and dispersion, these global cities are organized around the place-based logics of agglomeration, concentration, and accretion. The idea of Bombay as co-terminal with Bollywood helps dampen – not obliterate – the techtonic grindings of space and place in the globalization of the culture industries. 'Hollywood' attempts to do the same through the promotional industries designed to produce a fictional locus of American media production even as its labor economy is dispersed throughout the world (see Miller *et al.* 2005; Goldsmith and O'Regan, 2005). The globalization of the culture industries operates through the deployment of a singularity that produces the global and the local as mutually imbricated forms. Sometimes, as with Bollywood and Hollywood, these spaces can refer to real places; but the 'Bombay' referenced by Bollywood is experiencing a period of intense transition as it disappears from bureaucratic and cinematic representation.

The Bombay referenced by Bollywood is no longer recognized by the Indian bureaucracy. In November 1995, in a maneuver that looked like a purging of the city's colonial past through the Hindu right-wing's evocation of a powerful local nativism, the city's name was officially changed to 'Mumbai.' However, the politics of Hindu exception that motivated the name change actually inscribed Mumbai as a vernacular marker of an indigenous urban modernity in support of Indian distinction in the global commodity space (Blom Hansen, 2001). Mumbai is deployed through a provincialism designed to exorcise Bombay of its Western past – what Salman Rushdie famously derided as its 'culture of remakes' – in order to realize its 'original' Indian identity in the global present (Varma, 2004). The recent launch of *Time Out Mumbai* magazine, designed to showcase the 'the changing mindset of people wanting to live well' (Borod, 2004), attests to the speed with which Mumbai has been branded and packaged in Indian consumer culture. Of course, this packaging is more than cosmetic, as it has been accomplished through the violent practices of slum clearance and forcible eviction that engender forms of cleansing and disappearance in the global city. While 'Bombay' may have disappeared from the government rolls, the emergence of Mumbai evokes the recovery of a primordial Indian identity that is, like other traditions of the national, both activated by and protected from the global present.

Furthermore, the rich tradition of referencing the city in Hindi popular cinema is also undergoing rapid transformation. Bombay has always resonated in the popular imaginary as a study in contrasts: between wealth and poverty; the skyline and the slum. Yet as Hindi cinema was a site for the vernacularization of Bombay, Bollywood creates a space for its dispersal through the narratives of global consumer mobility. As Mazumdar (2006) argues, Hindi cinema invoked the city through the representation of the street, the city crowd and the footpath. In many of Bollywood's globally marketed films beginning in the 1990s, these classic representations of Bombay's everyday life at the street level have been anesthetized and supplanted by the symbolic spaces of commodity consumption like the shopping mall and the multiplex, as well as the modern interior designs of the upper-middle-class Indian home. These spaces represent the projection of India into the global commodity fantasy.

The globalization of Bollywood is clearly situated within a Bombay defined by these institutional and aesthetic 'strategies of disappearance' (Abbas, 1997). This alignment is defined by the preservation of a locality and its trans-literation into the global entertainment space. Following the economic 'liberalization' initiatives of the late 1980s, the new objective of Indian audiovisual policy has been, as Mukherjee (2003: 17) notes, 'to strike a balance between the preservation of the rich cultural heritage of the nation and increased efficiency and global competitiveness of that sector through privatization and foreign investment.' Bombay provides a nodal point for Bollywood's articulation of popular cinema to Indian transnationalism. What better place to represent Bollywood's global linkages than the reimagination of Bombay as real and imagined space?

The permanency of crisis

The cover of a recent issue of *Outlook* magazine is emblazoned with a dramatic statement of crisis: '132 Films, 124 Flops – This is Bollywood's WORST year ever.' Inside we read about the sorry state of affairs: director Karan Johar has sworn off making yet another 'crying, singing, dancing, happy movie.' In a year marked by the extravagance of *Devdas*, producers and critics openly indict a hit-driven industry run amok with bloated star salaries, marketing, and publicity budgets; distributors refuse advance bookings in favor of commissions; social scientists claim that 'Bollywood's mythmaking is collapsing'; there are calls for the rationalization of budgets, a greater degree of professionalization, and attention to scripting as process; 'everyone's in the panic room,' says writer/director Anurag Kashyap (Joshi, 2002).

As with most Bollywood narratives, there is something familiar about this story. At the 1998 conference that announced the formalization of the film industry, the president of the Federation of Indian Chambers of Commerce and Industry (FICCI) – an organization founded in 1927 to consolidate countercolonial calls for greater indigenous management, participation, and ownership in Indian industry – implored attending Ministry of Information and Broadcasting officials to recognize Bollywood's patriotism: 'whenever there has been a crisis . . . be it war with Pakistan, or in times of great national tragedy, we have seen that people from this sector have come forward and given all help to the nation' (Modi, 1998). What the FICCI president failed to mention – mere hours before the onset of India's nuclear tests at Pokhran – was that Bollywood not only responds to national crisis, but actually functions in *a state of permanent crisis*. The permanence of crisis is partly due to the fact that commercial Hindi cinema operates in an economy of risk management that is different from that of the other global culture industries. Contemporary Hollywood, for example, balances cost and predictability through a cybernetic system of budgetary rationalization enabled by market research and the feedback between audience preference and box-office returns. Faced with the severity of state discipline in the shape of entertainment and income tax, however, the Indian film industries have never invested in Hollywood-style administrative competency via auditing and other technologies of corporate enumeration. In fact, the Indian state creates a disincentive to the collection of institutional statistics or systematic data. This lack of systematic or verifiable data is a constituent feature of Bollywood's improvisational mode of production.

Crisis is therefore part of the melodrama of Bollywood as a culture industry – but like one of its classic heroes, Bollywood reemerges in the face of predation and dire odds. Even the crisis of 2002 has been supplanted by the success of new 'crossover' films that boosted the fortunes of the Indian box-office in 2005. The historiography of crisis is punctuated by a before-and-after tipping point that often takes the shape of single, 'industry-altering' films such as *Lagaan* or *Devdas*. While crisis is both the engine of Bollywood's innovation and the explanation for cliché, it also presents a way for Bollywood to extend its own boundaries. As Marx famously observed, crisis structures the global mobility of capital through a process of internalization: 'the tendency to create the world market is indirectly given in the concept of capital itself. Every limit appears as a barrier to overcome' (Marx, 1973: 408).

Posing Bollywood as a perennial problem in constant need of a solution systematizes a set of demands and proliferates a series of disparate connections: between the business and industrial community (give us more stable forms of investment!); the state and the film sector (recognize our industry as legitimate!); management and cultural labor (give us a more disciplined star and script system!); enforcement authorities and distributors (curtail media piracy!); and producers and foreign investors (come and help us!). In this way, the issues presented as critical in the industry create strategic opportunities for Bollywood to present itself in perennial threat of irrelevance at home in order to justify its growing relevance in the world. The speech genre of crisis is motivational, it inspires a proliferation of connections in the exhortation of transformation. Bollywood's crisis is what allows its biggest movie star to claim in our opening epigraph that so many Hollywood films are Hindi films too.

Bollywood, inside and out

In the mid-1970s, the Indian film industries repeatedly failed to meet annual export targets of $15 million, often falling as much as 50 per cent short. While some traditionally strong film-importing nations, like Singapore, Syria, Lebanon and Jordan had begun to view Indian cinema imports as a threat to the development of their own industries, blame for soft export figures was also cast on a complex regulatory apparatus, the length of Indian films, and a difficulty in translating 'local' forms into 'universal' themes that could travel well. Throughout the 1970s and the 1980s, the government attempted to rationalize the export of Indian cinema under a single regulatory agency, but individual Indian film exporters found a more piecemeal, country-by-country approach that could generate the greatest possible revenue (especially with video and television rights).

By the early 1990s, bolstered by export markets in the Middle East and other places hostile to US film distribution, Indian film exports were up to $20 million, but it was not until the turn of the century that the export market topped $100 million. While these numbers are clearly speculative, they nonetheless indicate a considerable exponential progression. Aamir Khan, the star and producer of *Lagaan*, a stirring tale of countercolonial agitation nominated for the foreign language Academy Award 45 years after another Oscar-nominated story of national integration (*Mother India*), gets at the heart of the rising fortunes of Indian film exports when he notes, 'I don't see the problem in addressing an international audience even from a business point of view' (personal interview, Bombay, 21 November 2002).

This business point-of-view is an amalgam of textual, spatial, industrial, and institutional strategies designed to maximize the potential of interconnectivity within the constitution of Bollywood and its drive for global relevance. Bollywood is serviced by a morphology that internalizes the movement between flow and counter-flow, while managing the universal and the particular in the projection of India into the global commodity space. The four commodity logics detailed in this chapter are not simply manifestations of Bollywood, but indicative of fundamental tensions at a time when the complexity and risk of cultures of circulation have elevated 'connectivity itself [as] the significant sociostructuring value' (LiPuma and Lee, 2004: 19). These tensions are part of the aftershocks of the displacement of the Keynesian state by the neoliberal market and the forms of transparency and account-ability that have emerged as a new ethic of corporate governance. Flow and counter-flow are critical to a Bollywood vernacular that is produced through complex strategies of appropriation, derivation, and difference. Yet in its engagement of informality, portability, singularity, and crisis, Bollywood's prioritization of linkage, transversality and assemblage pursues the flexibility that is 'both the product and condition of late capitalism' (Ong, 1999: 240).

This flexibility has its rewards, of course, but also its price. If Bollywood remains committed to achieving global relevance through the nostalgic pro-ject of recovering primordial national sentiment, then it will be drowned out by the plodding, martial strains of majoritarian triumphalism. On the other hand, if Bollywood can move along the frictional trajectories inscribed in its name, well, that's a beat more of us might dance to.

Acknowledgments

Many thanks to Denise McKenna, John McMurria, Ranjani Mazumdar, and Bhaskar Sarkar for their comments and suggestions. Also, thanks to the South Asia Center at the University of Pennsylvania for their support in pre-senting part of this material at the *Cinema South Asia* conference in early 2006.

References

Abbas, A. (1997) *Hong Kong: Culture and the Politics of Disappearance*. Minneapolis: University of Minnesota Press.

Aftab, K. (2002) 'Brown: the new black! Bollywood in Britain', *Critical Quarterly*, 44 (3): 88–98.

Blom Hansen, T. (1999) *The Saffron Wave: Democracy and Hindu Nationalism in Modern India*. New Delhi: Oxford University Press.

Blom Hansen, T. (2001) 'The proper name', *Violence in Urban India: Identity Politics, 'Mumbai', and the Postcolonial City*. New Delhi: Permanent Black, pp. 1–19.

Borod, L. (2004) 'A passage to India', *Folio*, 1 August: 8.

Canby, V. (1964) 'Indian film industry here; many vexations, lack of theatres; diffi-culties in breaking even', *Variety*, 21 October.

Chakrabarty, D. (2000) 'The two histories of capital', *Provincializing Europe: Post-colonial Thought and Historical Difference*. New Delhi: Oxford University Press, pp. 47–71.

Dalton, S. (2002) 'Meet the Khan-do guy', *The Scotsman*, 14 August, p. 5.

Das Gupta, C. (1968) 'The cultural bias of Indian cinema', in C. Das Gupta, *Talking About Films*. New Delhi: Orient Longman, pp. 3–18.

Ganti, T. (2002) '"And yet my heart is still Indian": the Bombay film industry and the H(Indianization) of Hollywood', in F. Ginsburg, L. Abu-Lughod and B. Larkin (eds), *Media Worlds: Anthropology on a New Terrain*. Berkeley: University of California Press, pp. 281–300.

García Canclini, N. (2001) *Consumers and Citizens: Globalization and Multicultural Conflicts*, trans. G. Yúdice. Minneapolis: University of Minnesota Press.

Goldsmith, B. and T. O'Regan (2005) 'Still at the center: studios and the United States', in B. Goldsmith and T. O'Regan, *The Film Studio: Film Production in the Global Economy*. Lanham, MD: Rowman & Littlefield, pp. 177–203.

Govil, N. (2005) 'Hollywood's effects, Bollywood FX', in Mike Gasher and Greg Elmer (eds), *Contracting Out Hollywood: Runaway Productions and Foreign Location Shooting*. Lanham, MD: Rowman & Littlefield, pp. 92–114.

Hardt, M. and A. Negri (2000) *Empire*. Cambridge, MA: Harvard University Press.

Indo-Italian Chamber of Commerce and Industry (2003) *Internationalisation of the Indian Film Industry*. Mumbai: IICCI/Bhalchandra Printing.

Iordanova, D. (2002) 'Bollywood calling: marketing in the global diaspora as exemplified by Bollywood cinema', trans. T. Jones, *Springerin*, 7(1).

Jameson, F. (1986) 'Third-World literature in the era of multinational capitalism', *Social Text*, 15: 65–88.

Joseph, M. (2000) 'Riverdale sonata', *Outlook*, 6 November: 42–51.

Joshi, N. (2002) 'Flop show: Bollywood's ship faces unfriendly trade winds at box office, prompting serious introspection', *Outlook*, 25 November: 48–56.

Keating, H. R. F. [1976] (1985) *Filmi Filmi, Inspector Ghote*. Chicago: Academy Chicago Publishers.

Khanna, A. (1998) 'Industry status for the film industry', remarks presented at the National Conference on 'Challenges before Indian Cinema'. Bombay, 10 May.

Lall, B. (1999) 'India opens up film to foreign firms', *Screen International*, 11 June.

Larkin, B. (2003) 'Itineraries of Indian cinema: African videos, Bollywood, and global media', in E. Shohat and R. Stam (eds), *Multiculturalism, Postcoloniality, and Transnational Media*. New Brunswick: Rutgers University Press, pp. 170–92.

Liang, L. (2005) 'Porous legalities and avenues of participation', in M. Narula, S. Sengupta, J. Bagchi and G. Lovink (eds), *Sarai Reader 05: Bare Acts*. Delhi: Sarai/CSDS, pp. 6–17.

LiPuma, E. and B. Lee (2004) *Financial Derivatives and the Globalization of Risk*. Durham, NC: Duke University Press.

McDowell, S. (1997) *Globalization, Liberalization and Policy Change*. London: Macmillan.

Marx, K. (1973) *Grundrisse: Foundations of the Critique of Political Economy*, trans. Martin Nicolaus. New York: Penguin.

Mazumdar, R. (2001) 'Figure of the "Tapori": language, gesture and cinematic city', *Economic and Political Weekly*, 29 December: 4872–80.

Mazumdar, R. (2006: forthcoming) *Urban Allegories: The City in Bombay Cinema*. Minneapolis: Minnesota University Press.

Miller, T., N. Govil, R. Maxwell, J. McMurria and T. Wang (2005) *Global Hollywood 2*. London: British Film Institute.

Modi, K. K. (1998) 'Introduction to Sushma Swaraj valedictory session', remarks presented at the National Conference on 'Challenges before Indian Cinema'. Bombay, 10 May.

Moulier Boutang, Y. (2000) 'A mutation of political economy as a whole,' *Mutations, Harvard Project on the City and Multiplicity*. Barcelona: ACTAR, pp. 70–83.

Mukherjee, A. (2003) *Audio-visual Policies and International Trade: the Case of India*. Hamburg: Hamburg Institute of International Economics.

Nandy, A. (1998) 'Indian popular cinema as a slum's eye view of politics', in A. Nandy (ed.), *The Secret Politics of Our Desires: Innocence, Culpability and Indian Popular Cinema*. New Delhi: Oxford University Press, pp. 1–18.

Naregal, V. (2001) 'The Mafia and the media get along: notes on contemporary media distribution and the public sphere in India', *Sagar: South Asia Research Journal*, 7: 37–48.

Ong, A. (1999) *Flexible Citizenship: The Cultural Logics of Transnationality*. Durham, NC: Duke University Press.

O'Regan, T. (1996) *Australian National Cinema*. New York: Routledge.

Orsini, F. (2002) *The Hindi Public Sphere, 1920–1940: Language and Literature in the Age of Nationalism*. New Delhi: Oxford University Press.

Pendakur, M. (2003) *Indian Popular Cinema: Industry, Ideology, and Consciousness*. Cresskill: Hampton Press.

Prasad, M. M. (1998) 'The State in/of cinema', in P. Chatterjee (ed.), *Wages of Freedom: Fifty Years of the Indian Nation-State*. New Delhi: Oxford University Press, pp. 123–46.

Prasad, M. M. (2003) 'This thing called Bollywood', *Seminar*, 525 (May): 17–20.

Rajadhyaksha, A. (2003) 'The "Bollywoodization" of the Indian cinema: cultural nationalism in a global era', *Inter-Asia Cultural Studies*, 4 (4): 25–39.

Sassen, S. (1994) *Cities in a World Economy*. New York: Pine Forge Press.

Sassen, S. (1998) 'The de facto transnationalizing of immigration policy', in C. Joppke (ed.), *Challenge to the Nation-State: Immigration in Western Europe and the United States*. Oxford: Oxford University Press, pp. 49–85.

Schlesinger, P. (2000) 'The sociological scope of "National Cinema"', in M. Hjort and S. MacKenzie (eds), *Cinema and Nation*. New York: Routledge, pp. 19–31.

Sundaram, R. (2002) 'About the Brazilianization of India', in Geert Lovink (ed.), *Uncanny Networks: Dialogues with the Virtual Intelligensia*. Cambridge, MA: MIT Press, pp. 122–31.

Thompson, K. (1996) 'Nation, national identity and the international cinema', *Film History*, 8 (3): 357–69.

Thrift, N. (1998) 'Virtual capitalism: the globalization of reflexive business knowledge', in J. G. Carrier and D. Miller (eds), *Virtualism: A New Political Economy*. New York: Berg, pp. 161–86.

Tsing, A. L. (2005) *Friction: An Ethnography of Global Connection*. Princeton: Princeton University Press.

Varma, R. (2004) 'Provincializing the global city', *Social Text*, 22 (4): 65–89.

Vasudevan, R. (2000) 'National pasts and futures: Indian cinema', *Screen*, 41 (1): 119–25.

Virdi, J. (2003) *The Cinematic Imagination: Indian Popular Films as Social History*. New Delhi: Permanent Black.

Chapter 6

Brazil and the globalization of telenovelas

Cacilda M. Rêgo and Antonio C. La Pastina

There is a difference between the fascination a telenovela exerts in Brazil and abroad. In Brazil it is more popular because it is an open work, because it is unfinished. It is alive, the audience knows that the story he [*sic*] is watching is unfinished and therefore it has a special charm for him. The viewer has even the impression that his reaction will in some way affect the plot. The characters start to come to life; to be real citizens involved in the daily life when a telenovela is successful. And the viewer includes them in his life and shares in the uncertainties of their fate because the novel is in the process of being written as it is being produced. The art form is completely open.

(Dias Gomes, 1990; telenovela scriptwriter)[1]

In the last few decades Brazilian and Mexican telenovelas, and to a lesser extent Venezuelan, Colombian and those produced in other Latin American countries, have been widely exported. Brazilian telenovelas have been aired – in dubbed and, sometimes, in edited versions – in more than 130 countries (Allen, 1995; Sinclair, 1996; Straubhaar, 1996). This international presence has challenged the traditional debate over cultural imperialism and the North–South flow of media products (Sinclair, 1996; 2003). Robert Evans has gone as far as to say that the export of telenovelas across the globe by Brazil can be viewed as an extension of cultural imperialism 'with Brazil surreptitiously spreading the United States culture to its audiences worldwide' (Evans, 2005).

Another way to look at the flow of the telenovela from Latin America is to consider its presence as a challenge to Hollywood's hegemony of cultural software exports. The Brazilian telenovela, for example, while adopting high production values and a star system not unlike the Hollywood standard, has strong local cultural roots. These serialized Brazilian melodramas discuss contemporary issues that cross national boundaries but also are firmly placed within the reality of a metropolis in the global South. In this chapter we will discuss the development of the telenovela genre and focus on the Brazilian telenovela, tracing its early history of borrowing and adapting from foreign sources to its insertion in the global market.

Primarily produced for the domestic market, Latin American telenovelas have been exported to Europe, Asia, Africa, the Middle East, and the United States since at least the late 1970s. Their worldwide success suggests that they are no longer a uniquely Latin American phenomenon, but a major global commercial force with extraordinary social and cultural importance. In this scenario, Brazil has cemented its place as one of the world's largest telenovela producers. Such recognition came in 2003 when TV Globo International was awarded two Latin ACE Awards for its telenovela *O Clone* [The Clone], the first ever to be sold abroad while it was still showing in Brazil. In the TV/ Dramatic Series category, Jayme Monjardim received the Latin ACE for Best Director, and Murilo Benício received the Best Actor award in the same telenovela. According to Helena Bernardi, director of marketing and sales for TV Globo International, *O Clone*, written by Glória Peres, 'is a continuation of Globo TV's tradition of excellence in telenovela programming, and the international success of this drama series shows that quality telenovelas possess a very strong appeal to viewers worldwide' (quoted in *Brazzil Magazine*, 2003). In 2004, TV Globo also received the Latin American award for the Best Telenovela Producer and Distributor worldwide (*Television Asia*, 2005). In the last 30 years TV Globo has produced more than 300 telenovelas, most of which sold in the international market in record numbers. *O Clone*, for example, was sold to more than 62 countries; *Laços de Família* [Family Ties] sold to 66 countries and *Terra Nostra* [Our Land] sold to 84. To this list one can also add past hits in the international market, such as *A Escrava Isaura* [The Slave Isaura], which was sold to 79 countries, and *Sinhá Moça* [Young Lady], which was shown in 62 countries (*TVMASNOVELAS*, 2005).

Globo's most important markets are Portugal, Russia, Romania, Hispanic United States, Chile, Peru, Uruguay, and Argentina. Although the key Asian markets, which include China, Indonesia, Malaysia, and the Philippines, have become increasingly important, they still represent a much smaller share of Globo's overseas sales, at only 0.5 per cent in 2003 (*Television Asia*, 2003; *Video Age*, 2005). Since the 1980s, Globo also has expanded its exports to the Middle East. In the past five years Globo has seen a growth of 70 per cent in program hours exported, totaling around 24,000 hours of programs every year. Such volumes of hours are due to the sale of telenovelas to over 50 countries, which account for 90 per cent of Globo's sales abroad. Movies and documentaries account for the remaining 10 per cent of sales in the international market (Mikevis, 2005). Understandably, Brazilian telenovelas – especially those produced by TV Globo – have maintained a near domination of the Portuguese market, which has served as a base for further expansion into the European market as well as the Portuguese-speaking African market, largely made up of former Portuguese colonies.

Despite its status as the fourth largest network in the world in terms of revenues and production capabilities, TV Globo is not the only influential telenovela producer in Brazil. The Sistema Brasileiro de Televisão (SBT), Brazil's second-largest television network, has consistently gained ground over its main competitor for the last two decades with telenovelas bought directly from Mexico's Televisa or with homemade remakes of telenovelas, especially from Argentina and Mexico. Like Globo, which has sold its highly polished telenovelas to more than 130 countries in the past 30 years, SBT – followed by other national telenovela producers such as Bandeirantes, Record, and Central Nacional de Televisão (CNT), which began telenovela co-production with Mexico's Televisa in 1996 – has aimed to expand its exports beyond the lusophone market (*Variety*, 1997; Filipelli, 2004).

According to Bernardi, a key factor in the success of Globo telenovelas in the international market is their high production values.

> Buyers have come to expect quality. A good story is always the beginning of a case of success, but buyers now know that audiences would not settle for only that. They demand that a good story is not only told in a good way, but it also must 'look good' on the screen. They define a 'good product' referring not only to the plot or story, but by production values, such as lighting, wardrobe, scenery, good-looking talent, etc. Globo is constantly investing in technology, infrastructure and creative talent; our products present the highest production value in their category, with great stories about universal themes.
> (Bernardi, quoted in Carugati and Alvarado, 2005)

Other Brazilian networks have also learned that high production values ensure a competitive edge at home and abroad. The broadcaster Record, for example, invested $10 million in state-of-the-art recording equipment to consolidate its position as one of the main telenovela producers in the country.

Aside from high quality, other factors have contributed to the success of the genre worldwide, as Bernardi notes:

> Our telenovelas travel around the world successfully because they talk about universal themes, the feelings of viewers, things such as love, emotion, contemporary conflicts and issues that affect women, families and society as a whole. Globo's telenovelas are successful because of their formula that brings social issues, sometimes long forgotten, sometimes issues that society, for one reason or another, has chosen not to face. A good example was the discussion of cloning in *El Clon*, a telenovela that also discussed cultural differences between Eastern and Western cultures and drug addiction. *Lazos de Familia* discussed leukemia and the lack of organ donors in the country, generating a nationwide campaign

to increase that number, a campaign that was replicated by Telemundo in the United States.

(Bernardi, quoted in Carugati and Alvarado, 2005)

Brazilian telenovelas have also experienced adaptations and changes to meet the tastes of international audiences. A rapidly rising trend, related to the expansion of the global telenovela market, is the sale of telenovela scripts by Brazilian writers to international broadcasters, who use their own actors, directors, and setting, with equal or greater success than imported telenovelas.

Telenovelas: locally produced, globally consumed

For the last 30 years telenovelas have dominated prime-time programming on Brazilian and most of Latin American television. Here Latin America refers to more than a geographic area. It entails a culturally constructed region that goes from the southern tip of South America to Canada and the United States, where the Hispanic community can watch daily telenovelas on several Spanish-language cable and satellite networks – namely, Telemundo, Gems Television (recently renamed MundoDos), TeleFutura, TV Azteca America, Univisión, and its affiliate channel, Galavisión.[2]

While telenovelas from Brazil and other Latin American countries cross national boundaries, and Latin American viewers pick and choose between Rio and Mexico City, glamor and down-to-earth ordinariness, fantasy and realism, it is becoming impossible to speak of the future of telenovelas except as part of the wider future of the new information and entertainment systems as they become globally interconnected. In the last decade, Latin America telenovela producers have confronted the advent of new technologies, the increasing neoliberalization of governments, and the opening of markets leading to greater competition from telenovela producers within and outside Latin America, such as Sony Pictures Television International (SPTI), Buena Vista International Television – a Walt Disney subsidiary – and Fremantle Media. Other strong competitors may soon be ABC, CBS, and Fox, three of the top English-language networks in the United States, which, after being outpaced by the Spanish-language networks in some major markets such as Miami and Los Angeles, announced in late 2005 their intention to create English-language versions of telenovelas in order to appeal to millions of younger second- and third-generation US Latinos/Latinas who speak English more frequently than Spanish (*New York Times*, 2006).

Some countries such as Germany, Romania, Portugal, Indonesia, Malaysia, China, and the Philippines, are also effectively venturing into local telenovela production, often in partnership with Latin American producers (Martinez, 2005; *Television Asia*, 2005). These local productions are now filling the prime-time slots that were once held by Latin American telenovelas (Jaspar, 2006).

The regional giants, Globo and Televisa, have had to deal with a more dynamic and diverse market in which their voices do not dominate the spectrum any longer, both within their own respective markets and in the broader regional market. According to Bernardi, 'the arrival of the majors [in the telenovela genre] makes it possible for new markets to open, markets where the telenovela genre is not that well accepted yet' (quoted in Carugati and Alvarado, 2005).

Of course, this can also work the other way around. Spurred by the success of Globo telenovelas abroad, especially in Eastern Europe, networks such as Romania's Acasa, which is entirely dedicated to telenovelas and other products from Latin America, have increasingly bought films produced by Globo solely on the strength of their cast, which include telenovela actors such as Giovanna Antonelli, Benício Murilo, Glória Pires, and Antonio Fagundes (de La Fuente, 2005). On the other hand, reality shows and game shows produced locally are considered the main competitors to Brazilian telenovelas in the international market, as they are generally low(er) budget productions. Even so, they are also thought to stimulate the habit of watching television and attracting potential viewers to those same telenovelas (*Television Asia*, 2005). As Bernardi says, what is important, in the final analysis, is that 'Globo's telenovelas are extremely ratings-oriented and are being perceived [by international broadcasters] as an important tool on the programming grid. In general, they occupy a strategic position in the afternoon, access and primetime grids' (quoted in Carugati and Alvarado, 2005).

While increasingly global, television remains primarily a national phenomenon and most television is still watched via national systems, despite the growth of transnational satellite systems. Further, unlike the situation observed in the early 1970s by Nordenstreng and Varis (1974), much of that television is also produced at the national level. However, most of this national programming is produced using regionalized or globalized genres or formats: Latin American telenovela is an example of the increasingly global commercial television reliance on soap opera. This contradiction echoes Robertson's (1995) idea that we are increasingly using globalized forms to produce the local, resulting in what he calls 'glocal' culture. TV Globo in Brazil and Televisa in Mexico are both far more powerful and important in their home markets than they were as partners in Sky Latin America, their Latin American regional broadcast joint venture with the very global Rupert Murdoch.

The genre and its roots

English-language soaps in the United States, Britain, and Australia have a well-established research tradition (Cantor and Pingree, 1983; Allen, 1985, 1995; Geraghty, 1991; Brown, 1994; Brunsdon, 2000; Hobson, 2003; Spence, 2005). In the last few decades, in different parts of the world, the production of serialized television fiction has spread and so has the academic interest in its format and its role in society. Egypt developed its own local production more than two decades ago, winning over local audiences, slowly increasing its penetration in the regional market and exporting to other nations in the region (Abu-Lughod, 1993, 1995; Diase, 1996). China (Wang and Singhal, 1992) and India (Singhal and Rogers, 1988, 1989a, 1989b) have been gradually increasing such productions for their national markets in the last decade.

Distinct from United States soap operas, Latin American telenovelas are broadcast daily, 'have very definitive endings that permit narrative closure' normally after 180 to 200 episodes depending on their popularity, and are designed to attract a wide viewing audience of men, women, and children (Lopez, 1991: 600). A teenage telenovela, *Malhação* (which can be roughly translated as 'Working out'), which began in 1995, is the longest-running telenovela in Brazil. Telenovela narratives are dominated by a leading couple of characters and rely on class conflict and the promotion of social mobility (Mazziotti, 1993). According to Aufderheide, 'Latin American television can be rich in wit, social relevance and national cultural style.' Brazilian *novelas* can tackle such issues as 'bureaucratic corruption, single motherhood and the environment; class differences are foregrounded in Mexican *novelas*; and Cuban *novelas* are bitingly topical as well as ideologically correct' (Aufderheide, 1993: 583).

Telenovelas and soap operas have common roots, but over time they have developed as clearly different genres. Within Latin American production centers, these distinctions have been emphasized, creating particularities in theme, narrative style, and production values. For Lopez (1995), the Mexican telenovelas are the weepies – ahistorical telenovelas with no context provided. Colombians are comical and ironic with a greater concern for context. Venezuelans are more emotional, but they do not have the 'barroqueness' of Mexican sets. Brazilians are the most realistic, with historically based narratives that have a clear temporal and spatial contextualization. Hernández (2001) distinguishes telenovelas as *blandas* (soft) or *duras* (hard), placing the Mexicans and Venezuelans in the first category and the Brazilian and Colombian in the second.

Recently, however, these divergences in style have been challenged by increasing competition within the two largest markets, Brazil and Mexico, from new networks such as TV Azteca in Mexico and SBT in Brazil. TV Azteca, located in the industrial north, close to the border with the United States, has produced politically charged telenovelas with a contemporary bend to their narratives, undermining Televisa. By contrast in Brazil, the more weepy melodramatic Mexican telenovelas aired by SBT and CNT are, as mentioned earlier, challenging Globo's dominance.

Apart from their differing styles, telenovelas are faithful to the melodramatic roots of the genre. Lopez argues that melodrama in Europe and the United States was discriminated against primarily due to its association with female audiences, while in Latin America, melodrama was devalued due to its class association that placed it in the realm of the popular. In this context of class identification, she explains how melodrama pertains to telenovelas:

> The telenovela exploits personalization – the individualization of the social world – as an epistemology. It ceaselessly offers the audience dramas of recognition by locating social and political issues in personal and familial terms and thus making sense of an increasingly complex world.
>
> (Lopez,1995: 258)

Furthermore, Mazziotti argues that

> [telenovelas] allow for the viewers an emotional participation in a set of fictitious powers that play with elemental human questions: honour, goodness, love, badness, treason, life, death, virtue and sin, that in certain ways has something to do with the viewer.
>
> (Mazziotti, 1993: 11)

Marketing soap in Brazil

Telenovelas have evolved in Latin America from the radio soap model developed in the United States by corporations such as Colgate-Palmolive, Proctor & Gamble, and Gessy-Lever. Seeing its success in reaching the female audience, the target consumer market for their products, these corporations invested in introducing the genre in Latin America, starting in Cuba and soon spreading to the rest of the continent. But it was in Havana in the 1930s that the Latin American version of the radionovela began its transition. In the next few decades, Cuba became the supplier of artists, technical personnel and, most importantly, the scripts for most of Latin America (Ortiz *et al.*, 1988).

The radionovela reached Brazil in 1941. The first to arrive was *A Predestinada* [The Predestined] on Radio São Paulo, after the artistic director of that station, Oduvaldo Viana, 'discovered' the genre while traveling in Argentina. This first radionovela, not surprisingly, was produced by Colgate-Palmolive. The success of the genre on Brazilian radio stations led to an increasing amount of time and resources devoted to radionovelas. The shows were produced and recorded in Rio de Janeiro and São Paulo and transmitted to the rest of Brazil. The leap from radio to television in Brazil took only a decade in the urban south, but in many rural areas the first TV set arrived in the late 1970s or 1980s.

Rede Tupi, the first TV station in the country, was inaugurated in São Paulo in 1950 and it aired the first telenovela, *Minha Vida Te Pertence* [My

Life Belongs to You], in 1951 twice a week live from its studios (Klagsbrunn and Resende, 1991). Throughout the 1950s, television stations in the country, primarily in São Paulo and Rio de Janeiro, broadcast short serialized programs live. They were mostly adaptations of foreign literary works and followed the melodramatic formula established by the Cuban radionovelas. It was only in 1963, due to the development of videotape technology, that telenovelas were recorded and broadcast daily (Klagsbrunn and Resende, 1991). Nevertheless, radionovelas and the early serialized TV shows had a fundamental role in establishing the genre in Brazil. Scriptwriters were trained in the melodramatic conventions, and once the technology arrived, they were ready to embrace the new medium. Telenovelas, however, did not evolve only from the radio matrix; other traditions in serialized fiction impacted the development of the genre. From the *feuilletons* in France to the locally produced serialized romances from the beginning of the century (Ortiz *et al.*, 1988; Meyer, 1996) to the *cordel* literature in Brazil, the genre evolved in each country within Latin America with certain peculiarities (Martín-Barbero, 1993).

Early serial telenovelas were part of a line-up that included ballet, opera, and theater designed to attract the elite audience that consumed TV in the 1950s. For most of its first decades in Brazil, television remained an elitist medium. Assis Chateaubriand created the first TV station in 1950, bringing 300 TV sets into the country to sell to the local elite that would allow for the creation of a small audience. By 1960 less than 5 per cent of Brazilian households owned a television. After the military takeover in 1964 and Globo's inauguration in 1965, the number of sets in Brazil was still small and mainly in urban and upper-income households. By 1970, with the broadcasting of the soccer World Cup, 24 per cent of the households had television. Many larger communities in the interior of the country already had public television sets on which viewers could watch images beamed from the urban south, mostly from Rio de Janeiro.[3] The Brazilian military regime saw in television a medium ready to promote national integration. The national telecommunications company, Embratel, created in 1965, had as its motto: 'Communication is integration,' reiterating the regime's objectives. But the tool to achieve those goals turned out to be TV Globo (Mattos, 1982).

Globo was inaugurated in 1965, spearheaded by media tycoon Roberto Marinho, owner of the daily *O Globo*, the largest circulation newspaper in Rio de Janeiro. Globo established a sophisticated technological infrastructure with the financial and technical support of the United States media group Time-Life. In 1969, pressured by the government, Globo bought Time-Life's share, becoming a totally Brazilian-owned company (Mattos, 1982). For four years the military regime that had taken over only a year before Globo network came into existence, had overlooked Globo's foreign backing, disregarding the country's constitution, which at the time forbade even partial foreign ownership of any media in Brazil.

At the same time that Globo was establishing itself, the competing networks were pressured by federal regulations. Excelsior, the then-leader in terms of audience share, had its license withdrawn by the military regime. Tupi held on until the end of the 1970s with steadily declining ratings. It closed in 1979 and its stations' licenses were divided between two media groups to create two networks: Manchete and SBT.[4] By the 1970s, Globo had established itself as the leading network in the country, attaining the highest audience ratings and benefiting from the largest segment of the advertising market, which at this point was heavily reliant on state-owned corporations (Ortiz et al., 1988). The main attractions at Globo remained the daily prime-time telenovelas and the evening newscast that came to be perceived as the official voice of the military regime (Lima, 1988; Mattos, 1982; Straubhaar, 1988).

Currently TV Globo's signal covers almost all the Brazilian territory (Amaral and Guimarães, 1994). In 30 years Globo became the main, if not the only, television voice available to all Brazilians. Several factors helped in this process. Embratel, following the military's goal of national unity, invested heavily in the development and expansion of the telecommunications infrastructure. Simultaneously, the production of TV sets in the country increased while consumer credit became available, leading to a boom in sales (Mattos, 1982). Finally, the government, through legislation and advertising support as well as favored use of the telecom infrastructure, allowed Globo to become a household presence in almost every corner of the nation. The Brazilian government also created the opportunities for Globo Network to become a vital player in the international media market and specially a leading voice in the lusophone market, filling the gap created by the end of the Portuguese colonial rule in Africa.

The 'Brazilianization' of the genre

Since the late 1960s and early 1970s the Brazilian telenovela has slowly evolved away from the general Latin American model. TV Globo, in particular, invested heavily in production values, increasing, for instance, the use of external shots that had been previously avoided due to production costs. The network also promoted a modernization of telenovela themes, including giving priority to texts produced by Brazilian writers. In this process, Globo created its own '*Padrão Globo de Qualidade*' or Global Pattern of Quality (Lopez, 1991).

Changes in style and format led Brazilian telenovelas to become more dynamic and closely associated with current events in the life of the nation (e.g. thematic inclusion of elections, strikes, and scandals that were happening in 'real' life). Events such as the killing of an actress by the actor who played her 'boyfriend' on the telenovela shocked the nation but also showed how reality and fiction blur in Brazilian life. Mattelart and Mattelart (1990) argue that Brazilian telenovelas are an 'open work' or an 'open genre'. During production, the telenovela's creators receive direct and indirect input from viewers and fans, theatrical productions, commercials, elite and popular press, institutional networks, audience and marketing research organizations, and other social forces in society, such as the Catholic church, the government, and civil society groups.

However, the genre was not so flexible in the early years of telenovelas. For several writers (Ortiz *et al.*, 1988; Mattelart and Mattelart, 1990; Mazziotti, 1993; Lopez, 1995), the landmark telenovela that started the redefinition of the genre in Brazil was *Beto Rockfeller* [Bob Rockfeller] aired by Rede Tupi in 1968–69. *Beto Rockfeller* escaped the traditional molds of the genre, presenting a telenovela in which artificial dramatic attitudes were abandoned and colloquial dialogue broke with the patterns of literary speech. But not only was the language different; the dramatic structure, narrative strategies, and production values were also modified.

Beto Rockfeller was the story of a middle-class young man who worked for a shoe store, but with charm and wit got himself mixed up with the upper class, passing himself off as a millionaire. To maintain his secret and status, he had to engage in many nefarious activities. The telenovela gained very high audience ratings, lasting for almost 13 months, much longer than the typical six to eight months (Fernandes, 1994). Globo, which up to that point had followed a traditional style of presenting telenovelas located in faraway places with exotic settings and plots, noticed the audience interest in *Beto Rockfeller* and took on this real style. In this process it reshaped the genre, distancing the Brazilian telenovela from the Latin American model.

However, according to officials from Mexico's Televisa, interviewed by *Variety*, Brazilian telenovelas did not truly reach the masses:

> Brazil's TV Globo produces esthetically better novelas but the content of Televisa's soaps is more understandable to the masses. Globo uses a lot of subplots and stories within stories, while our scripts are more direct and the themes more universal. Television is a mass communication medium. Cinema can be elitist but not television.
>
> (*Variety*, 1986: 105)

The gap between the telenovela styles of Globo and Televisa is crudely summarized in the quote above, but it stretches beyond diversity of plot lines. Globo has included in its telenovelas the reality of the country, thus grabbing the attention of the majority of Brazilian households by incorporating contemporary social and political issues. During the military regime (1964–85), television became a space in which, even when censored, writers managed to stretch the limits of what was acceptable in the repressive atmosphere of the period, possibly also benefiting from the prevailing view that telenovelas were designed for a female audience. Telenovelas did not break completely with their melodramatic roots but rather incorporated a national voice. They introduced a popular language, using colloquialisms and characters rooted in the daily life of the Brazilian metropolis, not unlike what cinema, theater, and popular music were trying to do. But this process, unlike those of other media, was limited by what was perceived to be the targeted audience's expectations.

In the first 40 years, more than 400 telenovelas were produced by Globo and other networks in Brazil. The telenovelas produced in this period predominantly centered on Rio de Janeiro and dealt with an urban middle-class lifestyle. Beginning in the late 1980s and continuing through the 1990s, as a result of the political *abertura* (opening) that started with the transition of the power from the military to the civilian government, telenovela writers increased the visibility of their social agendas and included national political debates in their narratives. The commercial nature of telenovelas also evolved, increasing the opportunities through which these programs are used to sell not only products targeting housewives, but sports cars, services, and any other consumer products. The melodramatic glue that has maintained their popularity with audiences has evolved and has been modernized. Nevertheless, these melodramas remained loyal to traditional topics such as romantic desire and conflict, social mobility, and the expected happy ending.

Global player

In 2005 alone, more than 30 Globo telenovelas were aired in 20 Latin American countries, totaling more than 10,000 programming hours. According to Bernardi, Globo intends to continue strengthening its presence in the Latin American market, and increasing its presence on TV channels throughout the world (Sofley, 2006). About 90 per cent of Globo's exports are telenovelas and mini-series, reaching a value of $30 to $32 million in 1998, while the remaining 10 per cent account for documentaries (Cajueiro, 1998).

As to the pricing of Globo telenovelas in the international market, Bernardi says that

> they change according to the realities of new territories, and their local economies. As with any programming options, prices are closely associated with the advertising investment in a particular client's station, which in turn influences that client's buying power. All this is subject to competitive pressures as well.
>
> (*Brazzil Magazine*, 2003)

TV Globo is interested in having a presence in the international market even if it has to make concessions in markets with less capacity to pay higher prices for its telenovelas. Moreover, according to Carlos Castro, director of sales for Televisa International,

Competition in Latin America is absolutely clear and transparent, as it is in the United States: forming alliances and agreements does not imply being disloyal. It is simply that commercial strategies have changed because times have changed, the audience changes and everything changes. The big players, Televisa, Venevision International, Coral, Tepuy and Globo, they all have a secure and deserved placed in the [telenovela] market.

(Carlos Castro, quoted in Herman, 2002)

To break into new markets, such producers and distributors as Televisa, Comarex, Globo, Coral International, Telefe, and Venevision, decided in 2003 to create an association called Asotelenovela (Large and Kenny, 2004). The idea behind Asotelenovela is to promote telenovelas in markets where the genre does not have a presence yet, such as in Japan, the key Asian target for the group. Other markets include countries in Western Europe, particularly Scandinavia.

Ulises Aristides, international sales director of Sistema Brasileiro de Televisão (SBT) argued that, as with many other companies, 'we [at SBT] weren't going to a number of markets because of the language.' SBT, operating since 1983, has began to search for overseas markets only in the last few years. 'We have very good quality material and markets such as Asia are almost virgin territories as far as knowledge of our products is concerned' (Conde, 2001).

The internationalization of Brazilian television, and Globo Network in particular, increased in the 1980s when the import of television programs into Brazil declined (Straubhaar, 1988; 1996) while Brazilian exports of programming increased. Recognizing this new trend, Globo set up an international division to support the export of its telenovelas. In the process of expanding internationally, in 1985 it bought 90 per cent of Telemontecarlo in Italy and, later, in 1992, purchased 15 per cent of Sociedade Independente de Comunicação (SIC), one of the newly created private channels in Portugal (Sousa, 1996). Since the mid-1990s Globo network has increased co-productions with foreign companies, at the same time focusing on successful domestic narratives that will have a greater appeal to foreign markets.

Another of Globo network's concerns is to increase its penetration among the upper classes in the domestic market, an audience traditionally resistant to telenovelas. In *Patria Minha* [My Homeland] Globo dealt with the increasing migration from Brazil, primarily to the United States, due to the persistent economic crises and consequent lack of opportunities for the well-educated upper classes. Since then other telenovelas have used central narratives located in foreign contexts such as Morocco, Japan, France, Argentina, Russia, the Czech Republic, and currently Greece, which are among the reliable consumer markets of Brazilian telenovelas.

In the 2005 hit, *America*, one of the main plots dealt with the increasing presence of illegal immigrants from Brazil in the United States. The US press covered the telenovela with interest, linking the increased apprehension of undocumented Brazilians attempting to cross the Mexico–United States border to the telenovela's popularity (Chu, 2005). Another 2005 telenovela, *Começar de Novo* [A New Beginning], partly funded by Petrobrás, the Brazilian oil company, centered on a Russian oil magnate who discovers he was originally from Brazil. This telenovela presents a positive image of the oil industry as well as a non-judgmental image of Russia and the former Soviet Union (Khalip, 2004). By introducing such cross-cultural themes, Globo is trying to extend its appeal in an increasingly competitive international market. It realized early in its attempts to secure access to foreign markets that it would have to repackage some of its telenovelas. In many instances, local content was too specific for an international audience, many product placement references had to be deleted and, in a few cases, some footage of Brazil was included to increase the visual appeal of the narrative (Filipelli, 2004).

In recent years, Globo and other telenovela producers in Brazil and other Latin American countries, such as Mexico, Argentina, and Colombia, have done more than just sell their telenovelas to other countries. They are also showing these countries, especially in Europe, how to develop their own telenovela industries. In fact, as pointed out by Melo (1995), Sousa (1996), and Matelski (1999), Brazilians are specially keen to sell their telenovela formats (including scripts previously shown in the country, with scene and costume descriptions likely to be molded to particular cultural contexts), and Brazilian telenovela writers are being contracted by other countries to write scripts for local productions, or even for those destined for the international market at large. One such example was the telenovela *Manuela*, written by Manuel Carlos, which was co-produced by an Italian-American company and successfully distributed in the international market (Melo, 1995: 9).

Traditionally, Brazilian telenovelas (except for those broadcast directly via satellite by TV Globo International) are dubbed into Spanish before they are aired in the United States and the rest of Spanish-speaking Latin America. *Vale Tudo* [Everything Goes], which was originally produced and broadcast in Brazil by TV Globo in 1988, was the first – and only, so far – Brazilian telenovela to be remade in Spanish (in a co-production with Telemundo) for the United States television market.

Between 2003 and 2005, the number of subscribers to TV Globo International jumped from 500 to 2 million. This is partly due to the fact that Globo started working with different time zones for different countries, motivating Brazilians who live abroad, especially in the United States and Europe, to sign up for the channel (*The Brazilians*, 2005: 15E). Many satellite packages also include other Brazilian channels, like Record, among the international selections. Although no subscription data are available, Brazilians living abroad also now have the ability to stream Brazilian programming from Globo Network online through a subscription service. This increased availability, coupled with the growing presence of Brazilians abroad and the strengthening of Globo's position in the international market as a reference point for telenovelas, has guaranteed a certain level of globalization for the Brazilian industry.

Nevertheless, as we hope this chapter has demonstrated, the history of Brazilian telenovelas is far from a clear case of an indigenous product becoming a global commodity. Rather, it can better be seen as the transformation and hybridization of a genre into a product that can appeal to a broad range of consumers both domestically and globally.

Notes

1 Dias Gomes, an already established playwright when telenovelas became popular, was influential in the development of the telenovela genre in Brazil. Quote from an interview with Dias Gomes conducted in 1990 by Klagsbrunn (Klagsbrunn and Resende, 1991, p. 23, authors' translation).
2 See Rodriguez (1999), for a discussion of the construction of a panamerican audience; Sinclair (1996), for an analysis of the Latin American cultural linguistic market; and La Pastina (1998) for the analysis of one specific case of a media product traveling within and between cultural linguistic markets.
3 For descriptions of communal viewing see Pace, 1993; Penacchioni, 1984.
4 Before closing its doors in the late 1990s, Manchete was owned by the Group Bloch, a family business that publishes magazines (specially *Manchete*) and owns radio stations. Silvio Santos who became a media tycoon due to the popularity of his day-long live Sunday variety show owns SBT.

References

Abu-Lughod, L. (1993) 'Finding a place for Islam: Egyptian television serials and national interest', *Public Culture*, 5 (3): 493–513.
Abu-Lughod, L. (1995) 'The objects of soap opera: Egyptian television and the cultural politics of modernity', in D. Miller (ed.), *Worlds Apart: Modernity through the Prism of the Local*. London: Routledge.
Allen, R. (1985) *Speaking of Soap Operas*. Chapel Hill: University of North Carolina Press.
Allen, R. (1995) *To Be Continued . . . Soap Operas around the World*. New York: Routledge.
Amaral, R. and C. Guimarães (1994) 'Media monopoly in Brazil', *Journal of Communication*, 44 (4): 26–38.
Aufderheide, P. (1993) 'Latin American grassroots video: beyond television', *Public Culture*, 5 (3): 579–92.
The Brazilians (August 2005): 15E (English edition).
Brazzil Magazine (2003) 'Let's hear it for Brazil's Globo'. May. Accessed on 3 February 2006: http://brazzil.com/2003/html/news/articles/may03/p105may03.htm.
Brown, M. E. (1994) *Soap Opera and Women's Talk: the Pleasure of Resistance*. Thousand Oaks, CA: Sage.
Brunsdon, C. (2000) *The Feminist, the Housewife and the Soap Opera*. Oxford: Oxford University Press.
Cajueiro, M. (1998) 'Globo gets global in new genres', *Variety*, 372 (7): M40.

Cantor, M. and S. Pingree (1983) *The Soap Opera*. Beverly Hills, CA: Sage.

Carugati, A. and M. T. Alvarado (2005) 'The business of love', *WorldScreen.com*. June. Accessed on 27 January 2006: http://www.worldscreen.com/featurescurrent.php?filename=0605novelas.htm.

Chu, H. (2005) 'Rising tide of Brazilians trying to enter United States', *Los Angeles Times*, 5 July.

Conde, P. (2001) 'The plot thickens', *Television Asia* (online). January. Accessed 27 January 2006: http://galenet.galegroup.com/servlet/BCRC?as1=telenovelas&ai2=KE&locID=ksstate.uka.

De La Fuente, A. M. (2005) 'Euro buyers lather up latino soaps', *Variety.Com* (online). 16 May. Accessed 7 January 2006: http://www.variety.com/article/VR1117922922?caterogyid=1443&cs=1.

Diase, M. (1996) 'Egyptian television serials, audiences, and the family house, a public health enter-educate serial'. Unpublished dissertation, University of Texas, Austin.

Evans, R. (2005) 'Research: TV Globo', *Media Matters* (online). Accessed 1 February 2006: http://journalism.cf.ac.uk/2005/MAJS/sjore/research1.html.

Fernandes, I. (1994) *Telenovela Brasileira: Memória*. São Paulo: Editora Brasiliense.

Filipelli, R. (2004) Responsible for Globo's exporting during the 1980s and 1990s. Personal interview.

Geraghty, C. (1991) *Women and Soap Opera: a Study of Prime Time Soaps*. Cambridge, MA: Basil Blackwell.

Herman, M. (2002) 'Telling tales', *Television Asia* (online). January–February. Accessed 27 January 2006: http://galenet.galegroup.com/servlet/BCRC?as1=telenovelas&ai2=KE&locID=ksstate.uka.

Hernández, O. (2001) 'A case of global love: telenovelas in transnational times'. PhD dissertation, University of Texas.

Hobson, D. (2003) *Soap Opera*. Malden, MA: Blackwell.

Jaspar, N. (2006) 'Falling in love . . . all over again', *WorldScreen.com* (online). Accessed 7 January: http://www.worldscreen.com/featurearchive.php?filename=0603novelas.txt.

Khalip, A. (2004) 'Petrobrás financia novela da globo' [Petrobrás finances Globo telenovela]. Accessed 11 April 2005: http://www.midiaindependente.org/pt/blue/2004/08/289184.shtml.

Klagsbrunn, M. and B. Resende (1991) *Quase catálogo: A telenovela no Rio de Janeiro 1950–1963*. Rio de Janeiro: UFRJ, Escola de Comunicação CIEC.

La Pastina, A. (1998) 'Crossing cultural barriers with children's television programming: the case of Xuxa', *Children's Literature Quarterly Journal*, 23 (3): 160–6.

Large K. and J. A. Kenny (2004) 'Latino soaps go global', *Television Business International* (online). Accessed 27 January 2006: http://galenet.galegroup.com/servlet/BCRC?as1=telenovelas&ai2=KE&locID=ksstate.uka.

Lima, V. A. (1988) 'The state, television, and political power in Brazil', *Critical Studies in Mass Communication*, 5: 108–28.

Lopez, A. M. (1991) 'The melodrama in Latin America: films, telenovelas, and the currency of a popular form', in M. Landy (ed.), *Imitations of Life: a Reader on Film and Television Melodrama*. Detroit: Wayne State University Press, pp. 596–606.

Lopez, A. M. (1995) 'Our welcomed guests: telenovelas in Latin America', in R. Allen (ed.), *To Be Continued . . . Soap Operas around the World*. New York: Routledge.

Martín-Barbero, J. (1993) *Communication, Culture and Hegemony: From the Media to the Mediations*, trans. E. Fox and R. White. Newbury Park, CA: Sage.

Martínez, I. (2005) 'Romancing the globe', *Foreign Policy* (online). November. Accessed 22 November 2005: http://yaleglobal.yale.edu/article.print?id=6442.

Matelski, M. J. (1999) *Soap Operas around the World: Cultural and Serial Realities*. Jefferson, NC: McFarland & Company.

Mattelart, M. and A. Mattelart (1990) *The Carnival of Images: Brazilian Television Fiction*. New York: Bergin & Garvey.

Mattos, S. (1982) *The Brazilian Military and Television*. Austin: The University of Texas Press.

Mazziotti, N. (1993) 'El estado de las investigaciones sobre telenovela lationoamericana', *Revista de ciencias de la informacion*, 8: 45–59.

Melo, J. M. (1995) 'Development of the audiovisual industry in Brazil from importer to exporter of television programming', *Canadian Journal of Communications*, 20 (3). Online Issue. Accessed 7 January 2000: http://infor.wlu.ca/-wwwpress/jrls/cjc/BackIssues/20.3/demelo.html.

Meyer, M. (1996) *Folhetim: Uma História*. São Paulo: Companhia das Letras.

Mikevis, D. (2005) 'Brazil's Globo: a soap opera global empire', *Brazzil Magazine* (online). Accessed 30 January 2006: http://www.brazzil.com/content/view/8919/76/.

New York Times (2006) 'Networks see telenovelas as maybe the next salsa', 5 January: C6.

Nordenstreng, K. and T. Varis (1974) 'Television Traffic – A One-Way Street?', *Reports and Papers on Mass Communication*, 70. Paris: UNESCO.

Ortiz, R., S. H. Simoes Borelli and J. M. Ortiz (1988) *Telenovela: História e Producão*. São Paulo: Brasiliense.

Pace, R. (1993) *The Struggle for Amazon Town, Gurupá Revisited*. Boulder, CO: Lynne Rienner Publishers.

Penacchioni, I. (1984) 'The reception of popular television in northeast Brazil', *Media, Culture & Society*, 6: 337–341.

Robertson, R. (1995) 'Glocalization: time-space and homogeneity-heterogeneity', in M. Featherstone, S. Lash and R. Robertson (eds), *Global Modernities*. Thousand Oaks, CA: Sage, pp. 25–44.

Rodriguez, A. (1999) *Making Latino News: Race, Language, Class*. Thousand Oaks, CA: Sage.

Sinclair, J. (1996) 'Mexico, Brazil, and the Latin world', in J. Sinclair, E. Jacka and S. Cunningham (eds), *New Patterns in Global Television: Peripheral Vision*. New York: Oxford University Press, pp. 33–66.

Sinclair, J. (2003) 'The Hollywood of Latin America. Miami as a regional center of television trade', *Television & New Media*, 4 (3): 211–29.

Singhal, A. and E. M. Rogers (1988) 'Television soap operas for development in India', *Gazette*, 41: 109–26.

Singhal, A. and E. M. Rogers (1989a) 'Educating through television', *Populi*, 16 (2): 38–47.

Singhal, A. and E. M. Rogers (1989b) 'Prosocial television for development in India', in R. Rice and C. Atkin (eds), *Public Communication Campaigns*. Newbury Park, CA: Sage.

Sofley, K. (2006) 'Globo brings new telenovelas to Natpe', *C21 Media.net* (online). Accessed 7 January 2006: http://www.c21media.net/news/detail.asp?area=1& article=28216).

Sousa, H. (1996) 'Portuguese television policy in the international context: an analysis of the links with the EU, Brazil and the US'. Accessed 7 January 2006: http:// ubista.ubi.pt/-comum/sousa-helena-portuguese-television-sydney.html.

Spence, L. (2005) *Watching Daytime Soap Operas: The Power of Pleasure*. Middleton, CT: Wesleyan University Press.

Straubhaar, J. (1988) 'The reflection of the Brazilian political opening in the telenovela 1974–1985', *Studies in Latin American Popular Culture*, 7: 59–76.

Straubhaar, J. (1996) 'The electronic media in Brazil', in R. Cole (ed.), *Communication in Latin America: Journalism, Mass Media and Society*. Wilmington, DE: Scholarly Resources Inc. Imprint.

Television Asia (2003) 'As the story goes'. Accessed 27 January 2006: http://www. tvasia.com.sg/new/mag/03.janfeb.teleoverview.html.

Television Asia (2005) 'Novela approaches: different novelas for different audiences'. Accessed 27 January 2006: http://galent.galegroup.com/servlet/BCRC?as1= telenovelas&ai2=KE&locID=ksstate.uka.

TVMASNOVELAS (2005) 'Globo shoots in exotic locations'. Accessed 30 January 2006: http://www.onlytelenovelas.com/Only.5/6.1.Telenovela.lat.hp.

Variety (1986) 'Telenovela is something else', 142, March 12.

Variety (1997) 'Sudsers scoring sales with Latino neighbors: Televisa S.A.'s multipart expansion strategy in Central and South America', 369, 8 December.

Video Age (2005) 'Telenovelas face mature market and new challenges', *Video age*, December, 25 (7). Accessed 27 January 2006: http://www.videoageinternational. com/2005/articles/Dec/telenovelas.htm.

Wang, K. and A. Singhal (1992) '"Ke Wang", a Chinese television soap opera with a message', *Gazette*, 49: 177–92.

Chapter 7

Challenger or lackey?

The politics of news on Al-Jazeera

Naomi Sakr

Conceptual versus geographical issues

Judged by appearances alone, few media outlets in the global South demonstrate contra-flow in action as effectively as the Al-Jazeera satellite channel. The headline 'Move over CNN: Al-Jazeera's view of the world takes on the West' (Cassara and Lengel, 2004) is fairly typical of countless examples portraying the Qatar-based 24-hour news channel as an influential challenger to a Western monopoly on international television news. If the significance of a particular source of contra-flow is measured in terms of this kind of brand awareness, then Al-Jazeera's high profile is not in question. The channel had been operating for just five years when it soared to international prominence in late 2001, after the US government responded to the 9/11 suicide attacks by bombing Afghanistan. As the only television station already in Afghanistan since 2000, Al-Jazeera had unique access to footage that was much in demand by Western media organisations. Thereafter, its coverage of events in Israeli-occupied Palestinian territory in 2002 and the US-led invasion of Iraq in 2003 elicited strong reactions, especially from interest groups in the US. Although it was still broadcasting only in Arabic at this time, these reactions were strong enough to turn Al-Jazeera into a global household name. An advertising industry website reported in January 2005 that a poll of nearly 2,000 advertising executives in 75 countries had identified Al-Jazeera as the world's fifth most recognised brand (Clark, 2005).

Al-Jazeera also fits media theory's concept of contra-flow as it applies to a reversal of old imperialist imbalances. By identifying the obstacles that developing country news organisations face in trying to establish a foothold in the world's core media markets, Boyd-Barrett and Thussu (1992: 138–9) highlighted the imperial powers' legacy of deep structural inequality in media as in other fields. If contra-flow occurs when countries once considered clients of media imperialism have successfully exported their output into the metropolis (Sinclair *et al.*, 1996: 23), then Al-Jazeera offers a textbook example of the empire 'striking back'. The peninsula of Qatar was part of the Ottoman empire from 1872 to 1914, coming under British tutelage through treaties signed with the local ruler in 1916 and 1934. Oil concessions made to Western companies under these arrangements determined the region's development from then on, since they obliged Gulf rulers to delineate their areas of influence in deserts that had previously been as open as the high seas, and served to strengthen the power of those rulers vis-à-vis other inhabitants (Said Zahlan, 1989: 17–20). Thus, instead of becoming part of a wider regional entity when British troops later withdrew from the Gulf, Qatar emerged in 1971 as a very small independent state. With a few notable exceptions, its early television programming was imported either from Egypt or the West (Graham, 1978: 295). Al-Jazeera was launched 25 years later, through the initiative and financial support of Qatar's third post-independence ruler.

For the contra-flow concept to have explanatory value in respect of a phenomenon like Al-Jazeera, it has to refer to changing power relations in the production and dissemination of media messages and not just superficial changes in the geography of media flows. Directional change alone can only tell part of the story; as Thussu points out (2000: 206–7), television flows from the periphery to the metropolitan centres of global media and communication industries may simply follow the pull of migration and the presence in these centres of migrants from the global South. Contra-flow as a category has more analytical purchase when it relates to programming from the South that is appreciated not only by migrants in the global North but by host communities too. Portuguese consumption of Brazilian soap operas shows that such appreciations occur (Nash, 1997).

Yet even then there may be a sense in which contra-flow potential remains unfulfilled if programming is inspired by imported models or is financed by regional hegemons, like India or Saudi Arabia, and thereby entrenches existing hierarchies. In other words, contra-flow in its full sense would seem to imply not just reversed or alternative media flows, but a flow that is also counter-hegemonic (Sakr, 2001: 149–53). Theories of hegemony suggest that counter-hegemonic media practices are liable either to be incorporated into dominant structures or marginalised in a way that neutralises the threat they pose to the status quo (Hall, 1977: 331–2).

Since Al-Jazeera qualifies instantly for contra-flow status purely on grounds of prominence and provenance, this chapter examines its performance against the stricter measure of whether or not it is counter-hegemonic. Counter-hegemonic contra-flow would, for example, reject unfair practices such as those reported in some US networks during the 2003 invasion of Iraq. The US group Fairness and Accuracy in Reporting (FAIR) monitored the nightly newscasts of ABC, CBS, NBC, CNN, Fox and PBS over a three-week period in March–April 2003 and found they were dominated by official voices that were also pro-war. Only 3 per cent of these newscasts' US sources were identifiably anti-war, whereas 27 per cent of the American population as a whole opposed the war at that time (Rendall and Broughel, 2003). Other studies have recorded self-censorship among respected US journalists in the name of patriotism (Jensen, 2005: 83) and examples of US reporting which, under a veneer of impartiality, helped to legitimise 'partisan political interests and goals' (Gasher, 2005: 210–11).

Assessments are mixed as to whether Al-Jazeera's own reporting has avoided or replicated practices like these. It is commonplace for the station to be credited with offering an alternative to dominant news agendas and news reporting available from the West, through its Arabic-language television channel and two websites, one in Arabic and the other in English. By late 2006 that alternative was also due to include an English-language television channel under the name Aljazeera International (*sic*). But the exact nature of the alternative it has offered has been hotly contested. Indeed, some strands of Arab opinion, far from agreeing that Al-Jazeera challenges the West, have accused it of serving a Western agenda in Arab states. The remainder of this chapter weighs evidence for and against three conflicting interpretations of Al-Jazeera's performance. Drawing on this evidence, it concludes by considering how far Al-Jazeera can qualify as a counter-hegemonic source of contra-flow.

Thesis One: challenging 'the West'

The notion of Al-Jazeera 'taking on the West' was so widespread less than a decade into its existence that the station's name had become almost synonymous with ambitious media innovation on behalf of the global South. When Telesur, a Latin American television network majority-owned by the Venezuelan government, started up in 2005 as a self-professed 'counter-hegemonic media project', its ambition to compete with CNN and other global giants instantly prompted comparison with Al-Jazeera (Hearn, 2005). As for African countries, forced onto world leaders' agenda by the Live 8 campaign of 2005, the UK's Foreign Policy Centre recommended creation of a pan-African broadcaster that could emulate the pan-Arab Al-Jazeera in enhancing transparency and improving links between home countries and the diaspora (Fiske de Gouveia, 2005). Similarly bold assessments of Al-Jazeera's significance were emblazoned on the covers of two books on the channel, one by Hugh Miles (2005) subtitled 'How Arab TV news challenged the world' and another by Mohammed El-Nawawy and Adel Iskandar (2002) with the subtitle: 'How the free Arab news network scooped the world and changed the Middle East'. For such assertions about a challenge to be justified, it needs to be demonstrated that Al-Jazeera consciously pursued a distinctive news agenda and that this agenda was knowingly obstructed in countries where globally dominant media are based.

Looking first at the news agenda, Al-Jazeera staff's occasional admissions of shortcomings in their performance are the corollary of the station's declared criteria for gathering and disseminating news. These have become more explicit over time. The original motto of 'Opinion and Counter-Opinion' was amplified some years later with explicit references to pluralism, professionalism, freedom of information and democracy. The English-language version of the organisation's Code of Ethics, formally adopted at an international media forum in Doha in July 2004, prioritised the 'journalistic values of honesty, courage, fairness, balance, independence and diversity'. It stressed accuracy, transparency, proactive avoidance of propaganda and the need for solidarity with journalistic colleagues who may be subjected to harassment or aggression. The Code's express purpose was to enable Al-Jazeera to fulfil a 'vision and mission' worded as follows:

> Al-Jazeera is an Arab media service with a global orientation. With its motto 'the opinion and the other opinion' it acts as a forum for plurality, seeking the truth while observing the principles of professionalism within an institutional framework.
>
> While endeavouring to promote public awareness of issues of local and global concern, Al-Jazeera aspires to be a bridge between peoples and cultures to support the right of the individual to acquire information and strengthen the values of tolerance, democracy and the respect of liberties and human rights.
>
> (Al-Jazeera, 2004)

The bridge metaphor in this mission statement points to a desire for two-way, not one-way, media flows. Jihad Ballout, head of Al-Jazeera's public relations until August 2005, confirmed this purpose when he said it was time for information to pass from East to West, on a communication bridge that had previously 'always been unidirectional – i.e. from West to East' (Miles, 2005: 417). The same metaphor also prescribes a mission of presenting the news from more than one side. Time and again after 2001, in the face of allegations that they were a mouthpiece for al-Qaeda terrorists, Al-Jazeera representatives insisted that any clip screened from tapes of Osama bin Laden or other advocates of violence against Western targets had always been followed by comments from US officials (Sakr, 2004: 158).

In late 2003, Washington bureau chief Hafez al-Mirazi repeated that Al-Jazeera had never broadcast a Bin Laden tape without first inviting an American official or commentator to the Washington studio to reply to the tape 'immediately' and 'point by point' (Lamloum, 2004: 50–1). Responding to criticism from political players, Al-Jazeera managers and editors cited the diverse sources of complaints as proof that they were successfully maintaining balance. They consistently justified the decision to show gruesome images of war victims by saying that viewers in countries involved in conflict have a right to know about casualties on all sides (Sakr, 2005: 151). According to Ahmad al-Sheikh, appointed editor-in-chief in 2004, a failure to report 'the ugly face of war' could imply that Al-Jazeera was shirking its duty to be honest (Reuters, 2004).

As preparations for launching Aljazeera International in English advanced in 2005, claims to a news agenda aimed at redressing global imbalances in the flow of information became much more frequent. Nigel Parsons, the new channel's managing director declared: 'We're the first news channel based in the Mideast to bring news back to the West' (AP, 2005). Parsons told a London audience that feedback from visitors to Al-Jazeera's English-language website, first launched in March 2003, had revealed 'mass disappointment' over dominant news organisations' 'dereliction of duty' in covering the Iraq war. People came to the English-language site, he said, because they were looking for 'the other side of the story' (Parsons, 2005). A channel hosted and financed by the state of Qatar had a particular advantage in presenting more than one side of any story, Parsons continued, because Qatar was far too small a country to project a domestic agenda onto the international scene. Thus, for Aljazeera International, every news item would effectively be a 'foreign story'. According to Parsons, the channel would not copy existing channels. It would make a unique contribution by offering more analysis of events behind the news and giving viewers more of a voice on air.

Parsons' declared objectives articulated practices already adopted by Al-Jazeera in Arabic. Giving the public a voice was the message behind an advertisement for the channel that started running in 2002, in which the slogan 'The right not to remain silent' accompanied a picture of a protest demonstration. During the Israeli siege of Palestinian towns and refugee camps in the spring of 2002, Al-Jazeera allocated an hour-long slot every day to Palestinian callers who wished to communicate their plight to the outside world. Significantly, it was one of Al-Jazeera's Palestinian correspondents, Walid al-Omary, who, after finally penetrating an Israeli blockade of Jenin, dispelled mounting fears that, amid the destruction of hundreds of Palestinian houses, hundreds of Palestinians had been killed (Miles, 2005: 191). When Palestinians then feared losing their daily slot on Al-Jazeera, the station responded with a new open discussion format, called *Minbar Al-Jazeera* (Al-Jazeera Pulpit), which it described as a 'platform for people without a platform'. From its inception, Al-Jazeera's live phone-in programmes provided audiences with a means to air their views.

Perhaps in response to criticism of the channel for ignoring Qatari affairs, the Qatari foreign minister took calls from viewers when he was interviewed live for 50-minutes on the weekly programme *Bila Hudud* [Without Limits] in June 2005.[1] Ahmad Mansour, the presenter, pressed the minister about a range of contentious issues, including Qatari relations with Israel. With the introduction of Al-Jazeera Live in April 2005, opportunities for public access to the airwaves were further increased. Jihad Ballout likened the project to C-Span in the US, which serves those who wish to influence public policy. He pictured Al-Jazeera Live as a means of bringing uncut parliamentary debates and press conferences into Arab homes.

Taken together, the ideals and aspirations of different elements in the Al-Jazeera network clearly aimed at an alternative approach to the ones shown earlier in this chapter to have been adopted by some US-based commercial media groups during and after the invasion of Iraq. However, mounting a challenge is one thing and making it effective is another. It became obvious during the 1990s that Al-Jazeera faced hindrance in a large number of Middle Eastern states.[2] But it took rather longer for the obstacles it faced in Western countries to become equally clear. In November 2005 the UK's *Daily Mirror* claimed to have seen a secret transcript of a conversation in which British Prime Minister Tony Blair, dissuaded US President George W. Bush from bombing Al-Jazeera's headquarters in Doha. As Wadah Khanfar, Al-Jazeera's director general, told an Italian news agency, the transcript, if true, would undermine claims that earlier US military attacks on Al-Jazeera offices in Kabul and Baghdad were accidental (AKI, 2005).

Basic news-gathering is fraught with difficulty for journalists, who risk physical attacks and imprisonment, not only by authoritarian Arab regimes but by supposedly democratic Western governments as well. When a US bomb destroyed Al-Jazeera's Kabul office in November 2001, the office was empty at the time. But when a US missile hit Al-Jazeera's Baghdad bureau on 9 April 2003, reporter Tariq Ayyoub was killed and a crew member, Zuhair al-Iraqi, was injured by shrapnel. The International Federation of Journalists (IFJ) estimates that a total of 75 journalists and media staff were killed in Iraq in the two years after the US-led invasion. So it cannot be said that Al-Jazeera was singled out when it lost a technician, Rashid Hamid Wali, during the filming of clashes between US troops and gunmen in May 2004. Yet few other news organisations had as many personnel imprisoned or interrogated by Western institutions in connection with events in Afghanistan and Iraq.

According to one estimate, 21 members of Al-Jazeera staff were arrested and released without charge in the weeks following the invasion of Iraq (O'Carroll, 2004). Of these, cameraman Salah Hassan, arrested in November 2003, said he was beaten, verbally abused and held in solitary confinement (O'Carroll, 2004; Miles, 2005: 321–2). A Sudanese assistant cameraman, Sami Mohieddin al-Haj, whom Al-Jazeera had sent to Afghanistan to cover the US-led bombing, was arrested in December 2001 and transferred to Guantanamo Bay, where he remained without any formal charges laid against him. Taysir Allouni, Al-Jazeera's Syrian-born correspondent in Spain, who interviewed Bin Laden while he was stationed in Afghanistan, was arrested in Granada in September 2003, charged with membership of a terrorist group and, after being bailed and rearrested, was sentenced in 2005 to seven years in jail. Suhaib al-Samarrai, an Iraqi cameraman working for Al-Jazeera, was detained by US forces in November 2004 and held for two months, including three weeks in the maximum security section at Abu Ghraib (AFP, 2004). Arthur Neslen, who worked for Al-Jazeera's English-language website in

2003–04, was detained by British special branch officers at Waterloo station after attending the European Social Forum in Paris. The officers questioned him about his employer and wanted him to provide information about other Al-Jazeera journalists and his work contacts (Neslen, 2004).

With suspicion of Al-Jazeera employees so widely reported, and few US or European media analysts able to understand the channel's Arabic-language content, Western publics were given the impression that this content was consistently partisan. Fouad Ajami, an Arab American, used a lengthy *New York Times* feature in November 2001 to accuse Al-Jazeera of 'Holly-woodiz[ing]' news, inflammatory coverage, and 'virulent anti-American bias' (Ajami, 2001). Much of Ajami's description dealt with talk shows rather than news. Yet charges of anti-Americanism against Al-Jazeera presenters, not just their guests, spurred US institutions to review their relations with Al-Jazeera. The New York Stock Exchange briefly banned the channel's reporters from its trading floor in 2003, even though they had been broadcasting daily from that vantage point for several years.

It also proved difficult for Al-Jazeera to get any of its journalists embedded with US or British troops during the invasion of Iraq. The US-led coalition would only embed reporters who had press accreditation with the authorities in Kuwait or Bahrain, which was denied to Al-Jazeera (Schleifer, 2003). Amr al-Kahky, the one reporter who was able to get accreditation because he had a Kuwaiti press card, was finally embedded just before the war began. But even then he was excluded from the morning briefing given by the commanding officer of the unit he was embedded with. According to Kahky, his complaint was countered first with the excuse that Al-Jazeera 'had a reputation' and then with a decision to replace the morning briefing with one-to-one interviews. 'It was very obvious to me', Kahky said later, that Coalition troops 'generally had a very biased attitude towards Al-Jazeera.' Other journalists did not share that attitude, he added. Colleagues in 'Reuters, BBC, AP Wire Service and others' were very supportive (ibid.).

Al-Jazeera's English-language website, which was due to be launched in March 2003, was kept out of action for six months by hackers. The original US hosting service, DataPipe, a brand name of Hoboken Web Services, said in March that it would cease hosting the site from the end of that month (Timms, 2003). The same electronic onslaught that crashed the English site hobbled the Arabic one too. Then US-based Akamai Technologies, brought in to help protect against hacking, cancelled its contract just as DataPipe had done, refusing to say why (Allan, 2004). John William Racine, who later admitted diverting traffic to a site called 'Let Freedom Ring', was sentenced to 1,000 hours of community service and a fine of $1,500 (BBC, 2003). Al-Jazeera staff remained convinced, however, that the extent of the hacking pointed to a well-resourced operation. In 2005, a civil defence group responsible for patrolling the border between Arizona and Mexico refused to let Al-Jazeera film a documentary in their area, saying it was 'the world's most prolific terrorism television network' (BBC, 2005).

Given this background and Al-Jazeera's loss of US advertising after 2001 (Sakr, 2004: 153–4), it was hardly surprising that Nigel Parsons, discussing plans for Aljazeera International in July 2005, predicted difficulties for the new channel in attracting advertising from US firms. There were also concerns about distribution, following a 2004 decision by the Canadian authorities to impose unprecedented restrictions on cable and satellite distribution of Al-Jazeera. By ordering distributors to monitor the channel for 24 hours a day and requiring them to alter or delete 'abusive comments', the Canadian Radio-Television and Telecommunications Commission effectively rendered distribution of Al-Jazeera in Canada uneconomic (Brown, 2005). Thus even some of the minority of Arabic-speakers in the West were to be denied access to the channel. It is true that Al-Jazeera found appreciative audiences in places like Malaysia, Indonesia and Pakistan, as well as moral support from international advocacy groups defending press freedom and journalists' rights.[3] Yet, in light of the obstacles it faced in North America, Europe and the Middle East, it would seem that headlines about Al-Jazeera 'taking on the world' put an unjustifiably positive spin on actual events.

Thesis Two: serving 'the West'

Strange as it may sound to Western ears, a portrayal of Al-Jazeera as challenging dominant Western media corporations is not universally accepted in the Arab world. As noted earlier, some Arab commentators have taken the view that, far from serving as a source of contra-flow, Al-Jazeera was created to reinforce a world order in which US and Israeli designs are imposed on the Arab region. According to this version, US hegemony is maintained through the preservation of corrupt and inert Arab dictatorships that depend on US military backing for their survival. Media liberalisation in these circumstances is seen as deception, giving a false impression that political reform is under way so as to distract attention from deep structures of political repression in individual Arab states.

Jordanian-born Salameh Nematt, who reported the Iraq war for *Al-Hayat-LBC* from Washington in March 2003, has put on record his total disagreement that Al-Jazeera acts as a bridge for communication between East and West. Asked to discuss the bridge analogy at a conference on Arab media in Berlin in 2004, Nematt said he had every respect for Al-Jazeera journalists but that Al-Jazeera as an institution was nothing more than a continuation of Nasser's radio propaganda machine, *Saut al-Arab* [Voice of the Arabs]. Just as *Saut al-Arab* was created to mobilise the masses but ended up giving them a false expectation of imminent victory in the 1967 Arab–Israeli war, so Al-Jazeera was focusing too heavily on pan-Arab causes and had inspired false hopes that Iraq could resist the US invasion. According to Nematt,

Al-Jazeera justified its lack of coverage of countries like Syria, Egypt and Saudi Arabia by saying that the governments of these countries placed too many obstacles in the way of its journalists. Instead, it concentrated on two sets of images: dead Palestinians and dead Iraqis. By doing this, he said, it sabotaged Israeli–Palestinian peace talks and the creation of a stable and united Iraq (Nematt, 2004).

Various manifestations of Nematt's argument that crop up in Arab political discourse incorporate the basic allegation that Al-Jazeera is a double bluff. That is to say, it provides an outlet for the expression of rampant anti-Americanism in a way that serves American interests because it prolongs Arab weakness and the regional status quo. For example, Israel is said to have benefited from heavy media exposure of Palestinian militancy and Arab hostility because this allegedly furnished a rationale for persistent Israeli crackdowns in the Occupied Territories and other measures attributed to security concerns.

The ruler of Qatar is meanwhile said to have enjoyed special US protection from the wrath of Saudi Arabia as a reward for pursuing diplomatic contacts with Israel.[4] Such Byzantine accounts of who benefits from Al-Jazeera, and how, carry weight with Arab intellectuals because of the striking ambivalence of US–Arab relations. The Bush Administration of 2001–04 purported to push for democratisation in Arab states while remaining deeply fearful of political Islam or any popular force that might destabilise unelected Arab governments and squeeze the supply of Arab oil. Complicated explanations for Al-Jazeera's existence, like those summarised here, are not to be confused with allegations often heard in Arab circles that Al-Jazeera is a Zionist channel because it gives airtime to Israelis, or is in the pay of the CIA because it interviews US officials. Rather, despite blatant internal contradictions, they contain an arcane logic that always comes back to entrenched US power over Arab affairs. Mohammed El Oifi, of the Institut d'Études Politiques in Paris, explains how some critics see Al-Jazeera as

> part of the global mediascape created by the American administration to contain the hostility of people in the Middle East against American hegemony and to legitimize the setting of American troops in the Gulf. . . . Advertising itself as a channel that presents the opinion and the other opinion, Al-Jazeera seems to be part of the American recipe for a media liberalism that is capable of producing political moderation.
>
> (El Oifi, 2005: 68)

It must be said, in defence of the 'American hegemony' argument, that the government of Qatar, which created and funds Al-Jazeera, is closely allied to that of the US. Washington led the way in recognising the government of Sheikh Hamad bin Khalifa Al Thani when he came to power through a palace coup in 1995. That recognition mattered greatly because the ousted emir, Sheikh Hamad's own father, was canvassing support for his reinstatement from other Gulf States. The US, meanwhile, had realised after the Iraqi invasion of Kuwait in 1990 that it should stop trying to balance Iran and Iraq against each other and put resources instead into preserving the independence of Gulf Arab oil producers against these two powerful neighbours (Indyk, 2004: 105–7). Qatar's 1992 defence pact with the US provided for prepositioning of US equipment. Its huge Al-Udaid air base was built up for US use, leading US Central Command to establish a forward headquarters in Qatar in 2002 (ibid.: 108). The 2003 US-led attack on Iraq was managed from a newer Qatari installation at Al-Sayliyah, the largest prepositioning base for US military equipment in the world (Bodi, 2005).

Later that year the US was confident enough about Al-Udaid and Al-Sayliyah to pull its troops out of Saudi Arabia and relocate them in Qatar. Against this background, it is not far-fetched to see the Al-Jazeera project as an attempt by Qatar's ruler to burnish his Arab nationalist credentials by financing a media outlet for denunciation of US policy in the Middle East. Shibley Telhami of the University of Maryland has reconciled close Qatar–US relations on one hand with US fury at Al-Jazeera on the other, by describing Al-Jazeera as a 'buffer' for the government of Qatar. It was helping them, he said, to withstand a lot of Arab anger arising from their role in the Iraq war (Telhami, 2004).

In discussing whether Al-Jazeera serves Western media hegemony, it should also be noted that it originated from a model developed by the British public service broadcaster, the BBC. Qatar's ruler, Sheikh Hamad, educated at Sandhurst military academy in the UK, watched the Arabic television news service that the BBC ran for the Saudi-owned pay-TV service Orbit, starting in 1994. Sheikh Hamad appreciated the fact that BBC journalists had interviewed him after he seized power in Qatar in 1995. When Orbit objected to BBC coverage of Saudi Arabia and the contract was ended in 1996, BBC-trained Arab journalists became available to help launch Al-Jazeera (Sakr, 2005: 148–9).

The potential for Western influence to be exerted through recruitment choices became much more obvious as appointments to the English-language Aljazeera International were announced during 2005. Nigel Parsons joined Aljazeera International as its managing director after spending 30 years working for organisations based in the UK, New Zealand and Italy, during which time he became a director of APTN. Parsons proceeded to build up a team that included former employees of the UK's ITN, BBC and left-wing weekly *Tribune*, and the Canadian Broadcasting Corporation. He brought in Steve Clarke who, besides directing news output at the Saudi-owned satellite channel MBC, had previously produced *Littlejohn*, the Sky News show presented by Richard Littlejohn, a columnist for Rupert Murdoch's tabloid daily the *Sun*. Riz Khan, senior anchor at CNN International and host of its show *Q&A*, was hired to present a similar style programme daily from

Washington. The veteran UK broadcaster, Sir David Frost, was snapped up after he retired from the BBC in May 2005.

A senior executive of Aljazeera International, privately acknowledging the large number of what he called 'white faces' in top positions, cautioned that many Europeans had grown bored and disillusioned in their former working environments and were eager for a more innovative news agenda.[5] Arab staff, in contrast, tended to judge appointments to the English-language channel in the context of management decisions already taken under US pressure. One such decision was the removal of Al-Jazeera's first managing director, Mohammed Jassem al-Ali, in May 2003. Ahmad Chalabi, leader of the US-backed Iraqi National Congress and a favourite of the Bush administration at that time, had accused Al-Jazeera under al-Ali of colluding with the government of Saddam Hussein (AFP, 2003). Later that year British journalist Yvonne Ridley was sacked from Al-Jazeera's English-language website, allegedly after protesting at the removal of two cartoons in response to US complaints (Bradley, 2003). Her departure followed Arab press reports that a committee representing the CIA, FBI, Pentagon and Congress had urged President George Bush to insist that the Qatari government should order Al-Jazeera to moderate its television output or be closed down.

Qatari compliance with US demands for the taming of Al-Jazeera surfaced openly in 2004. After meeting US Vice President Dick Cheney and Defense Secretary Donald Rumsfeld at the White House in April 2004, Qatar's foreign minister, Sheikh Hamad bin Jassim, said he would instruct Al-Jazeera to be more professional and avoid 'wrong information' (BBC, 2004). In May 2004, Al-Jazeera journalists underwent a training course paid for by the Media Outreach Center at the American Embassy in London and run by Search for Common Ground, a non-governmental organisation specialising in conflict transformation.

As part of the training, Al-Jazeera staff were encouraged to choose a new vocabulary when reporting suicide bombings, Palestinian casualties and hostilities in Iraq. It was after this that the channel adopted its Code of Ethics, sharing it with about 100 media professionals at an international conference in Doha in July 2004. One clause in the code pledged that Al-Jazeera would 'give full consideration to the feelings of victims of crime, war, persecution and disaster, their relatives, our viewers, and to individual privacies and public decorum' (Al-Jazeera, 2004). One of the channel's best-known presenters said this clause belonged to a 'code of the meek' (Qassem, 2004). After the July conference it emerged that the consultancy firm Ernst & Young had been retained to advise on selling the Al-Jazeera group to private buyers. It was unclear whether Qatar's ruler was using the prospect of privatisation to deflect further US pressure or whether the venture really would be exposed to the market censorship pressures that often accompany commercialisation.

Despite such obvious impact of US pressure, US officials themselves do not appear to have regarded Al-Jazeera as a conduit for US control over Arab affairs. On the contrary, a former media adviser to the Coalition Provisional Authority in Iraq alleged even after the changes that Al-Jazeera journalists were in 'cahoots with terrorists' and suggested that Qatar's funding of Al-Jazeera constituted 'state sponsorship of terrorism' (Smith, 2005). As for criticism of Al-Jazeera for focusing on pan-Arab issues at the expense of local ones, programmes to refute this are too numerous to list. Obvious examples include Al-Jazeera's December 2003 documentary on atrocities in Darfur, screened before the crisis there had captured the world's attention. They could also include the channel's extensive coverage of the US presidential election campaign in 2004, which staff at the Washington bureau described as an opportunity to educate Arab viewers about the practice of democracy. It was US Democrats who had doubts about such intentions, as shown by their refusal to let Al-Jazeera display its banner at their Convention.

Thesis Three: an Arab force in Arab politics

Had the US government regarded Al-Jazeera as a benign influence in Arab affairs, it would have had no call to launch the Arabic-language television station al-Hurra with state funding in early 2004. Al-Hurra's creation might even be cited as evidence of Al-Jazeera's success as a credible source of counter-hegemonic contra-flow. But here another set of questions must be asked as to whether Al-Jazeera, by self-consciously articulating a rationale for its own existence based on building bridges, moved from being a transparent media outlet to becoming a political actor in its own right. This was the path taken by, for example, Inter-Press Service (IPS), which succeeded in putting development concerns on the UN agenda but, in doing so, morphed from news agency to pressure group (Thussu, 2000: 252).

In classic models of representative democracy, the media are theorised as part of a triangular relationship that also includes government (or sometimes politicians generally) and the public (or electorate). In a democratic system, all three forces theoretically have the means to set the political agenda – through investigative journalism and inclusion of under-represented sources in the media's case. In practice, as Gaber has argued (1998: 409), at different times and in different societies, politicians have gained ascendancy over the media as agenda setters. Nevertheless, whoever is in the ascendant, this three-way model contrasts starkly with a non-democratic system, where the media are routinely subordinate to the control of ruling elites, and where elections are either non-existent or rigged. By contrasting the three-way model with what has traditionally been a one-way model in Arab political systems, it becomes possible to visualise Al-Jazeera as playing one of two roles. Either it has thrust its way between Arab rulers and the Arab public and helped to form the beginnings of a three-way political system by providing an unprecedented medium through which governance can be monitored and public opinion expressed. Or, conceivably, as a government-sponsored vehicle for alternative media content, the station has been a foreign policy plaything of Qatar's political leadership. If the latter, then Al-Jazeera could be said to have reinforced a long-standing, one-way model in which Arab political agendas are determined principally by ruling elites.

Those Arab media commentators who have described Al-Jazeera as 'the only political process' in the Middle East, have seemingly opted for the first of these two conflicting assessments. Muwaffaq Harb, director of al-Hurra, takes this line. He says that, where the mosque once served as a primary forum for information and views, Al-Jazeera has now 'hijacked' that role (quoted in Kinninmont, 2005). Similarly, Al-Jazeera's own M'hamed Krichen has quipped that the channel is 'the most popular political party in the Arab world' (quoted in Lamloum, 2004: 17). But Hazim Saghiye, a columnist for the daily *Al-Hayat*, sees the same situation in a negative light. For him, it is a cause for concern that Arab satellite channels have become the 'sole, or virtually sole, instrument for politicization' (Saghiye, 2004).

As for the alternative assessment, Al-Jazeera is often dismissed as an appendage of the state of Qatar. Supporters of this view say that the 'enlightened autocrats' who govern Qatar, a 'rich, small, weak country caught between three potentially deadly neighbours: Iran, Iraq and Saudi Arabia' (Boniface, 2004), rely on Al-Jazeera's global presence to enable their emirate to 'punch above its weight' in international affairs. Some Saudi princes delight in referring to Qatar's foreign minister as the 'foreign minister of Al-Jazeera' (*Al-Watan*, 2002). There are many disagreements between Qatar and Saudi Arabia that are exacerbated by friction over the content of Al-Jazeera broadcasts. Saudi officials are alleged to have supported a coup attempt by Qatar's ousted emir in 1996, while Saudi Arabia accuses Qatar of supporting Saudi dissidents in exile. In 2002, Riyadh responded to Al-Jazeera panelists' criticism of the Saudi ruling family by recalling the Saudi ambassador from Doha and placing an indefinite bar on entry to the kingdom for Al-Jazeera crews. Saudi Arabia then blocked construction of a gas pipeline and a causeway between Qatar and other Gulf States, ostensibly because of a border dispute.

In view of the detrimental effect of Saudi anger on both the Qatari economy and Al-Jazeera's news-gathering, two points emerge to weaken the argument that Al-Jazeera exists to help the Qatari government set its own political agenda. One is that the government of a small state next to a big one might be expected to play safe and put its commercial interests first. Instead, the leadership in Doha appears to have done the opposite, courting trouble rather than a quiet life. The second point is that any agenda-setting undertaken via Al-Jazeera is supposed to happen under the banner of 'Opinion and counter-opinion', which serves as a constant reminder that politicians are not the only agenda setters. Far from Al-Jazeera being created as fundamentally different from dominant Western media, the station's first managing director explained in 1998 that it intended to emulate news-gathering practices that were taken for granted in the West. In 'telling the truth', he said, Al-Jazeera was 'not doing anything different from what others do in Europe and the US. Maybe it's unusual in the Third World, but not elsewhere' (Al-Ali, 1998).

Conclusion

Unlike Telesur or IPS, the original Al-Jazeera channel in Arabic was not primarily conceived as a source of counter-hegemonic contra-flow. It was based on a widely accepted model of pluralistic reporting espoused by, among others, the BBC. However, because it broadcast in Arabic and had access to sources that were not available to Western media, Al-Jazeera had an image problem. As world politics evolved and opinions polarised, from 9/11 to the invasion of Iraq, certain groups came to regard Al-Jazeera itself as no less of a threat to their interests than some of the political players represented in Al-Jazeera news bulletins and panel debates. Being allied to the US, the Qatari ruling family was put on the defensive in a way that seems to have altered the nature of the Al-Jazeera project. Talk of Al-Jazeera building a communication 'bridge' came after its crews and their output had been subject to physical, legal and verbal attacks; so too did expansion of the network to include the high-profile English-language Aljazeera International, with its mandate to 'bring news back to the West'. From its initial purpose of delivering news in Arabic according to criteria of newsworthiness widely accepted in the West, Al-Jazeera's role was adjusted to include promoting certain values (Al-Jazeera, 2004) and reporting the 'other side of the story' from that covered by dominant news media (Parsons, 2005).

Changes in Al-Jazeera's purpose and self-image over time cannot be understood in isolation from world politics or the varied and often conflicting assessments of its performance that have been summarised in this chapter. Well before it launched into broadcasting in English, the station was routinely credited by Western observers with having 'taken on the West', even though broadcasters in languages other than Arabic could never have competed for the same Arabic-speaking audience. The station's supposed challenge to Western media was magnified in these reports at the very time when its staff were being harassed, imprisoned and even killed and its access to sources and audiences was being blocked. In the Arab world, meanwhile, smear campaigns portrayed the station as a lackey of US neo-imperialism or a plaything of Qatar's ruler, whereas its actual achievement was to create an unprecedented space for pan-Arab public discussion. To the extent that these depictions misrepresented reality, they suggest that Al-Jazeera's original Arabic-language operation did pose a threat to hegemonic interests and was predictably subject to processes of neutralisation and exclusion.

Notes

1 Sheikh Hamad bin Jasim bin Jaber Al Thani, Qatar's first deputy prime minister and foreign minister, was interviewed on *Bila Hudud* on 22 June. According to BBC International Reports (Middle East) on 24 June 2005, calls to the programme came from Qatar, Saudi Arabia and the UAE. One caller asked why the programme had been cut from its usual length of 90 minutes.
2 The list includes Algeria, Bahrain, Iraq, Iran, Jordan, Kuwait, Saudi Arabia, Sudan and Tunisia.
3 The IFJ, Committee to Protect Journalists and Reporters sans frontières are among organisations that have defended the rights of Al-Jazeera journalists.
4 For details on meetings between Qatari and Israeli officials, the opening of an Israeli trade office in Doha and talks about the supply of Qatari gas to Israel, see Da Lage (2005: 57–8).
5 Private communication to the author, London, 15 July 2005.

References

AFP (2003) 'Al-Jazeera TV chief sacked', *Middle East Times*, 30 May.
AFP (2004) 'US forces in Iraq release Al-Jazeera cameraman', *Middle East Times*, 30 January.
Ajami, Fouad (2001) 'What the Muslim world is watching', *New York Times*, 18 November.
AKI (2005) 'Al-Jazeera demands White House denial of alleged attack plans', AdnKronosInternational online at http://www.adnki.com. Accessed 26 November.
Al-Ali, Mohammed Jassem (1998) Author's telephone interview, 27 May.
Al-Jazeera (2004) *Al-Jazeera Code of Ethics*. Doha: Al-Jazeera.
Allan, Stuart (2004) 'Conflicting truths: online news and the war in Iraq', in Chris Paterson and Annabelle Sreberny (eds), *International News in the 21st Century*. Eastleigh: John Libbey, pp. 285–99.
Al-Watan (2002) 'Al-Jazeera's foreign minister', *Al-Watan* website: http://www.al-watan.com. Accessed 28 July.
AP (2005) 'Al-Jazeera prepares to launch English-language channel'. Online at http://ap.org/pages/indnews/index.html. Accessed 9 July.
BBC (2003) 'Al-Jazeera hacker pleads guilty'. Online at http://news.bbc.co.uk. Accessed 13 June.
BBC (2004) 'Qatar pledges Al-Jazeera review'. Online at http://newsvote.bbc.co.uk. Accessed 30 April.
BBC (2005) 'Al-Jazeera shelves US border film'. Online at http://newsvote.bbc.co.uk. Accessed 1 July.
Bodi, Faisal (2005) 'The price of a protection racket', *Guardian*, 22 March.
Boniface, Pascal (2004) 'Qatar: buying into a different future', *Le Monde diplomatique*, June: 14–15.
Boyd-Barrett, Oliver and Daya Kishan Thussu (1992) *Contra-flow in Global News: International and Regional News Exchanges Mechanisms*. London: John Libbey.
Bradley, John R. (2003) 'Fit to print?', *Al-Ahram Weekly*, 666, 27 November–3 December.

Brown, DeNeen L. (2005) 'In Canada, exceptions are the rule for Al-Jazeera', *Washington Post*. Online at http://washingtonpost.com/wp-dyn/articles/A14009–2004Jul25.html. Accessed 30 July.

Cassara, Catherine and Laura Lengel (2004) 'Move over CNN: Al-Jazeera's view of the world takes on the West', in Ralph Berenger (ed.), *Global Media Go To War*. Spokane, WA: Marquette Books, pp. 229–34.

Clark, Matthew (2005) 'Apple ousts Google as top brand'. Online at http://www.electricnews.net. Accessed 24 July.

Da Lage, Olivier (2005) 'The politics of Al-Jazeera or the diplomacy of Doha', in Mohamed Zayani (ed.), *The Al-Jazeera Phenomenon: Critical Perspectives on New Arab Media*. London: Pluto Press, pp. 49–65.

El-Nawawy, Mohammed and Adel Iskandar (2002) *Al-Jazeera: How the Free Arab News Network Scooped the World and Changed the Middle East*. Cambridge, MA: Westview/Perseus Books.

El Oifi, Mohammed (2005) 'Influence without power: Al-Jazeera and the Arab public sphere', in Mohamed Zayani (ed.), *The Al-Jazeera Phenomenon: Critical Perspectives on New Arab Media*. London: Pluto Press, pp. 66–79.

Fiske de Gouveia, Philip (2005) *An African Al-Jazeera?* London: Foreign Policy Centre.

Gaber, Ivor (1998) 'Parliamentary politics', in Adam Briggs and Paul Cobley (eds), *The Media: An Introduction*. Harlow: Longman, pp. 392–411.

Gasher, Mike (2005) 'Might makes right: news reportage as discursive weapon in the war on Iraq', in Lee Artz and Yahya Kamalipour (eds), *Bring 'Em On: Media and Politics in the Iraq War*. Lanham, MD: Rowman & Littlefield, pp. 209–24.

Graham, Helga (1978) *Arabian Time Machine*. London: Heinemann.

Hall, Stuart (1977) 'Culture, the media and the "ideological effect"', in James Curran, Michael Gurevitch and Janet Woollacott (eds), *Mass Communication and Society*. London: Arnold/Open University Press, pp. 315–48.

Hearn, Kelly (2005) 'El Jazeera'. Online at http://www.alternet.org/story/21988. Accessed 27 July.

Indyk, Martin (2004) 'US policy priorities in the Gulf: challenges and choices', in Emirates Center for Strategic Studies and Research (ed.), *International Interests in the Gulf Region*. Abu Dhabi: Emirates Center for Strategic Studies and Research, pp. 103–30.

Jensen, Robert (2005) 'The problem with patriotism: steps towards the redemption of American journalsm and democracy', in Lee Artz and Yahya Kamalipour (eds), *Bring 'Em On: Media and Politics in the Iraq War*. Lanham, MD: Rowman & Littlefield, pp. 67–83.

Kinninmont, Jane (2005) 'Qatar draws up plan to sell off Al-Jazeera', *Guardian*, 27 April.

Lamloum, Olfa (2004) *Al-Jazira, miroir rebelle et ambigu du monde arabe*. Paris: Editions la Découverte.

Miles, Hugh (2005) *Al-Jazeera: How Arab TV News Challenged the World*. London: Abacus.

Nash, Elizabeth (1997) 'Brazil's soaps wash away the mother tongue of Portugal', *Independent*, 7 May.

Nematt, Salameh (2004) Address to the conference on Neue Kommunikationsmedien in der arabischen Welt. Berlin: Haus der Kulturen der Welt, 26 June. Author's transcript.

Neslen, Arthur (2004) 'Reality television', *Guardian*, 21 April.

O'Carroll, Lisa (2004) 'US makes Al-Jazeera complaint'. Online at http://media.guardian.co.uk. Accessed 28 April.

Parsons, Nigel (2005) Address to the Regional Media Leaders' Forum of the Association for International Broadcasting. London, 15 July. Author's transcript.

Qassem, Faisal (2004) Remarks to the conference on Media and Political Change in the Arab World. Cambridge: Cambridge Arab Media Project, 30 September. Author's transcript.

Rendall, Steve and Tara Broughel (2003) 'Amplifying officials, squelching dissent', *Extra!*, 16 (3): 12–14.

Reuters (2004) 'Al-Jazeera adopts a new code of accuracy and good taste: http://www.nytimes.com/2004/07/14/international/middleeast/14jaze/html. Accessed 14 July.

Saghiye, Hazim (2004) 'The war of the Arab satellite TV stations' [in Arabic], *Al-Hayat*, 5 May. Translation in *Middle East Economic Survey*, 31 May 2004: C3.

Said Zahlan, Rosemarie (1989) *The Making of the Modern Gulf States*. London: Unwin Hyman.

Sakr, Naomi (2001) 'Contested blueprints for Egypt's satellite channels: regrouping the options by redefining the debate', *Gazette*, 63 (2/3): 149–67.

Sakr, Naomi (2004) 'Al-Jazeera satellite channel: global newscasting in Arabic', in Chris Paterson and Annabelle Sreberny (eds), *International News in the 21st Century*. Eastleigh: John Libbey, pp. 147–68.

Sakr, Naomi (2005) 'The changing dynamics of Arab journalism', in Hugo de Burgh (ed.), *Making Journalists*. London: Routledge, pp. 142–56.

Schleifer, Abdullah (2003) 'Interview with Ibrahim Helal and Amr al-Kahky', *Transnational Broadcasting Studies*, 11 (Fall/Winter). Online at http://tbsjournal.com.

Sinclair, John, Elizabeth Jacka and Stuart Cunningham (1996) 'Peripheral vision', in John Sinclair, Elizabeth Jacka and Stuart Cunningham (eds), *New Patterns in Global Television: Peripheral Vision*. Oxford: Oxford University Press, pp. 1–32.

Smith, Dorrance (2005) 'The enemy on our airwaves', *Wall Street Journal*, 25 April.

Telhami, Shibley (2004) Remarks on US National Public Radio programme *Talk of the Nation*. Accessed 4 May: http://www.npr.org/features/feature.php?wfld=1870703.

Thussu, Daya Kishan (2000) *International Communication: Continuity and Change*. London: Arnold.

Timms, Dominic (2003) 'Al-Jazeera websites "hit by hackers"': http://media.guardian.co.uk. Accessed 26 March.

Part III

Regional perspectives on flow and contra-flow

Chapter 8

The rising East Asian 'Wave'
Korean media go global

Youna Kim

Since the late 1990s South Korea (hereafter Korea) has emerged as a new centre for the production of transnational popular culture, exporting its own media products into Asian countries including Japan, China, Taiwan, Hong Kong and Singapore. While its popularity is mainly concentrated in neighbouring Asian markets, some of the products reach as far as the United States, Mexico, Egypt and Iraq.

This is the first instance of a major global export of Korean popular culture in history. Its impact has reached into communist North Korea: in 2005, a 20-year-old North Korean soldier defected across the demilitarized zone and the reason given, according to South Korean military officials, was that the soldier had grown to admire and yearn for South Korea after watching its TV dramas which had been smuggled across the border of China (*New York Times*, 2005).

The spread of Korean popular culture overseas is referred to as the 'Korean Wave' or '*Hallyu*' – a term first coined by Chinese news media in the middle of 1998 to describe Chinese youth's sudden craze for Korean cultural products. Initiated by the export of TV dramas, it now includes a range of cultural products, including Korean pop music (K-pop), films, online games, animation, mobile phones, fashion, cosmetics, food and lifestyles. This growing interest in the Korean popular culture, especially TV dramas, has further triggered a drastic increase in foreign tourists visiting the locations where their favourite dramas were filmed.

In the past, national images of Korea were negatively associated with the demilitarized zone, division and political disturbances, but now such images are gradually giving way to the vitality of trendy entertainers and cutting-edge technology (*New York Times*, 2005; *Chicago Tribune*, 2005). The success of Korean popular culture overseas is drawing an unfamiliar spotlight on a culture once colonized or overshadowed for centuries by powerful countries. The Asian region has long been under the influence of Western and Japanese cultural products, and the sudden popularity of the Korean Wave culture has presented a 'surprise' and triggered a question and a possible answer: why has it taken off so dramatically at this point? 'The popularity of Korean stars is establishing Korean ethnic features as a standard of beauty across the region. Some sociologists see a subtext in the craze: a rebellion by Asian people against the images of Caucasian good looks that dominate much of the international media' (*Wall Street Journal*, 2005).

While not denying the obvious power of Western, particularly American, dominance over the international media landscape, the purpose of this chapter is to draw attention to the rise of a new player in regional media flows – Korean popular culture – and to provide an overview of its scope and impact across Asia and beyond. With a particular focus on the transnational mobility of Korean TV drama, the chapter will explore its significance at socio-cultural and political levels. It will, first, present a current overview of Korean media export; second, explain the political context of its development, especially globalization of Korean culture industry; third, survey the trans-national circulation and consumption of Korean TV drama; and finally, address its meanings and significance in various locations.

This chapter will suggest that the transnational mobility of Korean popular culture is a facet of decentralizing multiplicity of global media flows today. It will also suggest that the Korean Wave phenomenon can be seen as a way to counter the threat of the Western-dominated media market. The postcolonial periphery is fast becoming a major centre for the production of transnational culture, not just a sinkhole for its transnational consumption (Watson, 1997).

Korean media export

Korea has recently experienced breathtaking export growth in its media production. The export of cultural contents stood at $800 million in 2004 (Korean Overseas Information Service, 2005); the amount was so insignificant before 1998 that the government could not provide figures. From 2000 to 2002, Korean cultural content export hovered at around $500 million, but began to pick up in 2003, when they rose to $610 million. Three cultural products, particularly – TV dramas, films and recorded music – showed brisk export growth. The size of the Korean culture industry, which began attracting considerable government investment only in the late 1990s, jumped from $8.5 billion in 1999 to $43.5 billion in 2003 (Korean Ministry of Culture and Tourism, 2004). Approximately $166 million of government investment was allocated to the culture industry in 2004. Korea's popular culture is now providing significant underpinning for the expansion of inter-national markets, generating $1.87 billion in value added for the country's economy from TV programme exports, films, merchandise sales and tourism revenue. The total economic effect of the Korean Wave phenomenon boosted Korea's GDP by 0.2 per cent as of 2004 (*Korea Times*, 2005c).

The one-way flow of American TV programmes has significantly decreased in recent years: Korea has reduced foreign cultural products since the mid-1990s while increasing its production and exports of domestic media products. The total amount of TV programme exports increased more than five-fold between 1995 ($5.5 million) and 2002 ($28.8 million). In contrast, imported TV programmes decreased by 70 per cent between 1996 ($69.3 million) and 2001 ($20.4 million). In 2002, exports of TV programmes exceeded imports of TV programmes for the first time (Korean Ministry of Culture and Tourism, 2004). By 2004, the exports of Korean TV programmes had reached $71.5 million, more than twice the level of imported foreign TV programmes which stood at $31 million (*Korea Times*, 2005b). Significant causes for the decrease in TV programme imports include the 1997 Asian financial crisis, the growth in the number of domestic programme producers, and an increase in the role of independent producers (Jin, 2004). Imports by cable TV companies have decreased dramatically since the 1997 Asian financial crisis. In 1998, terrestrial television channels reduced broadcasting airtime by two hours while reducing foreign programme imports. The total units of imported TV programmes in 2001 were 4,581, about one-third of those in 1995 (Korean Ministry of Culture and Tourism, 2004).

Exports of Korean TV programmes are maintaining an average increase of 40 per cent every year, with the drama genre constituting nearly 92 per cent of total exports in 2004. The three nationwide TV networks – MBC, KBS and SBS – lead overseas sales for their dramas. China has rapidly emerged as the largest cultural market in Asia. In 1997 China accounted for a nearly 6 per cent of Korean TV programming sales, but in 2001 it made up the largest share touching 25 per cent, followed by Taiwan (just over 20 per cent). Korean dramas comprised over a quarter of all foreign dramas and movies shown on the Chinese television screens in 2003 and 2004 (*Television Asia*, April 2005). Since 2004, the leading importers of Korean TV dramas have shifted: Taiwan (nearly 25 per cent), Japan (19 per cent), China (nearly 19 per cent), Hong Kong (more than 3 per cent) and Southeast Asian countries (Korean Ministry of Culture and Tourism, 2004).

In 1999, at the early stage of the Korean Wave phenomenon, the average price of a Korean TV drama was $750 per one-hour episode in overseas market: the range in 2005 was $15,000 to $20,000, more than a twenty-fold increase (*Korea Times*, 2005b). In 2000, Taiwan's Gala TV (GTV) paid $1,000 for one hour of a Korean TV drama, compared with $15,000 to $20,000 for a Japanese one: by 2005, a Korean TV drama commands $7,000 to $15,000, and a Japanese $6,000 to $12,000 (*New York Times*, 2005). In the Asian markets, Korean TV dramas are even more expensive than those of Hollywood and Japanese production, although the average production cost is only about one-sixth that of Japan (*Korea Herald*, 2005b). Korean dramas have now become so popular that each one-hour episode can even cost overseas TV stations $40,000, the amount SBS commands for its 24-episode drama *All In*.

The popularity of TV dramas has also boosted tourism in Korea. In 2004, an estimated 3 million Asian tourists visited Korea, and two-thirds of the Asian visitors were influenced by Korean TV dramas (Korean National Tourism Organization, 2005). As picturesque romance dramas like *Winter Sonata* and *Autumn in the Heart* have dominated TV screens across Asia, the snow slope and the beach where the memorable scenes were filmed have become popular tourist destinations. In past decades, Korean TV stations and drama producers were often accused of putting too much focus on dramas at the expense of other programming, but now they are honoured for bringing home foreign currency (*Korea Times*, 2004b).

The growing popularity of Korean dramas, music and movies was the main factor for the first annual increase in foreign tourists in six years. The economic effect of the Korean Wave on the tourism industry amounted to $825 million in 2004 (Korean National Tourism Organization, 2005). To capitalize on the *Hallyu* phenomenon, a $2 billion entertainment centre called Hallyuwood will be built in Korea by 2008 to attract foreign tourists and house a variety of media centres dedicated to the production of movies, music, TV shows and animation. 'Hallyuwood will ultimately create an East Asian culture that will hold its own against a Western culture that is championed by Hollywood' (*China Daily*, 2005a).

The growing export of Korean media has also improved the national image and led to heightened market awareness of general Korean products. Overseas sales of Korean consumer goods, including televisions, mobile phones, cars, clothing and cosmetics, have risen sharply in recent years from the strategic appropriation of popular culture. For instance, in communist Vietnam, where Korean dramas are among the highest-rated shows, a Korean electronics company has provided the latest Korean TV dramas to local broadcasting stations free of charge, even covering the cost of dubbing. A Korean cosmetics company has become a market leader in Vietnam with the largest share, as more and more Vietnamese youth have become influenced by trendy images of Korean TV dramas. Korean products are reaping benefits from the enhanced Korean brand value springing from the success of this cultural export. In the widest possible sense, the Korean culture industry 'commodifies the country', exporting its culture as a national brand (*Asia Media*, 2006). The export of Korean media has seen influence at cultural, economic and political levels.

Context: globalization of Korean culture industry

The Korean culture industry was developed for economic and political reasons in the late 1990s. Since the 1997 Asian financial crisis, the Korean government has targeted the export of popular culture as a new economic initiative, one of the major sources of foreign revenue vital for the country's economic advancement (*Financial Times*, 2001). Korea, with limited natural resources, sought to reduce its dependence on a manufacturing base under competitive threat from China. Trade experts have called for the nation to shift its key development strategy to fostering overseas marketing for culture, technology and services – including TV programmes, online games, movies and distribution services. The government has striven to capitalize on Korean popular culture and given the same national support in export promotion that was once provided to electronics and cars.

To a large extent, the global circulation and popularity of Korean popular culture is the consequence of Korean national policy. Korea may be the first nation to consciously recognize and, more importantly, form official policy and take action towards becoming a dream society of icons and aesthetic experience (Dator and Seo, 2004). The culture industry has taken centre-stage in Korea, with an increased recognition that the export of media and cultural products not only boosts the economy but also promotes the nation's image. The government has actively supported the spread of Korean popular culture to increase the 'nation's brand power' (KBS World Radio, 2006). The immediate profits or effects created by the Korean Wave phenomenon are important but the improvement of the national image, though intangible, is considered as more important. The Korean Wave started from the efforts of private sectors but the government has played a key role in the speed of growth. A systematic political infrastructure set by the government and institutional strategies developed by the industry have combined to produce the preconditions for the rise of the Korean Wave.

The rise of Korean popular culture was also facilitated by the opening of the Korean market to global cultural forces. Such opening had long been accompanied by the fear of Western cultural invasion, 'a kind of cultural totalitarianism' (Tomlinson, 1997: 130), and the fear was amplified by the uncertainty of the competitiveness of Korean popular culture. In addition, Japanese popular culture was equally feared and banned in Korea due to colonial history. Only in 1998, more than 50 years after Japanese colonial rule ended, did the Korean government begin to lift a ban on cultural imports from Japan. At the same time, in 1998, the government carried out its first five-year plan to build up the domestic culture industry and encourage exports. By the time nearly all restrictions on Japanese culture had been lifted (January 2004), the Korean Wave had spread across Asia. It is worth noting that the sense of crisis coming from the opening of the market to the West and Japan has rather strengthened and benefited the Korean culture industry. The threat of a foreign cultural invasion was dispelled 'not by protecting but by opening up' the domestic market (Iwabuchi, 2002: 87). The Korean culture industry has been developed as a national project competing within globalization, not against it.

The recent policy discussion in Korea continues to utilize culture as a resource for promoting economic and political interests in the era of globalization. Culture, as a transnational commodity and capital, is taken to be the very platform which could usher in an era of $30,000 per-capita income. To think of new ways to promote Korean popular culture, the government activated an advisory committee composed of key cultural experts, joined by the Ministry of Culture and Tourism and the Ministry of Finance and Economy (*Korea Times*, 2005a). Focusing on the so-called three Cs – Content, Creativity and Culture – the government has encouraged colleges to open culture industry departments, providing equipment and scholarships. The number of such departments rose from almost zero to more than 300 by 2004. The Ministry of Culture and Tourism has created various sections fostering media and culture, from the aspects of policy and technology to the development of cultural contents, exportation and promotion.

For instance, each year the Korean government sponsors a concert in Los Angeles, flying in major Korean music (K-pop) artists. The event draws up to 20,000 concert-goers, reportedly making it the largest Asian music event in the US (*San Jose Mercury News*, 2005). In 2004, the government organized a 'Korea Promotion' free tour for journalists from Asian countries, inviting them to tourist attractions, entertainment industries and interviews with the celebrities who had been creating the *Hallyu*. In 2005, the Ministry of Culture and Tourism launched the tourist-friendly, multilingual website called 'Hello! Hallyu' (www.hellohallyu.com) listing information on Korean popular TV dramas, movies, filming locations and celebrities – in Korean, English, Chinese and Japanese.

The Korean Wave was a laboured coincidence and amalgamation of strategic export at a time when the globalized consumer culture instigated a demand in the localities for the exports (Leung, 2004). The Asian media market is rapidly growing, fuelled by the rising affluence of the middle class. The global entertainment and media market is estimated to be about $1.1 trillion: Asia accounts for about 20 per cent, with an estimated market of $215 billion (*Asia TV Forum*, 2002). To meet the rising demand, Asia is producing more local media content. Increasingly, rich Asians look for new sources of entertainment, or alternative cultures, not necessarily American or European. While Japanese popular culture, for example TV drama, may appear 'too Westernized' for consumers of Southeast Asia, Korean cultural products are perceived to have the right amount of modernity and Asian traditions to meet their tastes (*Korea Now*, 2001). The emergence of the affluent urban middle class in Asia has provided a catalyst for the transnational circulation and consumption of Korean popular culture.

Transnational mobility of Korean TV drama

Japan

Nowhere is the popularity for Korean TV drama stronger than in Japan. The Korean Wave reached its peak in Japan when the Korean romance drama, *Winter Sonata*, became a national phenomenon in 2004. It was first broadcast by NHK in 2003 and has been screened four times due to popular demand. Almost 40 per cent of the entire Japanese population has seen the drama at least once (*Korea Herald*, 2005b). Most of the Korean romance dramas are broadcast late at night in a time slot that used to be the preserve of American imports. *Winter Sonata* proved so popular that its lead actor was nicknamed by the Japanese as '*Yon-sama*' (a deferential word reserved for royalty). A survey by Japanese newspaper *Asahi* revealed that '*Yon-sama*' was ranked as the most popular word of the year in Japan. The Japanese prime minister even said, 'Yon-sama is more popular than me'. Thousands of middle-aged women turned up at Tokyo's airport to see Yon-sama's visit: 'Now I can die happy' said a 48-year-old Japanese woman (*Asia Cable*, 2005). This explosive popularity of the Korean drama has baffled the Japanese media, entertainment commentators and social analysts.

Winter Sonata, a 20-episode romance drama produced by KBS, has been exported to 16 countries (*Korea Herald*, 2005b). This tragic love story has captured hearts everywhere, perhaps most intensely in Japan. The drama features beautiful winter scenery and pure love between a young woman and her boyfriend suffering from amnesia. The hero is not only handsome, intelligent and successful, but sensitive, caring and understanding towards women. The appeal of the hero is that 'he always says the exact thing that women want men to say' (*Japan Times*, 2004), which is not surprising since the script was written by two women. To Western eyes, this kind of Korean drama seems 'old-fashioned' and the hero of *Winter Sonata* 'might be written off as a wimp in a Western drama' (*Financial Times*, 2004). Contrary to Western popular culture, particularly American drama, with its strong emphasis on sex appeal, the Korean drama depicts 'love in its purest form without any nude or lustful contents to mitigate the essence of true love' (*Asia Cable*, 2005).

The hero's unconditional love for a woman – faithful and devoted to one lover, sensitive and understanding of woman's emotional needs – captivated many women in Japan. Fans of *Winter Sonata* in Japan are particularly women in their thirties to fiftiess, and the depth of their adulation for the hero is striking: 'If there was ever such a man in Japan, then I wouldn't be suffering like this' (*Japan Times*, 2004).

Some Japanese women have even registered with matchmaking agencies to get a Korean husband and many have visited the places featured in *Winter Sonata*. About 2 million Japanese travel to Korea every year. 'Watching the drama, I just wished I could understand what he was saying in Korean' (a female fan, quoted in *Yomiuri Shimbun*, 2004). The drama has prompted an interest in learning Korean, and the number of private language schools that teach Korean has mushroomed in Japan. 'It was kind of like an awakening. I started to learn about South Korea through the boom, and then I wanted to know more and more' (a female fan, quoted in *Japan Economic Newswire*,

2005). The consumption of Korean TV drama has created a new awareness among the Japanese and allowed for their self-reflection.

What can TV drama do? This cultural phenomenon signifies more profound political implications. *Winter Sonata* has done more politically for Korea and Japan than the FIFA World Cup co-hosted by these two countries in 2002 (Leung, 2004). In an effort to overlook their colonial past, both governments promoted cultural exchanges before the World Cup event, but it was the huge success of *Winter Sonata* which triggered growing interest among the Japanese in their close neighbour. The producer of the drama has received the Korea–Japan Friendship Contribution Award in Japan and the Presidential Prize in Korea for his work and achievements. The drama is said to have built a bridge between Korea and Japan, which politicians and diplomats have been unable to achieve. 'If the two countries ever went to war again and Yon-sama joined up in Korea, Japanese women would riot, bringing any conflict to an immediate end' (*Smart TV*, 2005).

China

Korean TV dramas were introduced into China in the early 1990s. China's rapidly growing media industries needed programmes to broadcast in their new channels. Korean dramas are among the favourite TV programmes in China: Chinese TV stations broadcast 359 Korean shows in 2003 and 2004, which made up a quarter of all foreign productions. Korea ranked second to the US, which had 487 shows or nearly 35 per cent of the total (*China Daily*, 2005b). A recent study shows that 53 per cent of the Chinese people surveyed enjoy Korean TV dramas, while only about 17 per cent liked domestically produced dramas (Sina.com, 2005). For East Asian audiences like the Chinese, things 'American' are dreams to be yearned for and conceptual forms to be pursued, but things 'Korean' are their 'accessible future', examples to be emulated and commodities to be acquired (Iwabuchi, 2001).

'The cultural mecca of China's Y Generation is now Seoul. It has replaced Europe and the US as a place of inspiration' (*China Daily*, 2005b). For the young generation, Korean dramas are inspirational – representing capitalist achievements, modernity, urban lifestyles and romance that many young Chinese admire. One feature they particularly like about Korean dramas is the way they can 'express their emotions freely, that it is a democracy' (*Financial Times*, 2005). Stars of Korean TV dramas have created a new standard of beauty, and fans emulate their fashion, hairstyle, makeup and pretty faces. Even dramatically, the soaring popularity of Korean TV dramas and stars has stimulated a desire for cosmetic surgery among Chinese young women, and cosmetic surgery is no longer considered as a cultural taboo (*China Post*, 2004).

Korean TV dramas integrate elements of both modernity and tradition, and this feature allows them to attract a wider age group in China. For the older generation, Korean dramas are appealing for their Confucian frame-work: 'We see a purer form of Confucianism and are refreshed by it because we feel a sense of belonging' (*China Daily*, 2005b). Some Chinese find neo-Confucian social concepts embedded in Korean dramas are awakening a respect for traditional values lost under communism. Traditional values are fading as the Chinese society undergoes restructuring and competition under the market economy. Korean dramas evoke a nostalgic longing for what China has lost.

A recent example is the popularity of Korean drama *Jewel in the Palace*, which proved even more popular than *Winter Sonata* in China. The Korean Wave reached a new peak with the airing of *Jewel in the Palace*, which 'has swept through living rooms all over Asia with tsunami-like intensity' (*Business Times Singapore*, 2005). The drama has earned $40 million worldwide since it was first broadcast in 2003, and Hunan TV paid $1.2 million to buy the Chinese distribution rights. Set in the Korea's Chosun Dynasty (1392–1910), *Jewel in the Palace* depicts a story about royal physician Jang Geum, who rose from an orphaned cook to become the king's first female physician. The heroine goes through tough times of palace politics, court intrigue and persecution, but she endures and upholds all the virtues of Confucian values. The persistence, self-sacrifice, optimism and hope projected on the Korean drama captures the Chinese living in a transitional society.

Hong Kong

Jewel in the Palace has become the most-watched television show in Hong Kong history. The series finale reportedly drew a record of 3.2 million of Hong Kong's 6.9 million potential viewers – more than 40 per cent of the total population (*Korea Times*, 2005b). Chinese New Year celebrations were cut short by many families rushing home before 10 p.m. in order to watch the final episode of the drama. Some even watched the drama with subtitles instead of dubbing, just to hear the leading character's voice (*JoongAng Daily*, 2005). This explosive popularity has intensified the Korean Wave phenomenon in Hong Kong – including a *Jewel in the Palace* theme park and restaurants that serve various Korean cuisine featured in the drama, and an increase in the number of tourists to Korea visiting the village where the drama was filmed (*Business Times Singapore*, 2005).

Viewing of Korean dramas in Hong Kong is more 'terrestrial' because local TV stations buy a substantial amount of Korean TV dramas (Leung, 2004). A terrestrial station (ATV) relies heavily on the imports of Korean dramas, which are shown in prime-time. The Hong Kong Cable TV, with the introduction of Korean romance drama *Autumn in the Heart* in 2000, ushered in the start of the Korean Wave. In addition, two other routes circulate Korean dramas into Hong Kong – one route from Taiwan in the form of VCDs and another from China, mostly pirated VCDs. VCD is a major source of the globalization of Korean dramas. The recorded nature of VCD tends to liber-ate viewers from the time–space restriction that terrestrial viewing imposes on its audience, and such alternative viewing is favoured by students and full-time workers. With VCD viewing, younger fans can 'own' the drama with a sense of autonomy and 'reclaim' the TV once they are left alone to indulge in their favourite Korean drama (Hung, 2006).

Taiwan

Since the mid-1990s Korean TV dramas have been exported to Taiwan and made increasingly into VCDs (with Chinese subtitles) and further circulated to Hong Kong. Gala TV (GTV) and Wei-Lai Drama Channel dedicate almost 24 hours to airing Korean dramas, and eight other channels broadcast Korean dramas. Star TV has also joined the competition of buying Korean dramas and broadcasting them at 9 p.m. Korean dramas have thus become a site for local media competition, which has led to sky-rocketing prices for Korean shows. Viewership ratings are high, as shown by an AC Nielsen survey: 'On one day in August 2004 more than 1.1 million people tuned into the Korean drama, *Jewel in the Palace*, as it aired on a local cable TV station' (*Taipei Times*, 2004). The success of Korean TV dramas in Taiwan should be understood in terms not only of their content appeal, but also in how they are promoted by the local TV stations' marketing strategies (Hung, 2006).

Since the late 1990s the growing success of Korean TV dramas has chal-lenged the domination of Japanese popular culture in Taiwan (Ko, 2004). Japan is no longer seen as a solo power in regional popular cultural flows. Taiwanese viewers now perceive Korean TV drama, which subtly depicts youth's love affairs in connection with family matters, as 'ours' even more than Japanese TV dramas (Iwabuchi, 2005: 33). Viewers like to savour the subtlety in the portrayal of love and romance in Korean dramas. *Autumn in the Heart* (dubbed as *Endless Love*) sparked the Korean Wave in Taiwan in 2001, as it filled the yearning for something other than Western or Japanese shows. Asians are often seen as being more reserved in the realms of expressing their love and sexuality, and this conservatism could be one common denomi-nator among audiences, the young and the old, who favour Korean dramas (Leung, 2004).

Southeast Asia

The Korean Wave has reached across much of Southeast Asia with the export of popular dramas like *Winter Sonata*, *Jewel in the Palace* and *Autumn in the Heart*. The importance of Korean media exports can be seen from its effects in Singapore. In 1999, the local monopoly that published all the major newspapers ventured into commercial television, one in English (I Channel) and the other in Mandarin (U Channel). The English-channel programmes, imported largely from the US, have been a failure and the studio shut down within two years of its establishment. On the other hand, the Mandarin channel has been able to carve out a significant slice of the audience population, by broadcasting imported Korean dramas and local variety shows (Chua, 2004). Every night, after the daily news, there is at least one Korean drama on Singaporean television stations. In Malaysia, the popularity of Korean dramas has heightened appreciation for Korean culture, language and fashion among the younger generation (*Korea IT Times*, 2006). In Vietnam, due to the popularity of the Korean drama *Jewel in the Palace* being broadcast at 10 p.m., the average bedtime for Vietnamese people extended much later (*Korea Times*, 2005b). Korean TV drama is one of the most highly rated forms of programming in the communist country, providing an enticing glimpse of the outside world.

Television can also act as trend-setter. Seasons are foreign to Southeast Asians living in hot, tropical weather all year round, which denies them the seasonal changes of fashion, especially 'layering' effects (Chua, 2004). The impact of Korean TV drama was felt on the streets of Southeast Asia by young people donning a wool scarf, as conspicuously worn by the leading characters in *Winter Sonata*. A much stylized cinematography and the elaborate use of beautiful settings underpinned by melodic music is a key feature of Korean drama (Leung, 2004). Scenery, as a marker of foreignness, constitutes a mode of visual tourism. Avid fans of Korean TV dramas have also become so enamoured by the scenery that the locations are 'must visit' places (Chua, 2004).

North Korea

The Korean Wave is finally making its way into communist North Korea despite tight controls set by the regime's authority. The biggest force driving the Korean Wave appears to be TV dramas. In 2005, a young soldier defected across the demilitarized zone as he had yearned for South Korea after watching its TV dramas with beautiful settings and lifestyles (*New York Times*, 2005). Copies of TV dramas, movie videos and music CDs are increasingly smuggled across the border of China into North Korea by those who have been abroad on business. In 2004, the regime launched a crackdown on illegal bootleg videos of South Korean TV dramas, according to North Korean defectors (*Time Asia*, 2004). The popularity of South Korean cultural products is mainly concentrated in three areas, including Pyongyang, which are relatively open to outside contact. North Korea's younger generation, especially the upper classes, are eager consumers of South Korean popular culture. The eagerness is spreading to the market where South Korean products (e.g. clothes, electronics) are becoming more popular than relatively cheap Chinese ones. Young North Koreans are competitively imitating fashion and hairstyles of the actors that appear in South Korean TV dramas (*New York Times*, 2005).

Iraq and Egypt

For the first time in the Middle East, Korean popular dramas have begun broadcasting. *Winter Sonata* hit the airwaves in Iraq in 2005 after an agreement with Kurdistan Satellite Channel, a broadcaster operated by the Kurdistan government. The goal was to generate positive feelings in the Arab world towards the 3,200 South Korean soldiers stationed in northern Iraq (*Korea Herald*, 2005a). Furthermore, the Korean government purchased the rights to provide Korean TV dramas free to broadcasting stations in more Arab countries in an effort to create a favourable image of the nation (*Korea Times*, 2004b). The Korean government also provided such popular dramas as *Winter Sonata* as well as *Autumn in the Heart*, to the state-run broadcaster ERTU (Egypt Radio Television Union) in 2004, paying for Arabic subtitles (*Korea Herald*, 2005a).

Mexico

The Korean Wave is gradually expanding to South America, including Mexico, Brazil and Chile, with the distribution of TV dramas, movies and popular music. Since a local cable company (Mexico TV) aired Korean drama *All About Eve* in 2002, Mexican audiences have turned to websites that offer information about Korean programming and stars. Fans have requested five broadcasting stations and the largest radio station in Mexico to screen more Korean dramas and music (*Korea Herald*, 2005a). Korea's Arirang TV started a 24-hour service through a local cable channel in 2005, becoming the first Asian TV station to broadcast its programmes in Mexico. Mexicans have become interested in Korean popular culture and their demand is publicly acknowledged. For instance, Mexiquense, a state-run television station, began broadcasting *Winter Sonata* with Spanish subtitles to mark the Korean president's visit to the country in 2005 (*Korea Times*, 2005e).

The United States

Korean TV dramas are broadcast to over 27 million households in the US (*PR Newswire US*, 2005). At least 30 stations are broadcasting Korean dramas in US markets, including Los Angeles, Hawaii, Chicago, New York and Washington DC: these can be seen nationally on cable channel AZN Television. In the Bay Area, more than 100,000 fans tuned in for the final episode of *Jewel in the Palace*, giving the Korean drama higher ratings than

ABC's *Extreme Makeover* or the WB's *Starlet* in that time slot (*San Francisco Chronicle*, 2005). American audiences – and not just those of Korean descent – are increasingly drawn to the emotional storylines set against the backdrop of historical and contemporary Korea.

Meanings and significance

Why is this so popular and why now? The extent of the Korean Wave has left observers in a state of surprise and puzzlement, searching for answers to explain the sudden craze for Korean popular culture. Even the local Koreans have trouble answering. However, the first common response in various transnational locations is that Korean TV dramas are emotionally powerful. 'The unique intensity of Korean emotion plays well to the more restrained cultures around the region' (Taiwan's Gala TV vice president, quoted in *Korea Herald*, 2005b). Many audiences from China, Hong Kong and Taiwan prefer Korean dramas because their local dramas do not offer them the same indulgence in the emotions that Korean dramas evince (Leung, 2004). The audiences enjoy savouring the subtlety in the handling of emotions, and Korean dramas are perceived to capture the delicacy of emotions by their adept direction techniques. While Korean producers do not pay particular attention to a 'global formula' for the success of TV drama, nevertheless they have found its 'affective' form useful to touch the sensibilities of disparate audiences.

Second, Korean TV dramas are infused with urban middle-class scenes as representations of modernization, yet effectively portray youthful sentimentality and provide an imaginary for an increasingly regionalized 'Asian modernity' (Erni and Chua, 2005: 7). Korea acts as a 'filter for Western values making them more palatable to Chinese and other Asians' (*New York Times*, 2006). In the urban cities of Asia, there are many young viewers whose desires and aspirations overlap with the way Korean TV dramas are presented – the beautiful urban environment, young and single professionals, aestheticized lifestyles, and the pure love which is still possible. The reality they perceive through cultural imports resembles their own reality, yet at the same time, the two differ. In this sense, the exoticism and foreignness of imported Korean TV dramas remain 'recognizably foreign' (Chua, 2004) to the local audiences' desires and viewing pleasure, simultaneously articulating 'familiar difference' (Iwabuchi, 2005: 21) and similarity.

The combination of subtle difference/distance and similarity/proximity creates interest and empathy on the part of the viewers. Audiences across different localities favour Korean dramas for the distant settings, which permit them to indulge in romantic illusions of idealized love, and for the way the dramas make them 'think' (Leung, 2004) about their own societies including gender issues, class and economic positions, thereby allowing them to engage with a 'dynamic process of becoming' (Iwabuchi, 2005: 28). TV dramas are often seen as a source of aspiration and reflexivity in transitional society, and globalized dramas can serve the function of extending the space for reflexivity (Kim, 2005).

Third, what also makes Korean TV drama appealing is its dramatization of 'Asian sensibilities', including family values and traditional emotive delicacies that are warmly embraced by cross-generational viewers in the Asian countries where full-fledged modernity has yet to arrive (*Korea Now*, 2001). It offers both a nostalgic reminder of what has been lost during modernization and an 'example of an Asian country that has modernized and retained its traditions' (*New York Times*, 2006). Global TV culture's focus on the urban, young and single professionals and aestheticized lifestyles has fostered a tendency to displace the central place of the family. However, 'Korean dramas are favoured because they are rich in the more traditional Confucian values, which place emphasis on familial relationship, filial piety and sibling love' (*China Daily*, 2005b).

Unlike American dramas such as *Friends* and *Sex in the City*, in which the focus is on romance between young lovers and the family has all but disappeared, Korean dramas are perceived by the Asian audience to embrace reality by dealing with diverse relationships in the Confucian familial framework. Unlike Japanese dramas where the urbanity and individual happiness are the themes, the conflicts between Confucian tradition and social modernity are some of the major cultural experiences in Korean dramas, with which the young audience engages deeply (Ko, 2004). Traditional moral ideals – placing the family before the self – alternate between an obstacle to and a refuge from modernity. Korean TV drama represents struggle over tradition and a common ambivalent experience of modernity in the region which 'American culture cannot represent' (Iwabuchi, 2002: 270), and therefore, a structure of feeling which the audience can relate to more readily.

Finally, Korea's historical colonial victimhood is pointed out as an intriguing reason behind the popularity of today's Korean Wave. As a Korean producer of popular film explains: 'For centuries Korea has been occupied by China, Japan or the US. We are not seen as a threat to anybody' (quoted in *Reed Business Information*, 2005). The success of Korean popular culture can be understood by global power relations and political sensitivities. 'Korea is surrounded by powerful neighbours. Throughout history, we have suffered and endured. Koreans keep hope inside and never give up' commented the producer of *Jewel in the Palace* (*San Francisco Chronicle*, 2005).

This suggests that the political conflicts and socio-cultural tensions of the divided nation have been used to good effect to create emotionally powerful content. Korean culture reflects the nation's unique sensibility, '*Han*' – a Korean word for a deeply felt sense of oppression and deep-seated grief: 'Korean dramas express sadness particularly well. The writer of *Autumn in the Heart* would cry when writing his script. The actors, during rehearsals, started crying too' (producer of *Winter Sonata* and *Autumn in the Heart*, quoted in *Time Asia*, 2005).

Thus, the reason behind the successful phenomenon is a combination of Korea's tragic history, the intensity of Korean emotive culture, and the non-threatening nature of its people. Often, the ambivalent nature of foreignness in imported Western cultural products can be perceived by two extremes – fascination and threat – but the threat is less manifested in the way Korean popular culture is received across Asia. Rather, the Korean Wave phenomenon is seen as a counterweight to Western cultural influence, or a 'periphery's talking back to the central West' (Hannerz, 1997: 13). There is a lingering anticolonial sentiment lurking in the hearts of people in many Asian countries, however, the acceptance of Korean popular culture appears to benefit from the sense of solidarity that the people have towards the country that shared a similar colonial past (Leung, 2004; Jin, 2004).

The rise of the Korean Wave phenomenon is seen as a 'long-awaited flowering of post-colonial Asian artistic expression', and a creation of a 'regional Asian cultural manifestation against the erstwhile domination of Western culture' (Dator and Seo, 2004). The postcolonial periphery has strengthened its national culture industry to compete against the dominant flow of Western media products. It is emerging as a new player for the production and circulation of transnational culture, while consolidating a relatively strong position in the regional market. This indicates a potential 'plurality of actors and media flows' (Chadha and Kavoori, 2000), and could be read as a 'symptom of the shifting nature of transnational cultural power in a context in which intensified global cultural flows have decentred the power structure' (Iwabuchi, 2002: 35).

Though the decentring tendency occurs within the context of global inequalities and uneven flows, a current image of global media flows may not be that of settled centres of economic and cultural power, but of a 'decentred network, in which the patterns of power distribution are unstable and shifting' (Tomlinson, 1997: 139). The transnational mobility of Korean popular culture is a facet of the decentralizing multiplicity of global media flows today. The significance of its popularity is reflective of a region-wide reassertion or imaginary of Asianism, and an alternative culture that is not necessarily American or European. The popularity of Korean TV dramas has spurred the confirmation of the power of Asian modernity, in terms of economic as well as cultural development, which might challenge the predominant hegemony of America and Europe (Leung, 2004). The Korean Wave phenomenon can be seen as a way to counter the threat and insensibility of the Western-dominated media market.

References

Asia Cable (2005) 'All you need is pure love', 18 February.

Asia Media (2006) 'A lesson from South Korea,' 11 January.

Asia Pulse (2004) 'Korean Wave hits Asia lifting S. Korean tourism',15 December.

Asia TV Forum (2002) 'Broadcast business'.

Business Times Singapore (2005) 'A Window to the Seoul', 23 September.

Chadha, Kalyani and Anandam Kavoori (2000) 'Media imperialism revisited: some findings from the Asian case', *Media, Culture & Society*, 22 (4): 415–32.

Chicago Tribune (2005) 'Asia rides wave of Korean pop culture invasion', 23 December.

China Daily (2005a) 'Hallyuwood to be built in ROK', 3 February.

China Daily (2005b) 'S. Korean soap opera sparks boom in China', 30 September.

China Post (2004) 'Cosmetic surgery booms in Taiwan', 19 January.

Chosun Ilbo (2004) 'Korean TV drama *Autumn in the Heart* gains popularity in Egypt', 24 September.

Chua, Beng Huat (2004) 'Conceptualizing an East Asian popular culture', *Inter-Asia Cultural Studies*, 5 (2): 200–21.

Dator, Jim and Yongseok Seo (2004) 'Korea as the wave of a future: the emerging Dream Society of icons and aesthetic experience', *Journal of Futures Studies*, 9 (1): 31–44.

Erni, John and Siew Chua (2005) 'Introduction: our Asian media studies?', in J. Erni and S. Chua (eds), *Asian Media Studies: Politics of Subjectivities*. Oxford: Blackwell.

Financial Times (2001) 'Artistic achievements bring a culture of rich success', 24 October.

Financial Times (2002) 'Seoul music strives for a global audience', 8 February.

Financial Times (2004) 'South Korea's soppy soaps win hearts across Asia', 14 December.

Financial Times (2005) 'South Korea's TV dramas express young people's yearning for greater freedom', 12 August.

Hannerz, Ulf (1997) 'Notes on the global ecumene', in A. Sreberny-Mohammadi *et al.* (eds), *Media in Global Context: A Reader*. London: Arnold.

Hung, Hsiu-Chin (2006) 'The Possibility of Regional Cultures: Intra-Asian TV Drama Flow'. PhD thesis, Goldsmiths College, London.

Iwabuchi, Koichi (2001) 'Becoming culturally proximate: The a/scent of Japanese idol dramas in Taiwan', in B. Moeran (ed.), *Asian Media Productions*. Honolulu: University of Hawaii Press.

Iwabuchi, Koichi (2002) *Recentering Globalization: Popular Culture and Japanese Transnationalism*. Durham, NC: Duke University Press.

Iwabuchi, Koichi (2005) 'Discrepant intimacy: Popular cultural flows in East Asia', in J. Erni and S. Chua (eds), *Asian Media Studies: Politics of Subjectivities*. Oxford: Blackwell.

Japan Economic Newswire (2005) 'S. Korean boom changing Japanese people's perceptions', 16 August.

Japan Times (2004) 'Korean Wave may help erode discrimination', 27 June.

Jin, Dal Yong (2004) 'Is Cultural Imperialism Over? Growing US Dominance vs. Emerging Domestic Cultural Market'. PhD thesis, University of Illinois at Urbana Champaign.

JoongAng Daily (2005) 'Korean "Royal Cooking" wave hits Hong Kong', 17 February.

KBS World Radio (2006) 'The Government's decision to globalize the ongoing *hallyu* or the Korean Wave by extending more active support', 18 January.

Kim, Youna (2005) *Women, Television and Everyday Life in Korea: Journeys of Hope.* London and New York: Routledge.

Ko, Yu-Fen (2004) 'From Hari to Hanliu', JAMCO Online International Symposium, February–March.

Korea Herald (2005a) 'Korean Wave spreading beyond Asia, showing greater Vitality', 2 June.

Korea Herald (2005b) 'Is it all over already?', 11 July.

Korea IT Times (2006) 'Malaysians embracing Korean pop culture', January.

Korea Now (2001) 'Cultural ambassadors (stars) on the rise: Asia dreaming of Korea's pop singers and actors', 11 September.

Korea Times (2004a) 'Korean TV dramas to be aired in Iraq', 21 February.

Korea Times (2004b) 'Television dramas spearhead Korean Wave', 7 April.

Korea Times (2005a) 'Keep Hallyu going', 17 February.

Korea Times (2005b) 'Is Hallyu a one-way street?' 22 April.

Korea Times (2005c) 'Hallyu boosts Korea's GDP by 0.2 per cent', 4 May.

Korea Times (2005d) 'TV drama *Winter Sonata* goes to Egypt', 1 June.

Korea Times (2005e) 'Hallyu links Korea to Mexico',11 September.

Korean Broadcasting Commission (2004) *The Annual Report of Korean Broadcasting Industry.* Accessed at: http://www.kbc.or.kr.

Korean Ministry of Culture and Tourism (2004) *Whitepaper of the Korean Culture Industry.* Accessed at: http://www.mct.go.kr.

Korean National Tourism Organization (2005) *Hallyu (Korean Wave) Research & Stats, Tourists Survey.* Accessed at: http://www.knto.or.kr.

Korean Overseas Information Service (2005) 'Korean Wave boosts exports of culture contents to $1 billion in 2005'. *Korea.net.* Accessed at: http://www.kois.go.kr.

Leung, Lisa (2004) 'An Asian formula? Comparative reading of Japanese and Korean TV dramas', JAMCO Online International Symposium, February–March.

New York Times (2004) 'What's Korean for "real man"? Ask a Japanese woman', 23 December.

New York Times (2005) 'Roll over, Godzilla: Korea rules', 28 June.

New York Times (2006) 'Korea's pop culture spreads through Asia', 2 January.

PR Newswire US (2005) 'Korean TV dramas rise in popularity in North America', 6 July.

Reed Business Information (2005) 'Asian market finds its Seoul', 9 October.

San Francisco Chronicle (2005) 'South Korea soap operas find large audiences', 28 August.

San Jose Mercury News (2005) 'The new cool: Korean pop culture', 9 October.

Sina.com (2005) 'ROK TV series grip Chinese viewers', http://www.sina.com. Accessed 16 October.

Smart TV (2005) 'World peace via Korean soap operas', 27 June.

Straits Times (2003a) 'K-mania still rules, ok?', 4 January.

Straits Times (2003b) 'Seoul survivor', 8 April.

Taipei Times (2004) 'Taiwanese going crazy over all things Korean', 15 October.

Television Asia (2005) 'Wave new world', April.

Time Asia (2004) 'He's still there', 6 December.

Time Asia (2005) 'South Korea: Talent show', 14 November.

Tomlinson, John (1997) 'Internationalism, globalization and cultural imperialism', in K. Thompson (ed.), *Media and Cultural Regulation*. London: Sage.

Wall Street Journal (2005) 'Korea's hip makeover changes face of Asia', 20 October.

Watson, J. (1997) 'McDonald's in Hong Kong: Consumerism, dietary change and the rise of a children's culture', in J. Watson (ed.), *Golden Arches East: McDonald's in East Asia*. Stanford: Stanford University Press.

Yomiuri Shimbun (2004) 'TV dramas melt hearts, thaw Japan–Korea relations', 7 December.

Chapter 9

South Africa as a regional media power

Ruth Teer-Tomaselli, Herman Wasserman and Arnold S. de Beer

The post-apartheid media landscape in South Africa provides an interesting example of the multiple and even paradoxical sets of power relations in which media industries in countries outside the global metropolises may be involved. In comparison with the global power houses of the United States and Britain, South Africa appears to be on the receiving end of cultural products carried by globalizing media. The country's channels are awash with news and entertainment produced elsewhere; newspaper and magazine columns are filled with information provided by international agencies ranging from news reports to entertainment gossip; local films struggle to find a space in a cinema circuit dominated by Hollywood products. As far as ownership is concerned, the influence of international media companies can also be felt, as in the case of Tony O'Reilly's multinational group, Independent Newspapers, which acquired a range of prominent print media titles soon after democratization in 1994 (Tomaselli, 2000: 284).

From this perspective, South Africa belongs to the margins of an imperialistic global media industry, falling prey to its homogenizing tendencies through the consumption of material and cultural products that may eventually lead to the erosion of local identities, cultures and ideologies (Chadha and Kavoori, 2005: 85). However, simplistic assumptions of media globalization as one-way traffic from the centre to the periphery have largely made way for more nuanced understandings of the multi-directionality of the process (ibid.).

Attention has been redirected to the ways in which countries outside of the global metropolises can contribute to a contra-flow and a disruption of the hegemonic tendencies underlying media globalization. Examples of this contra-flow do exist in the South African media environment post-democracy, as this chapter will seek to illustrate. The relationship between the global and the local, therefore, is more complex than a crude version of media imperialism, which seems to belong to older debates such as those within UNESCO in the 1970s about a New World Information and Communication order regarding inequalities between the 'information-rich North and the information-poor South' (Boyd-Barrett, 1998: 165; Thussu, 1998: 64).

This is not to deny that those inequalities still exist, but to emphasize the need for a more complex understanding of how these inequalities take on different forms. Such nuance is provided by Boyd-Barrett (1998: 159) in his 'generic' model of media imperialism, which 'acknowledges the multi-dimensionality of media forms . . . and degrees of dependence/imperialism'. According to this model, media practices within nation-states, territorially or inter-ethnic, inter-cultural and inter-class (ibid.: 160), also may be analysed to lay bare imperialistic tendencies, even while such nations occupy a peripheral position within the global media arena. Similarly, these nations may also exercise imperialistic influence over other countries in their respective regions. Such a definition of media imperialism recognizes that 'imperialism could vary between different media and between different levels, dimensions or spheres of activity within any one sector of the media industries. The definition in itself refers to ownership, structure, distribution or content' (ibid.: 166).

According to this nuanced definition of media imperialism, the South African media may be seen as involved in contradictory, or at least varied, processes of globalization. While the South African media occupy a marginal position in the global media arena, as a market for media products owned and produced outside its borders, they extend their influence (albeit on a much smaller scale) as a powerful role-player into the region and further on the continent. The penetration of South African media into Africa, and the concomitant spread of content originating in South Africa or the relaying of content produced outside Africa, also have implications for the way in which the South African media's position within the globalization/imperialization debate is viewed.

Furthermore, the South African media are marked by unequal flows internally, so that it also becomes necessary to examine the ways in which the structure and operation of the media perpetuate unequal power relations on a national level. Chadha and Kavoori point out that, despite the exaggerated 'rumours of the death of the nation-state' (Chadha and Kavoori, 2005: 86), national governments still exert a crucial influence on media structures, institutions and regimes. In post-apartheid South Africa, the influence of the state and regulatory agencies (such as the Independent Communications Authority of South Africa and the Media Diversity and Development Agency) on the structuring of the media can be noted, as well as the role that self-regulatory bodies such as the Broadcasting Complaints Commission and the Press Ombudsman play in the professional ideologies of media workers and journalists. Furthermore, developments such as the liberalization of the public broadcaster and the increasingly commercial nature of the mainstream print media have raised questions about the limitations of, and structural inequalities within, the post-apartheid mediated public sphere.

When the South African media are analysed in relation to the creation of counter-flows in the processes of globalization, the above multi-dimensionality of their position globally, regionally and internally should be taken into account. In the subsequent discussion of various media sectors in the country, these various aspects therefore will be taken together to provide a glimpse into the complexity of the South African media's position within multi-directional global media flows.

Broadcasting: transnational in an African context

Both television and radio are less developed in Africa than on any other continent. Fewer people have a TV set at home and there are fewer stations transmitting per head of population than on any other continent.[1] For the most part, broadcasting in the sub-Saharan countries is state owned and controlled, frequently in local languages that do not travel well. For this reason the old colonial languages – English, French, Portuguese and to a lesser extent, German – provide a 'common-carrier' medium. Most broadcasters carry a significant amount of imported content. Lack of financial means and poor infrastructure result in little local audio-visual content, neither is there much inter-African cooperation in production, exchange and marketing (Mytton *et al.*, 2005).

In contrast to radio, which crossed national boundaries from its earliest days, for many years television was broadcast within the boundaries of a particular country. The exceptions to this rule were channels that spilled over national boundaries: people in Botswana and Lesotho could watch South African television long before they had their own national television stations. Aside from these, most services are contained within the boundaries of the nation-state. Advances in technology, together with a relative liberalization of the media and the phenomenon of globalization, led to the growth of transnational activity in Africa during the last decade of the twentieth century. The synergies between telecommunications, information technology and electronics all increased the possibilities for satellite media in Africa. The more liberal atmosphere necessary for transnational broadcasting to grow was slow to develop in many parts of Africa and is yet to emerge in some countries. But in most of the 48 sub-Saharan states, deregulation of some kind has lifted restrictions on broadcasting activities, formerly a government monopoly in every African country.

MultiChoice Africa

Within a single decade one provider, MultiChoice has become the preeminent content carrier in Anglophone Africa. It emerged from M-Net, South Africa's first private channel and has expanded horizontally, moving from a terrestrial pay-platform in a single country, to a multi-platform provider across the African continent. M-Net, a terrestrial channel available only in South Africa, which began broadcasting in 1986, was a joint venture of four newspaper publishers,[2] breaking several decades of SABC's broadcasting monopoly. An analogue service, distributed via satellite, was launched to more than 20 African countries in 1992. Its subscriber management division became so successful that the company launched it as a separate venture called MultiChoice Limited (MCL) in 1993. Digital satellite services were offered across Africa in 1995, utilizing the C-band on PAS4 satellite. With the delivery via satellite, the bouquet of channels was enlarged significantly.

The first transnational joint venture was entered into with Namibia in 1993. This was the beginning of DSTV (Direct Satellite), a subsidiary of MultiChoice. At this point, M-Net and MultiChoice were formally separated, with the latter changing its name to MultiChoice Investment Holdings (MIH). During the next few years, MultiChoice expanded beyond Africa: into Greece in 1995, Thailand two years later and China in 1999. That year, the transmission moved to PAS7 satellite and in 2000 the launch of the Eutelsat W4 satellite opened up the Ku-band services to sub-Saharan African and the Indian Ocean Islands. The year also heralded the launch of Indian and Portuguese bouquets on the DSTV satellite service in southern Africa.

MultiChoice operates two distinct systems of distribution – encrypted terrestrial broadcasting and encrypted broadcasting via satellite. The latter is available on both the analogue and digital platforms, although strong moves are being made to 'migrate' all subscribers onto the digital platform. Multi-Choice operates from three satellites over Africa: PAS7 for Ku band coverage of southern Africa, PAS10 for C band coverage of sub-Saharan Africa, and Eutelsat W4 for spot beam coverage of Nigeria and broadband coverage of the rest of Africa. Further capacity of Ku band services was recently rolled out on the back of the Eutelsat W4 at a cost of $10 million. The Ku band operates at a much higher frequency than the older C-band, and has a much smaller footprint with more power. This means that it covers a smaller area across the continent, requiring a greater number of transponders. However, the advantage of the Ku band is that it requires far smaller (and less expensive) satellite dishes than other bands, allowing for a greater consumer uptake of satellite technology.

MultiChoice Africa is a broadcast-publisher and subscription manager. In its former guise, MCA packages channels, some fully imported from the United States, Europe or Asia, others compiled from imported programming together with locally commissioned programming through its sister company, M-Net, and broadcasts these as channel 'bouquets' to subscribing clients. These clients are served with programme guides, both printed in magazine form as well as electronically available on-screen. As a subscription manager, the company administers contracts with, and receives payment from, subscribers; operates a call centre for subscriber service; and coordinates the supply and servicing of decoders to subscribers.

The parent company, MIH, operates subscription services across the whole of Africa, as well as the Middle East, Greece and Thailand. At the time of

writing, MIH owns operations that span over 50 countries, providing entertainment, interactive and e-commerce services. The group employs over
6,000 collaborators, 690 of whom are based in their South African headquarters. The group claims over 2 million paid-up subscribers in Africa, the
Mediterranean and Asia, 1.25 million of whom are in Africa. Fifty-seven per
cent of African customers subscribe to the digital platform (DSTV): 705,000
households in South Africa and a further 251,518 in the remainder of sub-
Saharan Africa. The analogue service accounts for 339,422 households in
South Africa, and 12,798 in the rest of Africa.[3] Critics point out that with an
annual monthly subscription of $60, the reception of these services is limited
to foreign nationals and the local elite, and thus they do not contribute to the
enrichment of the local states, either culturally or economically. Prices are
very much higher for this service than for a comparable service in Francophone Africa, with the result that access to transnational television within
Anglophone Africa has so far been much lower. The only available detailed
audience data for MultiChoice services by satellite applies only to the South
African portion of the viewership. They confirm that viewers are mostly to be
found among the high-income earners, government officials and expatriates.

Under a joint venture model, MIH undertakes a partnership with local
entrepreneurs or state broadcasters, in which each party has a partial shareholding and a joint management strategy. Joint ventures trade under the
name of MultiChoice and the country, e.g. MultiChoice Zambia, and have
full access to MultiChoice Africa's nerve centre outside Johannesburg
through satellite communication, allowing for technology transfer and fully-
staffed, customer-service support. Franchises carry a MultiChoice identity,
while the parent company provides management, infrastructure, training
and marketing support. As with joint ventures, they are facilitated through a
fully online connection to the central computer system. Independent agents
comprise a network of entrepreneurial agents who sign up subscribers and
install DSTV. These companies trade under their own business names, while
also promoting the MultiChoice Africa brand.

One of the advantages of digitalization is the opportunity to exploit the
content over a number of different delivery platforms, notably the Internet.
As part of the MultiChoice Investment Holdings Ltd Group, the content
acquired by M-Net and DSTV is used to cross-promote the African M-Web
Internet operation. Interactivity is in its infancy, exemplified mainly through
the electronic programme guides, however some territories do have access to
embryonic services in e-mail, gaming and home shopping, all of which are
planned for future development.

Growth in the satellite television market will be determined most directly
by the expansion of the middle classes, able and willing to afford the subscription fees for the service. Beyond this, there will be an increase in band-
width capacity, which will allow the delivery of high-speed, bulk data on a

point-to-point basis, while at the same time, facilitating a drop in the cost of transmission services. Another growth area will be interactive applications, such as e-mail using the satellite connection, which will encourage a diversification of the services on offer to consumers, adding value and creating greater demand.

M-Net

M-Net, also owned by MIH, is a broad-spectrum entertainment channel, available on the terrestrial service in South Africa. MIH, through M-Net, has three wholly owned, 'proprietary' brands: K-TV for children's programming, Super Sport for sports coverage and Movie Magic for movies. Each of these channels is made up of both commissioned local programming together with programming produced elsewhere and dubbed or subtitled into the local language. The Movie Magic service acquires exclusive pay-TV rights to premier movies, notably from the Disney, Columbia Tri-Star/Sony, Warner Brothers, Fox, MCA/Universal, Paramount, MGM and DreamWorks Studios. Further channels provided by M-Net include the partially interactive reality TV show, *Big Brother*, which in 2003 was produced as *Big Brother Africa*, with an all-African cast, living together in a game house until all but one is eliminated.

The analogue and digital services available via satellite are delivered as DSTV, a direct-to-home service, and these provide various 'bouquets' of channels. In addition to those already mentioned, fully imported channels such as Discovery, The History Channel, National Geographic, Hallmark, BBC Prime and Cartoon Network are also included. Twenty-four-hour news channels – BBC World, CNN International, Sky News and CCTV-9 – provide a mainstay of programming. Some of the channels are of international standards, while others are created by their sellers for specific world regions. BBC Prime, for instance, is a 24-hour entertainment channel offering a selection of the best British domestic programming emanating from the BBC. The line-up of programming is decided by the BBC and sold as a package, tailored for different regions of the world, thus obviating the necessity for the carrying satellite service to apply for individual programme rights. CNN too has an international edition tailored for Africa. Foreign language programming in French (including Canal+ and TV5), Italian and German is available as a standard part of the bouquet, while specialist bouquets, provided for an additional fee, for Indian, Portuguese and Arabic viewers are also available.

SABC Africa

Another prominent South African channel beamed across the sub-continent is SABC Africa, the external service of the South African Broadcasting Corporation, South Africa's state-owned broadcasting body. The channel was created by an amalgamation of two previously separate channels. Its name-sake, SABC Africa, was a news, current affairs and documentary channel beamed at the rest of the continent, while Africa-2-Africa, an all-entertainment channel, was launched in September 2000, in order to provide a satellite channel broadcasting entertainment made in Africa, for Africa. On 1 April 2003 a hybrid channel was launched, drawing programming from both sources. The channel is housed on the DSTV platform operated by Multi-Choice, reaching 49 countries.

The channel also serves as an overnight feed on SABC2, one of the three domestic SABC terrestrial channels. In terms of content, the channel has a dual content strategy – to provide news and current affairs, as well as enter-tainment programming. Most of the weekly programming is based on the news/current affairs format, while weekends are predominantly entertain-ment. The stated philosophy is to 'celebrate the positive side of Africa and being African'. Some programming, approximately a quarter of the airtime, particularly lifestyle, news and current affairs programmes, is especially com-missioned for the channel, while a special effort is made to source African movies. Two African-produced dramas are broadcast every week, represent-ing countries such as Tunisia, Egypt, Burkina Faso, Zimbabwe, Guinea Bissau, Cameroon and Ethiopia. For the most part, however, the programmes are re-broadcasts of material shown on the terrestrial channels in South Africa. The majority of programming is broadcast in English, with considerable sub-titling in African languages, French and Portuguese.

Detailed audience data for SABC Africa are available only for the South African viewership.[4] The audience profile is predominantly male and pre-dominantly middle-aged. The channel attracts the top two socio-economic groups on the Living Standards Measurement index, i.e. those with a monthly income of over $2,500 per household.

Sales of programming into Africa[5]

Apart from direct broadcasting by South African organizations into the con-tinent, there is also a substantial flow of programming sold for re-broadcast on national terrestrial channels. Most of this originates from the SABC or M-Net, which have been selling locally produced programmes into Anglo-phone Africa since 1995. In 2004, 2,800 hours were sold in Africa, the Seychelles, Jamaica, Barbados and the United Kingdom. Soap operas were the most popular genre, with *Siding* and *Generations* (SABC), as well as *Egoli* (M-Net) heading the list of bestsellers. They are sold to the following countries: Kenya, Zambia, Namibia, Tanzania, Uganda, Botswana, Swaziland, Malawi, Nigeria and Ghana. Ethiopia and Zimbabwe were buyers until about 2002, but deteriorating economic circumstances in those countries have meant they can no longer afford to buy imported programming.

Where the original programme is multilingual, using more than one South African language in the sound track, an all-English version is fashioned for the African market. The all-Afrikaans soap opera, *7de Laan,* is sold into Namibia, where a substantial Afrikaans-speaking population lives. Other drama offerings include comedies (*Suburban Bliss*; *Going Up*); drama (*Justice for All*; *Behind the Badge*; *Slavery of Love*; *Emzini*). An example of South African programme popularity is illustrated in Zambia, where *Isidingo* was originally broadcast five times a week, but since 2004, has been re-scheduled to run seven times a week. A similar pattern occurred in Namibia with *Generations.* These programmes are extremely popular because they depict African situations, African locations and African actors, increasing the level of empathy on the part of viewers.

Substantial numbers of non-drama programmes are attractive to the African market, including wildlife series (*Secrets of Nature*; *The Last Edens*; *Nature on Track*; etc.), documentaries (*The President and the Prosecutor*; *The Man who Drove Mandela*; *The Life and Time of Chris Hani*) and magazine programmes (*Africa Within*; *Top Billing*). Religious programmes are particularly popular (*Hosanna*; *Tapestries*; *An African Pesach*; *Issues of Faith*). Finally, there is also a market for children's programmes (*Pula and Friends; Amagagu*).

Transnational radio from South Africa – Channel Africa

Channel Africa is the 'foreign service' wing of South African state broadcasting, and was designed specifically to broadcast beyond the borders of the country. Initially it was available only on shortwave, and today the shortwave broadcast covers the south, east, central and west Africa. At the present time it is also broadcast via satellite on PAS10 across the entire sub-Saharan region, although with sufficient amplification, it can be picked up as far away as London. Within the boarders of South Africa it is available on shortwave and through SENTECH's vivid decoders, a 'free' satellite distribution system designed to 'fill-in' spaces left by the terrestrial broadcasting network, but available throughout the country. Additionally, Channel Africa's programmes are 'streamed' on the Internet throughout the world.[6] The radio station produces and broadcasts in six languages, making it accessible to a large number of people across the continent. The three common ex-colonial languages form the backbone of programming (English, French and Portuguese) while three commonly spoken African languages (Chinyanja, Silozi, Kiswahili) are also used.

Once the apartheid regime's propaganda mouthpiece in the African continent, Channel Africa, as with the rest of the broadcasting landscape in South Africa, has undergone a thorough-going transformation of purpose and content. It has self-consciously reinvented itself with the stated purpose of acting as 'a major role player in the field of continental and international broadcasting'.[7] News and current affairs programming is the mainstay of content on the radio station. In this sense, the channel provides a viable alternative to northern and western-based broadcasters, many of whom have been long-established on the African continent. In its vision, Channel Africa states that it is committed to the production of 'world class programmes by a profes-sional staff' and will strive to be 'the number one international broadcaster in Africa' promising 'accurate, impartial and authoritative programming' to the rest of the continent.

An examination of the schedules on Channel Africa illustrates a strong commitment to talk radio, highlighting issues such as building democratic institutions, promoting a culture of respect for human rights, as well as pro-moting economic development on the continent. The philosophical idea of the 'African Renaissance' is a guiding thread throughout the programming, with the stated mission of the channel 'to reinforce Africa's dignity, pride and sense of self worth'. This is achieved not only through developmental pro-grammes, but also by showing art, culture and of course, music. *Afro Gig* is an African 'musical odyssey'. Each week the programme focuses on a particular region within Africa, showcasing both established and new talent. In the words of the channel's own publicity, it 'reflects and expresses an African experience – an experience of togetherness! An experience of forgetting the differences!' *Music of the World* takes African listeners beyond the continent, featuring international music from the fringes, particularly those from under-exposed international artists.

Print

One of the first significant events pointing to the South African media's re-introduction to the global media sphere after the demise of apartheid took place on the level of ownership. In 1994, just before the first democratic elec-tion in the country took place, the Irish-based Independent Newspapers plc – endorsed by then president-in-waiting Nelson Mandela on the understand-ing that black shareholding and participation would be increased – bought 31 per cent of the shares in Argus Newspapers Ltd. This included the *Cape Times*, the *Natal Mercury* and a 45 per cent share in *Pretoria News*. This initial deal was later followed up by a second phase, thereby consolidating Indepen-dent's hold over much of the English-language print media (Tomaselli, 2000: 285; Horwitz, 2001: 311). This led to the opening up of South African media to global competition and contributed to the increasing tensions between the local and the global economies (Tomaselli, 2000).

Through global shifts in ownership such as these, issues confronting the media in Western countries around the interaction between locality and globality in the public sphere (Sparks, 2000: 74), are also increasingly raised in the South African media context. This is because these economic changes, facilitated by technological developments, form part of a shift in which public affairs are now more commonly centred outside the state, in institutions of global political and economic governance and linked to forces of trans-national capital (ibid.: 76). This entry of a foreign multinational into the South African media landscape meant increased commercial pressures on the titles in that group, because local media now had to be commercially compe-titive in a global marketplace and show profits in foreign currency. On this level, it would seem as if globalization has worked to the detriment of the local print media sector and that foreign capital has in this instance performed an imperialistic function.

The nuanced cultural imperialism thesis mentioned above, however, also necessitates a look at the power relations of the media in the country intern-ally. The post-apartheid print media have inherited market structures and ownership patterns, including distribution networks, which had been oriented towards white audiences (Horwitz, 2001: 286). These structures acted as a limitation to transformation in the print media industry, and the power rela-tions within this industry could therefore also be seen as imperialistic in nature – still favouring lucrative audiences that were mostly white. Since the mid-1990s, and after two inquiries into racism in the media (by the Human Rights Commission and the Truth and Reconciliation Commission), the editorial make-up of South African print media has changed significantly. The most influential print media publications now have black editors, includ-ing the *Mail and Guardian, The Star, The Sunday Times, City Press and Sowetan.* The Afrikaans media seem to lag behind as far as racial transformation on the executive editorial level is concerned. Although black Afrikaans journal-ists ('coloured', in terms of apartheid nomenclature) are widely represented in Afrikaans print media publications, the executive positions at these outlets are still dominated by white journalists, leading to criticism that the institu-tionalized value system in print media still privileges whites (Du Plessis, 2005).

It is against this background that the establishment of the Media Diversity and Development Agency should be viewed, namely as a way to increase diversity in the print media sector through subsidies to publications (such as community newspapers) that would not be viable if approached only from a commercial perspective that insists on profitability. An ostensibly major shift in the make-up of the print media industry occurred with the introduction of tabloids aimed at a mass black market. These commercially very successful print outlets reverse the imperialistic structure that the print media have inherited from the apartheid dispensation – in other words, a contra-flow of sorts, albeit internal to the country only (and although still subject to the commercial logic referred to above, instead of originating among the com-munity itself). However, on another level, these tabloids also may be seen as the result of the globalization of media. They mirror the so-called 'red tops' of Britain as far as style and approach are concerned. As such they represent an example of the global expansion of media formats developed in the West and applied to other contexts, as Chadha and Kavoori mention with reference to programming. In the case of the tabloids, this is not a direct imitation; however the domestication of global formats by local exponents should be acknowledged (Chadha and Kavoori, 2005: 97).

There is not much to report regarding a contra-flow of print media from South Africa outwards, to reach across the country's borders. The local media conglomerate Naspers (formerly Nasionale Pers, associated with Afrikaner capital under apartheid) has restructured after democratization (see Tomaselli, 2000) and has explored a number of ventures abroad. Earlier in this chapter, the company's ventures into broadcasting were mentioned. On a much smaller scale, it has also started exporting some of its print media products; a number of its magazine titles have been launched in East Africa. In this sense, the South African print media sector provides a contra-flow to the barrage of international media content on the African continent. At the same time, however, questions may also be asked regarding the hegemony of South African cultural products facilitated through the media on the African continent – mostly by the broadcast media, as mentioned above, but also on a still small scale by the print media. As such, the contra-flow increasingly created by South African media introduces new issues around power relations on the continent.

Notes

1 Accurate and reliable statistics for Africa are hard to find. The BBC's international research department estimated in 1999 that there were 29 million TV sets in sub-Saharan Africa, about one for every 20 people. This compares to Asia and North Africa where there is one set for every six people. See Graham Mytton, 'From Saucepan to Dish', in Richard Fardon and Graham Furniss (eds), *African Broadcast Cultures* (Oxford: James Currey, 2000). As far as TV transmitting facilities are concerned, there are several African countries with only one terrestrial domestic broadcaster. In many countries, satisfactory reception can only be obtained in and around the major urban areas. See *World Radio TV Handbook* (Oxford: WRTH Publications, 2004).
2 Nationale Pers (Naspers) owned the greatest share, while Republican Press, Allied Publishing, and Times Media Limited held equal shares. In 1998 Naspers acquired control over MIH from the other press groups and in 2002 the MIH conglomerate including MultiChoice, M-Net and M-Web became a wholly owned subsidiary of Naspers.
3 http://www.multichoice.co.za/ourbusiness.
4 SAARF TV audience data 2003.
5 We are indebted to Veena Lala-Naidu, International Sales, SABC Content Enterprises for the information in this section.
6 http://www.channelafrica.org.
7 http://www.channelafrica.org.

References

Boyd-Barrett, O. (1998) 'Media imperialism reformulated', in D. K. Thussu (ed.), *Electronic Empires – Global Media and Local Resistance*. London: Arnold, pp. 157–76.

Chadha, K. and A. Kavoori (2005) 'Mapping interactions in policies, markets and formats', in J. Curran and M. Gurevitch (eds), *Mass Media and Society*. London: Hodder Arnold, pp. 84–103.

Du Plessis, C. (2005) 'Die behoefte aan bruin media? Ek sê my bra, die Ekstra is sat (enkele gedagtes rondom die behoefte al dan nie aan 'n Bruin Media)' [The demand for coloured media?], *Vrye Afrikaan*, 2 June 2005. Accessed 6 June 2005: http://www.vryeafrikaan.co.za/lees.php?id=232.

Horwitz, R. B. (2001) *Communication and Democratic Reform in South Africa*. Cambridge: Cambridge University Press.

Mytton, G., R. Teer-Tomaselli and A. Tudesq (2005) 'Transnational television in sub-Saharan Africa', in J. Chalaby (ed.), *Transnational Television Worldwide: Towards a New Media Order*, London: I. B. Tauris, pp. 96–127.

Sparks, C. (2000) 'The global, the local and the public sphere', in G. Wang, J. Servaes and A. Goonasekera (eds), *The New Communications Landscape – Demystifying Media*. London: Routledge, pp. 74–95.

Thussu, D. K. (1998) 'Infotainment international – a view from the South', in D. K. Thussu (ed.), *Electronic Empires – Global Media and Local Resistance*. London: Arnold, pp. 64–82.

Tomaselli, K. G. (2000) 'South African media, 1994–7: Globalizing via political economy', in J. Curran and M. Park (eds), *De-Westernizing Media Studies*. London: Routledge, pp. 279–92.

Chapter 10

Flows and contra-flows in transitional societies

Terhi Rantanen

The concept of 'flow' has a relatively long history in international communication studies. First, there is a long tradition of comparative news flow studies which started in the 1950s (see, for example, IPI, 1953; Kayser, 1953; Schramm, 1959; Hester, 1971, 1974; Sreberny-Mohammadi *et al.*, 1985). Second, there are studies on comparative television programme flows (see, for example, Varis, 1973; Nordenstreng and Varis, 1974; Varis, 1985) introducing the term one-way (Nordentreng and Varis, 1974) or uni-directional (Boyd-Barrett, 1977) flow. And finally, there is the concept of counter- or contra-flows (see for example, Boyd-Barrett and Thussu, 1992; Thussu, 2000: 206) which challenged the position of earlier theorists who claimed that the flow was only one-way.

All empirical studies on news and television flows have been based on methodological nationalism (Beck, 2002: 21) in which nation-states are seen as an unchallenged departure point for analysis. This position, which was dominant in international communication studies, has been challenged by many globalisation theorists, most notably by Arjun Appadurai, who himself has been using the concept of flow, but in a broader way. He talks about *global cultural* flows between five scapes, of which the mediascape is only one (Appadurai, 1998: 33), and shows the complex and multi-directional character of flows:

> The critical point is that both sides of the coin of global cultural processes today are products of an indefinitely varied, mutual contest of sameness and difference on a stage characterized by radical disjunctures between different sorts of global flows and the uncertain landscapes created in and through these disjunctures.
>
> (Appadurai, 1990: 308)

Hence, much has happened theoretically in the study of global media since the television flow studies. The research done on globalisation in many fields outside media and communication studies has challenged the previous theoretical analysis based on the dichotomy between the national and the international, and has introduced more layers, the most important of which are localisation and cosmopolitanisation. But, despite the paradigm change, most globalisation theories still relate to the West and speak to the West. But what about the media in those non-Western countries, such as Russia or China, that are also major political powers?

Defining Russia and China from inside and outside

Even before we start doing research on China and Russia, we need to define a term we can use to justify a joint analysis. As Elena Vartanova has remarked, it does not make sense to talk about post-communist media, because communism was never established anywhere. The term post-communist was thus inadequate from the beginning, but came to be used widely in the West. I am also guilty, since the subtitle of one of my books was *Media and Communications in Post-Communist Russia* (Rantanen, 2002).

Not only was that term incorrect in relation to post-socialist countries, but it also limited our view. China, for example, is not post-communist or even post-socialist, since the Communist Party continues to hold power. Still, it shares many similarities with post-socialist Russia, even if their current political systems are different. The term I will suggest here, instead of post-communist or post-socialist media, is *media in transition*, since this term is wide enough to cover all kinds of media systems that are in transition, no matter what the current political system is within which they operate.

One could, of course, counter this by saying that almost every media system anywhere is currently going through significant changes, such as globalisation, no matter what the political system. However, my argument is that socialist media systems that were earlier insulated on purely political grounds against globalisation encounter globalisation in a different way from those countries in which globalisation was never opposed for political reasons (see Rantanen, 2002). The main feature is that the media and communications systems in these countries have gone through a significant transformation where the *national* media and communications systems, formerly owned and/or controlled almost exclusively by one national party/government, are changing into media systems combining the national and the global. This is what Ulrich Beck (Rantanen, 2005a: 257) calls a 'both and' approach compared to an 'either or' approach that sees the relationship between the national and the global purely in dichotomist terms.

From inside

The 'either or' approach has dominated research in media and communications studies and is clearly seen in the attempts to study the development of and change in media systems. The most famous is of course the *Four Theories of the Press*, based on theories that lie behind the different kinds of press and which divided media into autocratic, libertarian, social responsibility and communist systems (Siebert *et al.*, 1956: 2). But it is not only Western scholars who have attempted to differentiate between media systems and to periodise them historically. A Chinese equivalent to the *Four Theories of the Press* is the three theories of (1) feudalistic, (2) capitalist-imperialistic and (3) socialist-communist media systems (Zhao, 2005). Apart from the obvious differences of opinion between the two models about the best possible media system, the two are strikingly similar. Both assume a complete transition from one model to the next in their respective societies and consider their own present media system to be the most advanced. Apart from the capitalist-imperialist stage, where imperialism is seen as the highest stage of capitalism with a territorial division of the whole world among the biggest Western capitalist powers (Lenin, 1917), both models see the development of media systems primarily as a national exercise.

From outside

Chalaby's (2005: 28–32) starting point is completely different. He has distinguished three phases in global media transition. The first is the *internationalisation* of the media that started in the nineteenth century when the first international markets emerged with the coming of the telegraph and submarine cables. The second, the *globalisation* of the media, took place from the 1960s, with innovations in telecommunications and computing and the emergence of a few global companies with a global reach. The third is the *transnationalisation* of the media, when market and audiences have become de-nationalised with the emergence and use of new media. Chalaby sees *cosmopolitanisation* as a distinctive feature of the third period. One could also argue that the cosmopolitanisation of the media will be the next phase.

Hence we have two ways to examine media in transitional societies: either from inside or from outside. The problem with both models is that they are not adequate in a situation where most media systems undergo a change that combines the national and the global. There is also a further problem in both approaches. The transformation of media and communications systems has often been defined solely from above as something that happens through institutions. My approach is different, since I want to include the users. I thus define the transition in media and communications as a process where media producers and users open up to the possible de-nationalisation of media and communications in a country where a national media system has been tightly controlled by the government and/or by a single party. These are not necessarily simultaneous processes that take place hand in hand, but there are junctions and disjunctions, to use Appadurai's (1998: 33–6) term, between institutions and individuals. As a result, the process is not fully controlled by institutions, but rather is unpredictable, depending on the junctures and disjunctures between institutions and individuals, and we have not yet seen a country where this process has been completed.

I speak not only about the media, but also include communications, in the sense that this is often defined as new media. Since it has become more and more difficult to separate media and communications, the distinction is not always necessary. But I do want to underline that I am speaking not only about traditional big media such as broadcasting, but also about small media (or communications) such as video, the Internet, etc.

The distinction I made in my research (Rantanen, 2002) between old and new media I still consider relevant, since one of my conclusions about the Russian media system was that the old media maintained their structures much longer and were more difficult to transform, while the new media were often left outside legislation and control. The old media are often considered the core media and are seen as particularly important objects for government or/and party control, while the new media are in the beginning seen as peripheral.

The phases suggested by Chalaby – internationalisation, globalisation, transnationalisation and cosmopolitanisation – are, as I see them, over-lapping and cannot be universally applied to different systems, since they are based on research done on the Western media. My argument is that in countries like China and Russia, they cannot be applied in the way presented by Chalaby, although there are similarities between his stages and what I am suggesting here. In China and Russia, I would argue that there have so far been three different stages. These are: (1) the cosmopolitanisation of the media; (2) the internationalisation of the media; (3) the globanationalisation of the media.

It is not only that the stages are different, but their reach is dissimilar. Where earlier models have assumed that the unit of analysis is a nation-state, I argue that the countries in question are internally divided and we should look at flows not only between countries but between cities and within countries. Some places in a country are more connected to similar places in other countries, while some are not. Equally, there is no simultaneous shift from one stage to the next, but countries can be internally divided.

The cosmopolitanisation of the media

Both Sassen and Castells have written about the importance of informational global cities (Castells, 1989; Sassen, 1994, 1998, 2002) in the current age of information. In this chapter, I use the concept of a cosmopolitan city to pinpoint the role of cities in the early phase of the cosmopolitanisation of the media. In most if not all countries, the first media were children of the big cities. China and imperial Russia were no exceptions, although compared to other countries their cosmopolitan cities were probably much more clearly divided from the rest of the country. Certain cities, primarily St Petersburg and to a certain extent Moscow in imperial Russia and Hong Kong, Guangzhou and Shanghai in China, operated as communication hubs for cosmopolitan elites who could speak several languages and had access to foreign-language newspapers and telegrams. The cosmopolitanisation of media had thus primarily to do with location and with individuals. These cities attracted individual cosmopolitans and became cosmopolitanised because of their connectivity to other cosmopolitan cities and the presence of these cosmopolitan individuals.

However, the individual cosmopolitans were privileged compared to the rest of the people both within and outside these cities. The cosmopolitans were primarily businesspeople, foreign government representatives, military officers, i.e., people with either a high political or high financial status, but also with a cultural status, such as intellectuals, artists and revolutionaries who were in contact with like-minded people in other cities, primarily abroad. For many reasons, including class and language, the cosmopolitans lived quite isolated lives from the rest of the country. This was a cosmopolitan lifestyle that only a few cities could provide, and only for a few people. In these cities transnational media, including foreign-language newspapers and telegrams from Western agencies, became available.

The cosmopolitan cities in China did not voluntarily become cosmopolitan. British troops forcefully opened up port cities in China to Western influence with the First Opium War (1839–42). Britain and other major Western powers forcibly Westernised these cities, which also became the media and communication hubs. The first telegraph line in China was built between Tianjin and Shanghai in 1881, and submarine cables were connected via Shanghai to inland telegraph lines (Yongming, 2006: 33, 71). By the end of the nineteenth century, foreigners had established more than 300 newspapers, most of them in Chinese and most published in Shanghai. They included *Shanghai Xinbao* [Shanghai News], *Wanguo Gongbao* [International Review], *Shen Bao*, *Xinwen Bao* [News Gazette] and *Min Bao* [People's Journal] (Chang, 1989: 7–8). These cities also had several foreign-language newspapers, and were locations for foreign correspondents and agents covering incoming and outgoing political and financial news.

The first newspaper in Russia, *Vedomosti*, founded by Peter the Great in 1704 in St Petersburg, was until 1756 the only paper to appear in Russian. St Petersburg, the new capital, became the media and communications hub of imperial Russia. The imperial court continued to grant privileges to foreign businessmen, artists, scientists and technicians to attract them to Russia. The Russian upper classes spoke several languages, primarily French, were much influenced by European, especially French, literature and arts and travelled frequently in Europe. Even those who resisted the system often ended up in exile in Europe. There were several newspapers that came out in different languages in St Petersburg, for example, *St Peterburger Zeitung* in German and *Journal de St Peterburg* in French. The main telegraph station was also located in St Petersburg in 1851, together with the telegraph agency in 1866. All foreign telegrams had to be sent and received via St Petersburg, where they were also censored (Rantanen, 1990: 71–2).

In this way, both St Petersburg and the port cities of China became cosmopolitan informational cities connected through news flows to other cosmopolitan cities such as London, Paris, Berlin and Vienna, and even to each other. They were seen as separate from the rest of the country due to their special position as locations where different languages were spoken and where different foreign cultures had a strong presence. The privileged position of the elites in these cities would be looked upon with suspicion by the rising national revolutionary movements, although even they benefited from the connectivity of these places.

Sassen (1998) talks about major new factors making claims to cities over the last decade, notably foreign firms that have been increasingly enabled to operate with the deregulation of national economies and the increasing number of international businesspeople. This phenomenon was already clearly visible in China's westernised ports and also to a certain extent in St Petersburg, although in an indigenised version where locals had the upper hand compared to foreigners. However, what was similar in all these cases was that both the production and the use of the media were mainly limited to these cities and to cities beyond China and Russia. The great majority of people outside these cities in Russia and China were not media-literate or could not afford to use the media.

The internationalisation of the media

The cosmopolitanisation of the media was to disappear with their nationalisation and internationalisation. The latter could not happen without the former, since there could be no international without the national. Nationalism as an idea was based on the unity constructed of territory, language and culture, and the media. With the rise of nation-states, comprehensive media coverage of a geographic area of a particular nation-state became more important for political and administrative purposes. This idea was reinforced by the process of internationalisation within which the media represented different nation-states. The concept was based on a homogeneity where the relationship between the media and a particular nation-state was not questioned, but was universally acknowledged as a basis for international co-operation.

In Soviet Russia, after the October Revolution of 1917, the task of creating all-national media was taken very seriously. ROSTA, later TASS, was established by the takeover of the St Petersburg Telegraph Agency in 1917 and its transformation in 1925 into an all-Soviet news agency under the Council of

People's Commissars of the USSR (Rantanen, 1994: 8; *O partiinoi i sovetskoi pechati, radioveschanii i televidenii*, 1972: 134–6). The Soviet model was a satellite model with the headquarters in Moscow and branch offices in the capitals of different Soviet republics (Bogdanov and Viazemsdkii, 1971: 136). Apart from the fact that this was a very centralised model, where the ultimate power lay in Moscow, there is clear evidence of early forms of *transnational* communication in a socialist context. This was a Soviet network society, for all its faults, where the national territory and the network society corresponded (Castells, 1998: 26–7), the influence of which cannot be underestimated. It was still based on the idea of the national, as was the Soviet Union itself, which acknowledged to a certain extent national differences and the sovereignty of Soviet republics, although the overall political system was highly centralised and vertical.

The nationalist movement in China started after the end of the First World War and resulted in the foundation of periodicals by the Communist Party. In 1931, during the Civil War, the communist regime founded the Red China News Press, which after the Republic of China was established became Xinhua [New China] News Agency. The Red China News Press released 'declarations and other documents of the Party Central Committee and the government, stories of constructions in the Soviet areas, communiqués on battles fought by the Red Army, and news about struggles carried on by the people in the Kuomintang-ruled areas'. Beginning in 1938, Xinhua established the Jin-Cha-Chi, North China, Shadong, Northwest Shaanxi and other offices (Chang, 1989: 17–21). Xinhua later adopted the TASS model for organising its operations, but gave its headquarters in Beijing centralised control over its branches (Xin, 2006).

This was the period when a new medium was introduced. Regular television broadcasts started in Moscow as early as 1931, but it was only by the 1960s that the number of television sets reached 4.8 million and then expanded rapidly. China began to experiment with television in 1956. The Soviet Union supplied most of the technical assistance and Beijing Television started experimental broadcasts on 1 May 1958. The break between China and the Soviet Union in 1960 affected the development of television in China. Only in the late 1960s did domestic manufacturing and the development of technical institutes lead to a resumption of the interrupted process (Howkins, 1982: 26–7). Television became a mass medium in the Soviet Union in 1970, when there were more than 70 million viewers. China's television audience, some 34 million in 1976, had grown to 590 million by 1987, and approached 1 billion by the late 1990s (Zhang, 2002). By 1994 television had reached 73 per cent of households in China and 98 per cent in Russia (UNESCO, 1997: 171, 187).

In both China and the Soviet Union, collaboration with foreign non-socialist media was restricted for ideological reasons. As a result, Soviet and Chinese media became one of the most self-sufficient media in the world. In

1971, the Soviet Union imported 5 per cent of its television programmes, while China imported only 1 per cent (Nordenstreng and Varis, 1974: 14). Ten years later, the Soviet Union still imported only 8 per cent of its programmes (Varis, 1985: 148). Most of the imported programmes were 'ideologically safe' – sports, music and cultural programmes and documentaries, but very few serials or films (see Table 10.1). The Soviet Union was, however, a major exporter: 24 per cent of imported programmes in Eastern Europe came from the Soviet Union (Varis, 1985: 36).

The national infrastructure was thus created for mass media that served primarily national and political purposes. The media system had to be controlled, centralised and vertical. Foreign journalists were viewed with suspicion; after 1949 all foreign correspondents were expelled from China. When a Reuters correspondent was allowed to return in 1956, for two years he was the only Western correspondent in China (Read, 1999: 449). The Soviet and

Table 10.1 Distribution of total imports in the Soviet Union by programme category and main countries of origin, between 31 January and 13 February 1983

Category	Total import minutes	Total import %	Country of origin	Minutes	%
Documentaries	145	7	USA	100	69
			USSR	12	8
			GDR	11	8
			Hungary	11	8
			Bulgaria	11	8
Cultural programmes	140	4	Spain	35	25
			Mongolia	30	21
			Sri Lanka	25	18
			Hungary	20	14
			USSR	10	7
			Bulgaria	10	7
			GDR	10	7
Children's programmes	60	5	Poland	30	50
			Hungary	15	25
			USSR	15	25
Cinema films	85	6	Mongolia	85	100
Music programmes	145	7	USSR	40	28
			Hungary	30	21
			Sri Lanka	30	21
			Poland	25	17
			Austria	20	14
Sports programmes	595	32	FRG	415	70
			Yugoslavia	100	17

Source: Varis, 1985: 59.

Chinese governments expelled several Western correspondents and tried to limit their personal contact with ordinary citizens (International Press Institute, 1953).

Although the audience had little direct access to foreign media and very little, if any, control over the content, they were provided with access to national *mass* media. In order to have some control over the content, the audience had to turn to small media such as the VCR in order to see the programmes they were denied for political reasons. Hence, in both China and the Soviet Union the globalisation of the media started from below rather than from above.

In the times when the media systems in the Soviet Union and China were controlled by their respective governments or communist parties, which sought to limit their citizens' access to media products that were considered politically or ideologically harmful, people found their own ways either to use the existing media in alternative ways or to get access to media and communications that were outside party and/or government control. The best-known example is *samizdat* in the Soviet Union, where people created their own media or combined existing media and communication for political purposes. But this was not only about politics: if Western or rock music was not available, it was copied and delivered from hand to hand. In China, students listened to their campus radio stations which played Western pop music (Rantanen, 2005b: 90). China has a quota of only ten foreign imported films a year, but American films are widely available even in the smallest towns, on pirated VCRs, VCDs and DVDs (Lull, 1991: 28; Rosen, 2003: 106). Western films were also widely watched in the former Soviet Union despite the fact that television did not show them (Rantanen, 2002: 55).

The 'globanationalisation' of the media

The official beginnings of transformation in the Soviet Union and China came officially six years apart: Deng Xiaoping's *gaige kaifang* (reform and opening up) began in 1979 (Kang, 2004: 1), while Mikhail Gorbachev's *perestroika* (restructuring) began in 1985, both resulting in ideological and cultural changes, including changes in the content of the mass media. In late 1979, China Central Television (CCTV) made China's first-ever purchase of a US series, *The Man from Atlantis*. Likewise, in 1979, CCTV bought two series from the BBC, *Anna Karenina* and *David Copperfield* (Chang, 1989: 214).

In both countries, the globalisation of the media started in big cities, but because of the mass national network created for political and national purposes, global media products soon spread all over the country. One of the unseen consequences of the socialist mass media system is that its mass orientation then provided a platform for global cultural flows to reach every corner of the country. When control was eased, there was nothing to hinder the effective spread of global, mostly Western, content.

Table 10.2 Imports of television drama into China by country of origin, 2004

Origin	Drama programmes	Episodes
US	86	256
Hong Kong	43	455
Taiwan	25	485
UK	24	66
Australia	14	28
Korea	13	164
France	13	26
Germany	12	24
Japan	10	28
Canada	5	10
Singapore	4	62
Monaco	4	8
India	3	42
Thailand	1	17
Spain	1	2
Sweden	1	2
Denmark	1	2
Italy	1	2
New Zealand	1	2
Total	262	1681

Source: SARFT.

In 1987, Soviet television showed a live ABC broadcast of the satellite Space Bridge, entitled *Capital to Capital*, which transmitted discussions between Soviet and American citizens. When Russian television started showing the Mexican soap opera *The Rich Also Weep* in 1992, it was estimated than 70 per cent of the population watched it regularly. The transformation of Russian television was enormous: in the early 1990s, Russian TV serials took up a mere 22 per cent of total air time, the rest being filled with US and Latin American soap operas. In 1997, of all Russian television programmes, 60 per cent were imported, and all serials were of foreign origin (Rantanen, 2002: 86), mostly soap operas from Brazil, Venezuela, Mexico, Europe and the United States. Of the domestic product, 90 per cent were old Soviet series of the 1970s and 1980s, like *17 Moments of Spring*. Russian series were shot on low budgets, were badly written and under-produced (Aksartova *et al.*, 2003: 75).

The popularity of Western TV serials had begun to decline by the mid-1990s and the number of foreign soap operas on Russian TV has shrunk dramatically. The leading channels replaced them with high-budget (in Russian terms), Russian-made crime drama series (Aksartova *et al.*, 2003: 75). The share of home-made serials on nationwide television has grown to 70 per cent. Industry estimates put the Russian TV serials market at $200 to $250 billion.

Table 10.3 The number of titles aired by top six Russian broadcasters, 1997–2001

Region	1997	1998	1999	2000	2001
Europe	111	132	144	120	134
Ex-USSR/Russia	103	111	116	139	175
USA	87	99	130	82	92
Others	38	39	46	38	45

Source: Aksartova *et al.*, 2003: 75.

The first commercially successful domestic productions were the costume dramas *La Dame de Monsoreau*, *Queen Margot* and *St. Petersburg Secrets*, with one minute of advertising time costing over $5,000. Advertising spots in Western productions became much cheaper – down to $800 per minute. In 2002, the total cost of home-made TV serials was $40 million; in 2003, $70 million, and in 2004, $150 million (Alyakrinskaya, 2005).

As several authors (Lee, 2003: 2–3; Rosen, 2003: 102; Kang, 2004: 9) have noted, globalisation has introduced the nationalist agenda into China's social discourses on the sovereignty of the nation-state and the nationalist project of modernisation. In Russia, we see a similar idea in the form of Great Russia (Zassoursky, 2000), where the national has been introduced in the name of law and order. In both cases, for different reasons, the national is back and has even replaced the socialist transcultural, whether this existed between socialist and developed countries or between Soviet republics. This is not only seen in production, as Tables 10.4 and 10.5 show, but also in the ratings of the most popular programmes in both Russia and China.

As many authors have shown, the changes in small and individual media had already started in the 1980s with the spread of small media and communications. The globalisation of the media is also different in Russia and in China, since in China the Communist Party still holds control. In Russia, two important structural factors gave way simultaneously: the state structures of the Soviet Union and the Communist Party control. However, in both countries most big media have remained mainly under government control. For example, although in Russia there are also private news agencies operating, ITAR-TASS and Xinhua have kept their status as official agencies for the government, and in Xinhua's case also for the Party.

Both in Russia and in China there have been recent attempts to provide global contra-flows in news, supported by the government. CCTV International (CCTV-9) the English-language, 24-hour news channel of China Central Television (CCTV), defines its role as 'China's contribution to greater diversity and more perspective in the global information flow'. Launched in 2000, CCTV International is dedicated to reporting news and information to its global audience, with a special focus on China (http://www.cctv.com/english/20040407/101796.shtml).

Table 10.4 Top ten Russian TV programmes, 8 to 14 October 2005

No.	Day	Begins	Ends	Programme	Channel	Share %	Rating %
1	Mo	19:01	19:59	Istselenye lyubovyu, serial (Russia-Ukraine)	Rossiia	39.9	11.2
2	Mo	17:59	19:01	Karmelita, serial (Russia)	Rossiia	44.2	10.9
3	Su	19:20	20:59	Lost, serial (USA)	First channel	35	10.4
4	We	20:00	20:29	Vesti, news	Rossiia	35.9	10.3
5	Thu	20:58	21:57	Neotlozhka, serial (Russia)	Russia	28	9.4
6	Fri	20:58	23:00	Krivoe zerkolo, concert	Rossiia	32.8	9.2
7	Su	21:00	21:25	Vremya, news	First channel	29	9
8	Mo	21:00	21:29	Vremya, news	First channel	27.9	9
9	We	21:57	22:59	Sarmat, serial	Rossiia	30	8.9
10	Su	21:25	24:01	Independence Day, film (USA)	First channel	33.1	8.8

Source: http://www.press-attache.ru/Section.aspx/ratings/tv/48/top100.

Table 10.5 Top TV serials in Beijing, August 2005

Ranking	TV series	Channel	Audience rating (%)
I	*The Spring Flower* (Chinese civil war)	BTV 2	8.4
2	*The Secret of the Country* (Chinese espionage)	CCTV 8	8.3
3	*The Grain Turns Yellow* (Japanese invasion)	BTV 4	7.3
4	*The Guerrillas* (Japanese invasion)	BTV 4	6.9
5	*The Fourth Route Army* (Historical kungfu)	CCTV I	6.7
6	*The Heroes in Northeast China* (Historical kungfu)	BTV 2	6.6
7	*The Sky of the History* (follows two soldiers' struggles against enemies, fate, and themselves from Japanese aggression to the cultural revolution (1966–76))	BTV Satellite	5.8
8	*Miss Mermaid 4* (Korean soap opera about a female writer's family)	CCTV I	5.8
9	*Heroes from the Yang Family* (Historical kungfu)	BTV 2	5.4
I0	*The Sixth Team 2* (Chinese police forces fighting against crime)	CCTV 8	5.I

Note:
The ranking is based on the feedback from the following channels: Sichuan Satellite, Hubei Satellite, Heilongjiang Satellite, Beijing Satellite, BTV 2, BTV 4, CCTV I, Guangxi Satellite, Shangdong Satellite and CCTV 8.

Source: http://www.csm.com.cn, trans. Hong Zhang.

In 2005, the Russian government launched 'Russia Today – From Russia to the World', a 24-hour, English-language television channel. This is the 'Russian equivalent to CNN or a kind of Russian BBC', offering international news 'from a Russian perspective', and broadcasting on cable and satellite throughout Europe, Africa, the US and parts of Asia, as well as in the former Soviet Union and Russia. The network is government funded, with an annual budget of $30 million, and draws heavily on the state-controlled RIA Novosti news agency.

Again, as before the revolutions, we see the emergence of cosmopolitan cities where foreign-language media are concentrated and where the latest communications technology is first used. In China, major metropolitan cities and economically more advanced regions have the best network facilities and most Internet users are based in Beijing, Shanghai and Guangzhou (UNESCO, 1999: 222; Hartford, 2003: 178). In Russia, the Internet spread first in Moscow and St Petersburg, but the most recent rapid growth has taken place in large academic circles. However, access is still mainly limited to big cities and many rural areas are not connected at all (Rantanen and Vartanova, 2003: 156–7).

Conclusion

The stages of transition in countries like Russia and China look different from those of many of their Western counterparts. The first stage, the cosmopolitanisation of Westernised (either by force or by class) cities has some similarities with the cosmopolitan cities of that era in the West, such as London, Paris, Berlin or New York. However, it is also remarkably different from these because of the huge differences outside these cities, in their respective countries. Precisely because of the disparity between cosmopolitans and others, access and connectivity beyond the national – whether this was linguistic, cultural, economic or political – became a source of suspicion and resistance.

However, the difference between the first and the second stage, that of internationalisation, is even more striking. The new period destroyed the special status of cosmopolitan cities, because they were considered suspicious if not dangerous. Socialist internationalisation, although taking place simultaneously with Western internationalisation, was a unique period not seen previously anywhere in the world. Although it was also based on the idea of sovereign nation-states, it celebrated collaboration between socialist nation-states and 'oppressed people', no matter what their location. In doing this, it developed a socialist version of transnationalism in which foreign audiences were de-nationalised across borders, while domestic audiences were tightly nation-bound with little or no access to Western programmes, but with access to programmes from other socialist and 'friendly' countries. In its division of the world into 'them' and 'us', it also became more inward- than outward-looking. However, it provided technological infrastructure, even if this did not always work perfectly, for the flow of *mass* media messages.

The third period, again, breaks away from the previous period, although not in an entirely similar way. In both China and Russia, the content of the mass media was globalised, with content and formats flowing from everywhere, but mainly from the West. The old forms of internationalisation were partly replaced by new forms of globalisation that opened up the content from its previous predominantly domestic or transnational production (although limited to other socialist countries) to global, mainly US, production. The audiences that had already found access to these products in the earlier period lost interest in them once they had become freely available and have now partly turned back to domestic content, but not to the early transnational content.

When both production and audience unite in what is being offered and what is being used, the result is often nationalism. In this situation, even with the re-emergence both in China and in Russia of cosmopolitan cities, one of the consequences has been the re-emergence of nationalism. Globalisation works in mysterious ways, and we can see one of its unexpected outcomes in countries like Russia and China. The outcome is not a de- but a renationalisation that turns its back even on the earlier forms of trans-nationalisation.

What is the next phase? Chalaby (2005) believes that the present period of transnationalism in Western countries carries in itself a seed of cosmopolitan-ism. Will China and Russia 'balance' the gap between the national and the Western (primarily US) flows with new forms of transnationalism that combine not only national but also other non-Western flows? Will they be able to provide significant contra-flows to the West? Or will their cosmopolitan cities unite with other cosmopolitan cities of the world through flows across their borders and give birth to new city states? Or will everybody, irrespective of location, become a cosmopolitan because of media and communications, because of global cultural flows?

So far what we have seen is that the media in transitional societies have developed their own forms of resistance, both from above and from below. Surprisingly, in China, where the Communist Party still holds sway, and in Russia, where the Communist Party has lost its power, the state has been able not only to hold on to its power but also even to increase it. This again shows the force of tradition: even if one period ends, there are elements that continue their life from one period to the next.

References

Aksartova, Sada, Floriana Fossato, Anna Kachkaeva and Grigory Libergal (2003) *Television in the Russian Federation: Organizational Structure, Programme Production and Audience. A report for the European Audiovisual Observatory.* Accessed 12 December 2005: http://www.obs.coe.int.

Alyakrinskaya, Natalya (2005) 'Home-made soaps dominate Russian TV', *The Moscow News*, 49, December 27. Accessed 27 December 2005: http://english.mn.ru/english/issue.php?2005-16-21.

Appadurai, Arjun (1990) 'Disjuncture and difference in the global cultural economy', *Public Culture*, 2 (3): 1–23.

Appadurai, Arjun (1998) *Modernity at Large. Cultural Dimensions of Globalization.* Minneapolis: University of Minnesota Press.

Beck, Ulrich (2002) 'The cosmopolitan society and its enemies', *Theory, Culture & Society* 19 (1–2): 17–44.

Bogdanov, N. G. and B. A. Viazemsdkii (1971) *Spravodchnik zhurnalista.* Moscow: Lenizdat.

Boyd-Barrett, Oliver (1977) 'Media imperialism: towards an international framework for the analysis of media systems', in James Curran, Michael Gurevitch and Janet Woollacott (eds), *Mass Communication and Society.* London: Edward Arnold, pp. 116–35.

Boyd-Barrett, Oliver and Daya Kishan Thussu (1992) *Contra-Flow in Global News. International and Regional News Exchange Mechanisms.* Acamedia Research Monograph 8. London: John Libbey.

Castells, Manuel (1989) *The Informational City. Information Technology, Economic Restructuring, and the Urban-Regional Process.* Oxford: Blackwell.

Castells, Manuel (1998) *The Information Age: Economy, Society, and Culture*. Oxford: Blackwell.

Chalaby, Jean (2005) 'From internationalization to transnationalization', *Global Media and Communication*, 1(1): 28–32.

Chang, Won Hu (1989) *Mass Media in China. The History and the Future*. Ames: Iowa State University Press.

Chin, Yik-Chan (2003) 'The nation-state in a globalizing media environment: China's regulatory policies on transborder TV drama flow', *Javnost*, 10(4): 75–92.

Hartford, Kathleen (2003) 'West Lake wired: shaping Hangzhou's information age', in Chin-Chuan Lee (ed.), *Chinese Media, Global Contexts*. London: RoutledgeCurzon, pp. 177–95.

Hester, Al (1971) 'An analysis of news flows from developed and developing nations', *Gazette*, 17(1–2): 29–43.

Hester, Al (1974) 'The news flow from Latin America via a world news agency', *Gazette*, 20(2): 82–91.

Howkins, John (1982) *Mass Communication in China*. New York: Longman.

International Press Institute (IPI) (1953) *The Flow of News*. Zurich: International Press Institute.

International Telecommunications Union (1999) *Challenges to the Network. Internet for Development*. Geneva: ITU.

Kang, Liu (2004) *Globalisation and Cultural Trends in China*. Honolulu: University of Hawaii Press.

Kayser, Jacques (1953) *One Week's News. Comparative Study of 17 Major Dailies for a Seven-Day Period*. Paris: UNESCO.

Lee, Chin-Chuan (2003) 'The global and the national of the Chinese media. Discourses, market, technology and ideology', in Chin-Chuan Lee (ed.), *Chinese Media, Global Contexts*. London: RoutledgeCurzon, pp. 1–31.

Lenin, V. I. (1917) *Imperialism, the Highest Stage of Capitalism*. Accessed 16 December 2005: http://www.fordham.edu/halsall/mod/1916lenin-imperialism.html.

Lull, James (1991) *China Turned On. Television, Reform and Resistance*. London: Routledge.

Nordenstreng, Kaarle and Tapio Varis (1974) *Television Traffic: A One-Way Street? A Survey and Analysis of the International Flow of Television Programme Material*. Reports and Papers on Mass Communication, no. 70. Paris: UNESCO.

O partiinoi i sovetskoi pechati, radioveschanii i televidenii (1972) *Sbornik dokumentov i materialov*. Moscow: Mysl'.

Rantanen, Terhi (1990) *Foreign News in Imperial Russia: The Relationship between International and Russian News Agencies, 1856–1914*. Helsinki: Federation of Finnish Scientific Societies.

Rantanen, Terhi (1994) *Howard Interviews Stalin. How the AP, UP and TASS Smashed the International News Cartel*. Roy W. Howard Monographs in Journalism and Mass Communication Research, no. 3. Bloomington: Indiana University Press.

Rantanen, Terhi (2002) *The Global and the National. Media and Communications in Post-Communist Russia*. Lanham, MD: Rowman & Littlefield.

Rantanen, Terhi (2005a) 'Cosmopolitanization-now. An interview with Ulrich Beck', *Global Media and Communication*, 1(3): 247–63.

Rantanen, Terhi (2005b) *The Media and Globalization*. London: Sage.

Rantanen, Terhi and Elena Vartanova (2003) 'Empire and communications: centri-
fugal and centripetal media in contemporary Russia', in Nick Couldry and James
Curran (eds), *Contesting Media Power: Alternative Media in a Networked World*.
Lanham, MD: Rowman & Littlefield, pp. 147–62.

Read, Donald (1999) *The Power of News*. Oxford: Oxford University Press.

Rosen, Stanley (2003) 'Chinese media and youth. Attitudes toward nationalism and
internationalism', in Chin-Chuan Lee (ed.), *Chinese Media, Global Contexts*. London:
RoutledgeCurzon, pp. 97–116.

Sassen, Saskia (1994) *Cities in a World Economy*. Thousand Oaks, CA: Pine Forge Press.

Sassen, Saskia (1998) *Globalization and Its Discontents*. New York: The New Press.

Sassen, Saskia (2002) *Global Networks, Linked Cities*. New York: Routledge.

Schramm, Wilbur (1959) *One Day in the World's Press: Fourteen Great Newspapers on a Day
of Crisis*. Stanford: Stanford University Press.

Siebert, Fredrick S., Theodore Peterson and Wilbur Schramm (1956) *Four Theories of
the Press*. Urbana: University of Illinois Press.

Sreberny-Mohammadi, Annabelle *et al.* (1985) *Foreign News in the Media. International
Reporting in 29 Countries*. Reports and Papers on Mass Communication, no. 93.
Paris: UNESCO.

Thussu, Daya Kishan (2000) *International Communication. Continuity and Change*. London:
Arnold.

UNESCO (1997) *The Media and the Challenges of the New Technologies*. World Communication Report, no. 759. Paris: UNESCO.

UNESCO (1999) *World Communication and Information 1999–2000*. Report no. 792.
Paris: UNESCO.

Varis, Tapio (1973) *International Inventory of Television Programme Structure and Flow of
TV Programmes between Nations*. Tampere, Finland: University of Tampere,
Research Institute Reports B 20.

Varis, Tapio (1985) *International Flow of Television Programmes*. Reports and Papers on
Mass Communications, no. 100. Paris: UNESCO.

Xin, Xin (2006) 'A developing market in news: Xinhua News Agency and Chinese
newspapers', *Media, Culture & Society*, 28(1): 45–66.

Yongming, Zhou (2006) *Telegraphy, the Internet and Political Participation in China*.
Stanford: Stanford University Press.

Zassoursky, Ivan (2000) 'The Rise and Transformation of the Media-Political
System'. Paper presented at the IAMCR Conference in Singapore, 17–20 July.

Zhang, Hong (2002) 'The Development of Press Freedom and Its Economic and Political Implications for PRC in the Era of Reform'. An unpublished MSc dissertation. The Institute of Communications Studies, University of Leeds.

Zhao, Xinshu (2005) A presentation at an International Conference on Chinese television and Globalization at Duke University, NC, 28–29 October.

Chapter 11

Chinese news in transition

Facing the challenge of global competition

Steven Guanpeng Dong and Anbin Shi

Following a lengthy ten-year consideration period within the decision-making circles of the Chinese Communist Party (CCP), China's first 24-hour news channel (CCTV-News) entered the media scene on 1 May 2003. However, this new development has not necessarily been matched by an increase in the quality of news provision. The move is also regarded as a direct reaction to the Hong Kong-based Phoenix TV's challenge in all aspects of television programming beyond the news. This chapter discusses the factors that led to the emergence of the new channel and also assesses problems associated with state-owned television networks in China. The discussion analyses the driving forces that underpinned the creation of the news channel (including demand for satisfactory coverage of news events, a change in the leadership of the CCP's 'thought work' regime, economic changes and CCTV's long-term strategic goals).

The weaknesses of these changes include the lack of original international coverage for news and failure to provide up-to-date news comparable to Western standards. Several challenges and limitations threaten CCTV's long-standing monopoly, including competition with other media providers – such as Rupert Murdoch's joint venture Phoenix Television, the growing imports of Korean television dramas and the increasing impact of the Internet. The prevailing attitude within Chinese media circles is that this intense competition will probably impinge on the remapping of the Chinese television industry and to a larger extent, delineate a new topography of the media landscape.

The need for a 24-hour news channel in China

On 1 May 2003 a significant development took place in China's media industry – the country's first 24-hour news channel (CCTV-13, more commonly known as CCTV-News) was launched, providing television coverage of events as they unfold. The channel provides news updates every hour, interspersed by in-depth coverage of news in four categories: Financial and Business, Culture, Sport and International Issues. The slogan of the channel is

'To keep the same pace with the world, to walk together with the times'. Impressively, almost every province in China was able to receive the channel after it had been on air for just one month.

Given the obvious benefits, indeed the necessity, of 24-hour news provision in China, it is perhaps surprising that CCTV-News emerged very recently. Discussions about creating a 24-hour news channel took place during the 1990s but lengthy consideration periods within the Central Propaganda Department meant that the channel remained only an idea until 2003. Several factors contributed to its conception. Perhaps the most important reason was increased criticism that CCTV received regarding its failure to respond to important news events in a timely and comprehensive manner. In particular, when big news stories (such as the 9/11 terrorist attacks) unfolded, CCTV did not report them quickly and news updates during the stories were inadequate. This lack of responsiveness caused widespread dissatisfaction throughout China, especially among the growing middle classes, comprised of white-collar workers, leaders of government agencies and social institutions, intellectual and professional elites, who were believed to be the emergent 'opinion leaders' in Chinese society. Further, there was potential for this dissatisfaction to escalate because the number of 'emergencies' reported by the Chinese media is increasing (although scholarly debate exists over whether this reflects a real increase in the number of actual emergencies or simply more open-mindedness on the part of the media). Satisfactory reporting of these events, especially breaking news stories, had not been achieved by the previous news structure and it was recognized that an exclusive news channel was needed: CCTV-News filled a niche within China's television industry.

Increased dissatisfaction with propaganda stories and viewers' concerns about lack of transparency of news also created demand for the 24-hour news channel. These issues centre on the tendency of the Chinese media to privilege positive news and abstain from criticism of the government or the party as well as the rather limited representative nature of news stories. Although this situation has existed for several decades, foreign channels are now available in China; viewers are sometimes confused by the different versions of events broadcast by national and international channels and some people feel they may be duped by state propaganda.

Competition from other stations motivated CCTV to improve the scope of its news provision. The market in China is large and lucrative: by 1999 China had about 320 million more television sets than the USA, and many media giants endeavour to enter China's vast market (Lawrence, 1999; Thussu, 2000). An example of a competitor that threatens the future success of CCTV is the Hong Kong-based Phoenix Television. The station, owned by News Corporation, was launched in China in 1996. Ma (2001) believes that Phoenix TV station is currently the only channel that can challenge CCTV. For example, Phoenix provided impressive news coverage during the

September 11 terrorist attacks whereas CCTV did not even report the inci-
dent during the initial 48 hours. Phoenix has successfully balanced the need
to provide comprehensive news about China without criticizing the central
government. Also, the company has been successful at transforming the
image of news presenters in China (until very recently, Chinese news presenters were simply considered to be providers of news whereas Phoenix television transformed their role into a celebrity status). In order to compete
with stations such as Phoenix Television, CCTV needed a channel devoted
exclusively to 24-hour news. It is evident, then, that there were several reasons
why the CCTV-News channel was set up. Unfortunately, the channel has
not met its expectation of being lively and groundbreaking – its news provision (in terms of quality and scope) does not match the standards set by
comparable news channels in the West.

Several driving forces contributed to the emergence of the 24-hour news
channel. An important change was the shift of decision-making powers from
the Chinese Communist Party (CCP) which ultimately controls CCTV.
This change allowed CCTV to exert greater control over the future direction
of their organization. The departure of President Jiang Zemin and the
appointment of the new standing committee members of the CCP Politburo
also had a direct influence. The previous leadership came to power following
a period of chaos in the late 1980s; the majority was promoted from provincial to state level directly and consequently their main priority was to
stabilize the socio-political arena. In contrast, the new leadership acquired
power at a time when the country was more stable and therefore it was possible to tackle politically sensitive issues such as reforming the state-owned
media. President Hu and his cabinet were also generally more amenable to
supporting reforms.

A second factor that prompted CCTV to launch a 24-hour news channel
was the improvement in the economy. In contrast to the 1990s, the media in
China were almost ready by the time China joined the World Trade Organization in 2001 to face the challenges of opening up the market to international investment (Brahm, 2002). The opening up of the Chinese economy
to foreign investors has resulted in competition – the business environment in
which CCTV now operates is completely different compared to a decade
ago (Hong, 1998). Both highlighted the changes in China's television industry, the most noteworthy of which is a proliferation of national, regional and
local stations (including cable television), an increase in leisure time (that is,
more viewing time), a growth in the number of foreign television services,
and also fiercer competition for audiences. Many Chinese viewers are now
able to receive foreign channels such as CNN, NHK, BBC and STAR TV
using satellite dishes and the Internet. Further, residents in Fujian and
Guangdong can receive broadcasts from Taiwan and Hong Kong without
the need for satellite dishes. Consequently, since the 1990s, television viewers
in China have become more selective about the programmes they watch

and, given the wide range of media in which news is communicated, it has become more difficult for television channels to attract and retain viewers (Hong, 1998).

Several other factors motivated CCTV to provide 24-hour news. The growing middle class is a new market demanding up-to-date news. Prior to CCTV-News, the only satisfactory news programme was available from *Xin Wen Lian Bo* (News Bulletin) on CCTV-1 at 7 p.m. everyday, but many professionals were not satisfied with this limited service. Further, increased numbers of young intellectuals, including those with an overseas education, entered the civil service (including CCTV) and influenced the culture of their workplaces. Additionally, leisure time has increased for most Chinese because, in the early 1990s, the six-day working week was reduced to five days and this change has led to a greater demand for better quality programming.

The creation of CCTV-News is part of CCTV's overall strategy to expand its media territory and to achieve its desired reputation as a world-class broadcaster. A channel that provides 24-hour news provision can be used as an indicator of success; conversely if CCTV cannot provide professional news coverage then such a situation could indicate that the organization is not a key player in the media industry. CCTV aims to become the first choice brand for media, perhaps a gold standard against which competitors are compared; all of these facts were reflected in the creation of CCTV-News.

The cornerstones of the 24-hour news channel

There were several cornerstones, however, which set the foundation for the establishment of the news channel. First, although it took a long time for the CCP to approve the channel, there were long-standing endeavours within CCTV's management division for blueprinting and launching the channel immediately, regardless of when the central government made a decision. This blueprinting, which reflects CCTV management's long-term prospect, facilitated the development of the channel quickly and smoothly once its approval was announced.

A second cornerstone was the timely reporting of the 2003 US invasion of Iraq and the impact the reporting had on CCTV's capabilities. The commencement of the war was reported on CCTV-1 only five minutes after it had begun and was announced on CCTV-4 a few minutes later. This was an important event because timely reporting was unusual for CCTV, and contrasts sharply to its previous responses to big stories. Efficient coverage of the Iraq War clearly demonstrated that CCTV was capable and ready to report news events immediately and accurately. When an anonymous decision-maker in CCTV was interviewed, he told us that CCTV wanted to show the government and the people that they were ready to report the news immediately. The interview also revealed that although CCTV had been previously criticized for delays in its reporting of important events, the situation was

not representative of its capabilities. In fact, most employees want to transform the way that CCTV reports news but realize that the changes cannot
take place quickly; indeed, CCTV boasts a workforce that is highly talented
and well qualified but the station is still the mouthpiece of the government
and its reporting needs to reflect this fact.

However, the coverage of the Iraq War helped to change the situation;
doubts both within the central government and among mass audience about
CCTV's ability to handle breaking news stories were assuaged because
during the war, CCTV's reporting was comparable to a rolling news channel.
Further, there was competition between CCTV-1 and CCTV-4 (both
channels with a large proportion of news programmes), with people debating
about which channel would be quicker to report events and which channel
would attract the majority of the audience. In other words, the idea of timely
and accurate news was put into the public arena for the first time, and in a
positive and non-threatening way. Zhao (2004) describes the positive feedback from the BBC and Japanese news agencies about CCTV's reporting of
the Iraq War. The BBC reported that the 'Chinese media's reporting on the
Iraq War is very balanced' whereas comments made by a Japanese newspaper stated, 'CCTV had an incredible coverage. It was really interesting
reporting. We believe Chinese media is on its way to change' (quoted in
Zhao, 2004: 41). Obviously, such positive comments about Chinese media
from renowned overseas news organizations were well received by CCTV
and the Chinese government, and demonstrated that CCTV could successfully report international news around the clock.

The creation of CCTV-News was set around several aims, including that
of being closer to the public; servicing the macro-environment, producing
news with Chinese characteristics, and achieving the highest professional
standards. The channel also follows the three 'closer' principles set by CCP's
leadership, all of which aim to transform the status quo of news media. They
are: closer to the practical, closer to the public, and closer to the everyday.
In other words, the principles direct news to be closer to the mass audience
than to the leadership. Moreover, the director of CCTV-News channel, Li
Ting, laid down his expectations of the channel. He insisted that the news
must be accurate and timely, that the background of the news should be
detailed and all-encompassing, that the news programming should be directed towards the official mainstream ideology, and that its format should be
audience-friendly (CCTV, 2003–04).

The success of another Chinese news programme, the 7 p.m. *News Bulletin*,
which celebrated its 25th anniversary recently, also influenced the decision
to go for a dedicated news channel. During those 25 years, the programme
has become a recognized leader of news reporting in China, has developed its
own brand image, and claims to have a viewership exceeding one billion.
The need to maintain and develop further a trusted and respected brand
motivated CCTV to consider breaking away from propaganda reporting

and to exploit the fact that the people trusted their news based on its brand reputation. The creation of CCTV-News was an opportunity to maintain, and enhance, the audience's brand loyalty to CCTV by pursuing more ground-breaking stories and styles. To aid this, CCTV-News took over a well-known controversial news programme called *Focus Interview* [*Jiaodian Fangtan*]. Following Prime Minister Zhu Rongji's earlier comment that 'if *Focus Interview* is not going to report on any negative news, I will not watch it', the programme has gained a reputation based on reporting critical news such as corruption. CCTV-News may, therefore, provide an avenue for CCTV to improve its general image.

The last cornerstone was a change in the leadership's attitude towards the reporting of their activities. On 28 March 2003, the Standing Committee of the Politburo passed new regulations (entitled 'On further developing and improving of Party Conference Reporting' and 'Top leadership activity report') which allowed greater reporting of the leadership's activities. After these resolutions, it became clear that the 'actual voice' of the leadership was being heard on CCTV for the first time rather than weak, voice-over interpretations of leadership activities.

The partisan vs. the commercial: limitations and challenges

Several of the factors that fuelled the conception of CCTV-News are actually double-edged swords because they also pose tough challenges to the future success, or even survival, of the channel. For example, although CCTV-News was partly created because of the increasing success of other media organizations such as Phoenix Television, these stations continue to offer tough competition. Another competitive threat is the Internet, as news is readily available online from both Chinese and foreign websites. It could be argued that the threat of the Internet is small because greater numbers of Chinese people have access to a television compared to the Internet: although China had 59.1 million Internet users in 2002, there were only about 27.6 computers per 1,000 people in the country (World Bank, 2004). In contrast, CCTV broadcasts to a much wider audience. Further, Internet users tend to be concentrated in three regions – Beijing, Guangdong and Shanghai, home to nearly 44 per cent of all Internet users in China (Brahm, 2001); in contrast CCTV-News has a much wider reach. However, competition from the Internet should not be underestimated as its usage is increasing exponentially every year due to changing attitudes, reduction in telecom charges, increased spending power, and plans for a Chinese-language software industry (Lewis, 2001; Yip, 2001). Indeed, Zhao Qizheng, the former minister of the State Council and Information Office, stated in 2001 that 'in terms of the time period from the introduction of one type of new electronic medium to the formation of 5,000 users, it takes 38 years for broadcasting, 13 years for wireless

television and 10 years for cable. It takes only four-years for Internet'
(quoted in CCTV, 2002). Undoubtedly, the Internet will revolutionize China
and its media over the next few years.

Another problem that CCTV-News needs to address is the quality of its
news, especially when compared to Western 24-hour news channels. Before
its launch, the media industry set high expectations for CCTV-News in the
hope that it would provide a livelier and more professional approach
currently lacking within the state-owned media. Unfortunately, these expectations have not been met. Also, although CCTV-News is theoretically a
24-hour news channel, in reality the same half-hour slot is continually repeated
throughout the day, even though many people want to watch the channel for
longer periods. Another quality issue is the lack of integration between
departments within CCTV. The CCTV organization can be described as
an 'under-developed land with many people wanting to cultivate'. Many
decision-makers are based in different departments and there is lack of communication between them; consequently many programmes overlap and are
repetitive.

It is also important to consider that foreign organizations, such as the BBC
and CNN, have different operational management philosophies. It is fair to
say that issues such as investment strategy, financial management, human
resource management etc., are more developed in Western organizations.
For example, Küng-Shankleman (2000) explained how the organizational
culture (as well as the interrelationships between quality and performance)
plays a major role in contributing to the success of the BBC and CNN.
However, fine-tuning the relationship between organizational culture and
performance is generally alien to Chinese organizations. Also, unlike
CCTV-News, global media organizations are very experienced in the competitive market, thus giving them an edge over CCTV. Phoenix Television
very effectively competes with CCTV and its success is partly based on Rupert
Murdoch's unmatched experience in media competition and his ability to
overcome the potential barriers that any market in China presents. For
example, the station localized Phoenix Television by ensuring that Chinese
professionals facilitate top management and decision-making. Phoenix Television has been sensitive to issues in China and has actively worked to smooth
relations with the government; for example, they removed the BBC from its
service following criticism over human rights abuses, cancelled another
potentially negative contract with HarperCollins, set up a joint venture with
the *Peoples Daily* newspaper, and organized a concert following the 1999
NATO bombing of the Chinese Embassy in Belgrade (Thussu, 2000).

Although Phoenix Television has successfully overcome the barriers of the
Chinese media market, CCTV remains bogged down by a failure to balance
party journalism and commercialization. Ma (2001) compared the Chinese
and international news broadcasting models. She described how the acceptance or rejection of news headlines is determined by political guidelines.

Consequently, headlines commonly include state leaders receiving visitors or a hero/model worker being introduced to the nation; in contrast, Western stations report the top stories dominating the world news. According to Ma, this major 'Chinese characteristic' means that 'a series of receptions and meetings are grandly pushed out into the news . . . obviously this style of news broadcasting – of highlighting politics – is different from the international, generally accepted news-broadcasting model' (Ma, 2001).

Another characteristic of the Chinese media is 'positive propaganda' which often results in the reporting of unnecessary news. For example, Li described how the reporting of floods in China was used to promote the image of the army; news pictures of the army working hard to save the Chinese people enhanced their public image. Other positive propaganda stories have included praising workers such as bus attendants and primary school teachers from remote areas. Although these activities have some merit, it is difficult to judge if viewers actually want to watch these events compared to breaking news stories available on other channels. The international models of news reporting adopted by competitors, particularly Phoenix TV, means that CCTV-News may be at a competitive disadvantage with regard to attracting audiences. Zhao (1998) discussed the intertwined nature of the commercialization of the media in China. Despite the commercialization of the media, and some reforms, urgent change is needed. She believes that values from commercial media in the West and Hong Kong are more informative and less didactic.

Another point to consider is that foreign news channels often provide critical commentary of governments whereas in the Chinese media there is a lack of critical evaluation of government policies and behaviours; this is exemplified by Schnell's (1999) interesting discussion of the lack of political cartoons in Chinese newspapers. Although political cartoons are common in the West they are rare in China, presumably because the government (which owns the press) does not want to be criticized or lampooned. The government has also expressed concern over the negative impacts of foreign television programmes, including the effects of movies on teenagers. For example, Lynch described how the leadership has previously set limits to the proportion of broadcasting time allocated to foreign programmes (in 1993 the government limited to 20 per cent the total air time allowed to foreign broadcasting, and in 1996, foreign programmes were suspended from prime-time television (Lynch, 1999)).

The partisan vs. the professional: global norms and Chinese characteristics

The catchphrase 'Chinese characteristics' has become a convenient cliché in dealing with the prevalent uncertainties and incommensurabilities for the global/local, China/the West and tradition/modernity encounters. However, such an all-encompassing yet vague notion as 'Chinese characteristics' cannot but patronize a 'don't ask, don't tell' escapism in the ideological realm of contemporary China, which undermines the further implementation of political and institutional reform, including that of the press and media. In this sense, China's entry into the WTO forces ideologues and policy-makers to abjure the banal pretext of 'Chinese characteristics' and to rationalize all the aforementioned dichotomies and discrepancies. The partisan/professional duality in Chinese news media reinforces the urgency and necessity for such rationalization in the face of global media's penetration into local arenas.

For decades, professionalism has been the central tenet of Western journalism, based on the belief that the media should stand outside and be detached from the subjects of their reporting. The norms of objectivity, impartiality and neutrality, which are all encompassed into this vague notion of 'professionalism', have been disseminated around the globe via the power of global communication. Journalists and media professionals – if they aspire to become professionals rather than partisans or government mouthpieces – are required to observe events and relate them to their audience as if from the perspective of 'God's eye' (Schudson, 2003).

The transformation of journalism from nineteenth-century partisanship to twentieth-century commercial-professionalism in the United States has become a universal norm for press/media reform in developing countries. Optimists foresee that the global media's entry into the Chinese marketplace would expedite, if not impose, the US model of transformation upon this largest 'un-democracy' in the world. In point of fact, such a process of transformation is far more complex than any ready-made prototype prescribed by a universal 'globality'.

In one of the most thorough studies and the most forceful argumentations thus far, Zhongdang Pan and Lu Ye have situated the Western model of professionalism into a 'discursive practice' in contemporary China. They aptly identify four discourses – namely, party-press, Confucian intellectual, professional, and market-economy – that Chinese journalists manipulate for their local recontextualization of the global norm of professionalism (Pan and Lu, 2003: 218–28). Put another way, contemporary Chinese journalists, to both authors, are manoeuvring strategies of Maoist 'guerrilla warfare' or Gramscian multi-directional 'war of positions' into their resistance to the doubly crushing power of partisan politics and market economy. Drawing upon Michel de Certeau's theorization of the everyday, and based upon a series of sociological surveys and ethnographic fieldwork, both authors attempt to draw a conclusion that the prototypical and idealistic model of professionalism is empirically dysfunctional and needs to be reinvented through Chinese journalists' everyday practices.

In many ways, Pan and Lu's study on Chinese specificities echoes their Western counterparts' increasing critique of professionalism in recent years.

As Michael Gurevitch succinctly points out, such a hallowed norm of 'apartness' as the central tenet of professionalism is all but a flawed myth, both empirically and conceptually. Journalists cannot 'extricate themselves from their societal context, either physically, socially or culturally, any more than other members of society' can. They cannot, therefore, claim – and hence should not pretend to – be able to 'observe the social world as if they were not part of it', as if from 'a position floating above it' (Gurevitch 1991: 178–80). By way of his study on the rapid globalization of television news, Gurevitch advocates the reinvigoration of the 'participatory' tradition of partisan journalism, wherein news media serve as a forum for discussion and debate.

Such doubt and challenge towards the ideal type of Western professionalism can be traced back to the early 1970s, when sociologists and political scientists conducted numerous ethnographic observations of newsroom practices, showing that media bias derives not from 'intentional perversion' but from 'professional achievement under the constraints of organizational routines and pressures' (Schudson, 1983: 5–7). Michael Schudson further identifies that the institutionalized application of professionalism is subject to five types of distortion in news media, namely: (1) event-centred, action-centred, and person-centred; (2) negative; (3) detached; (4) technical; and (5) official. Ironically, according to Schudson, both partisan and professional journalism converge on an overreliance on legitimate public sources, usually high-ranking government officials and a relatively small number of experts (Schudson, 2003: 48–55). This is even more so in post-9/11 US journalism, wherein 'patriotism through journalism' has turned into an accepted reality both for media professionals and for the general audience. On a global scale, the recent decade has witnessed news media's shift to cynicism and infotainment, or what Dutch media scholar Liesbet van Zoonen calls the 'intimization' of the news (1991: 217–35).

Admittedly, Western media's penetration into Third World nations has turned professionalism into a global norm, which has to be recontexualized in various local contexts. Moreover, the globalization of news media under global media's patronage has also shown that the US model of transforming the partisan into the professional is universally applicable. However, the aforementioned scholars, by way of drawing upon Western or non-Western experiences, all attempt to deconstruct the hyperbolical myth of professionalism. Relating the issue to the Chinese context, we may draw the following hypotheses on the basis of their empirical studies and/or theoretical argumentations:

1 Professionalism is never a fixed, unitary category, but rather consists of 'necessary constructions in necessary situations' (Weeks, 1991: 3).
2 Professionalism, especially the US model of commercial-professionalism, is not necessarily conducive to press freedom and media democratization.

3   In the case of Chinese press/media reform, the tradition of partisan journalism should not be completely relinquished, but rather should be reinvented as a complementary resource to the ongoing reform.
4   As long as CCP maintains the treatment of news media as its 'mouthpiece' (*hou she*, literally, throat and tongue), the negotiation between the partisan and the professional should be undertaken to find out an alternative model for Chinese journalists' 'discursive practice'.

A Chinese version of public/civic journalism?

The discursive negotiation between partisanship and professionalism all but reflects the fundamentally structural tension between the CCP-dominated press system and the ongoing media commercialization in contemporary China. Remaining central to such tension is the 'mouthpiece' theory, which CCP commissars employ to legitimate its firm control of the press and media in the past five decades. Following in the same vein as Jiang Zemin's open-ended theory of the 'Three Represents', Chinese scholar Tong Bing has attempted to redefine the role of news media along the following three dimensions:

1   The right to know and the right to communicate are basic human rights which are constitutionally legitimate.
2   News media can serve as the mouthpiece both for the Party and for the general public.
3   News media can be defined both as an Althusserian 'state ideological apparatus' and as an integral part of the profit-oriented 'service industry' (Tong, 2003: 18–20).

Its empirical contradictions and theoretical ambiguities aside, Tong's re-definition can be read as another typical manifestation of 'post-politics' prevalent in the ideological domain of contemporary China. The term 'post-politics', coined by Chinese critic Chen Xiaoming, embodies a condition wherein 'everything is political and nothing is political at one and the same time; politics is everywhere, and yet it subverts itself at any moment' (Chen, 2000: 222–3). Obviously, such post-politics reflects CCP's current agenda in cultural/ideological domains, that is, to shift decidedly away from Maoist revolutionary legacies and towards pragmatic objectives for maintaining order and stability, or the status quo (Liu, 2004: 19–28).

For Chinese journalists and media professionals, Tong's redefinition of the news media's role lends legitimacy to their experimentation of negotiating the partisan/professional. Post-politics is characterized by their eclectic motto, 'Helping but not making trouble' (*bamang bu tianluan*), that is, to help the public voice their concerns while not making trouble for top Communist Party leadership. This approach has been central to the development of public/civic journalism. Since 1 April 1994, Chinese Central Television (CCTV) aired *Focused Interview*, a 15-minute in-depth news programme in the mould of CBS's *60 Minutes* segments. At the core of the programming are interpretation of current affairs, investigative reportage, and watchdog journalism. The programme has gained official endorsement from topmost leadership, high ratings from general audiences and considerable revenues from advertisers, which has led to a boom in public/civic journalism in the Chinese news media.

We need, however, to rethink what 'public/civic journalism' means in different global/local contexts. The notion surfaced primarily at a group of American mid-size daily newspapers in the late 1980s. Davis 'Buzz' Merritt, one of the advocates in this campaign and editor/vice president of the *Wichita Eagle*, has defined key aspects of civic journalism as follows:

- It moves beyond the limited mission of 'telling the news' to a broader mission of helping public life go well, and act out that imperative.
- It moves from detachment to being a fair-minded participant in public life.
- It moves beyond only describing what is 'going wrong' to also imagining what 'going right' would be like.
- It moves from seeing people as consumers – as readers or non readers, as bystanders to be informed – to seeing them as a public, as potential actors in arriving at democratic solutions to public problems (Merritt, 1995: 113–14).

Obviously, Merritt's idealistic model of civic journalism finds fault with the norm of apartness, which remains central to professionalism and prevails in contemporary American journalism. Moreover, he also attempts to resuscitate the participatory nature and the overriding concern with political/public issues, as manifested in the bygone tradition of partisan journalism. Interestingly enough, Sun Yu-Sheng, the founder and then producer of *Focused Interview*, shares a similar approach in defining the guidelines for his news programming, which can be read as a tentative definition of a Chinese version of public/civic journalism:

- To maintain a correct standpoint in our observation, interview, analysis and programming; do not 'give vent to outrage and be killed'.
- Social conflicts and problems remain the core to our news programming while a positive standpoint must be adhered to, that is, to construct but not to destroy.
- The topical selection, interview skills, shooting, editing, and programming must conform to the criteria of television newsworthiness (Sun, 2003: 5–6).

To a non-Chinese observer, Sun's vision appears to be a far cry from Merritt's model of public/civic journalism. We should bear in mind, however, that Sun, as a senior editor with one of the topmost CCP's 'mouthpieces' rather than a liberal intellectual, cannot but state his reformist ideas in line with official rhetoric. His euphemistic wording, such as 'a correct or positive standpoint' and 'criteria of television newsworthiness', points to a departure from the conventions of partisan journalism, and to the efforts of recontextualizing the global model of public/civic journalism in indigenous Chinese discursive practices.

According to the leading theorist of public/civic journalism, Jay Rosen, 'the idea is to frame stories from the citizen's view, rather than inserting man-in-the-street quotes into a frame dominated by professionals' (Rosen and Merritt, 1995: 15). Both Merritt and Sun, despite their different ways of expression, converge on such news framing from a public/civic perspective. In fact, CCTV's *Focused Interview*'s contribution to the ongoing press/media reform lies precisely on its reliance on the public/civic sources as the basis of news framing and production. It is estimated that the editorial department receives over 2,300 news sources every day from all around China, via various channels of correspondence, phone calls, e-mails, and mobile-phone text messages (Chen, 2004). The programme has received a new lease of life under the current Communist Party leadership: *Focused Interview* was granted a quota of no less than 50 per cent of 'muckraking' reportage in its annual programming; the ratio by April 2004 had already exceeded 50 per cent, perhaps a positive sign for media reform (Chen, 2004).

The Chinese recontextualization of public/civic journalism has taken a notable new turn in recent years. A new concept of 'plebeian journalism' (*minsheng xinwen* or 'news about citizens' life') surfaced to encompass public participation in news production, which originated in *Zero Distance from Nanjing* [*Nanjing ling juli*, hereafter *Zero*], a prime-time live news show in a provincial Jiangsu Television's Urban Channel. If CCTV's *Focused Interview* attempts to negotiate partisanship with professionalism, *Zero* aims to displace official discourses into a more playful, intimate and interactive plebeian culture.

As well as having the audiences call in directly to provide news sources, *Zero* enlists more than 1,000 amateur onsite correspondents and cameramen into their newsroom and constantly updates news polls and sampling during the course of the telecast. The majority of *Zero*'s news items are comprised of live reportage of various incidents and disasters, public policy-making, as well as urban residents' call-in complaints and investigative reportage, ranging from outages of electricity supply to mistreatment by government officials. Obviously, *Zero*'s discursive practice aims to construct 'plebeian journalism', news about ordinary people's mode of living and psychological stances (Wang and Wu, 2003).

The socio-political vicissitudes of *Focused Interview* and *Zero* cannot but testify to the dialectics and contradictions in the course of China's media reform, which deserves a book-length project for a detailed account and in-depth analysis. What remains to be seen is how far such experimentation with public/civic journalism can go and to what extent the goals of public/civic journalism can be achieved within the current framework of the para-doxical partisan-cum-marketing system. With global media's further pene-tration into the Chinese media arena, it is no surprise that the news media are torn between opposing forces of partisan control and market economy. Emergent cheque-book and yellow journalism, for instance, have already drawn attention from conscientious media scholars and professionals. The negotiation between the partisan and the professional still constitutes the core of the agenda of post-WTO Chinese media reform. The Chinese experi-ence, as the attempts at recontextualizing public/civic journalism have suggested, points to the directions in which we may engage the problematic of globalization (read Americanization) and the search for its cultural and social alternatives.

The challenges and changes of television journalism in contemporary China discussed in this chapter point to the urgency and necessity of transfer-ring the focus in the current studies of global communication and China, namely, from the central theme of 'What can media/cultural globalization do to China?' to that of 'What can China do to media/cultural globaliza-tion?' The practices and experiments by CCTV-News and Phoenix, as well as local television stations, are emblematic of the remapping of Chinese media topography in response to the prevailing media/cultural globalization. In a foreseeable future, negotiating between the partisan, the commercial and the professional will remain the central tenet of this ongoing 'glocaliza-tion' in Chinese media sphere. Not surprisingly, the end of a propaganda state seems to be consequent upon the negation as such. What remains to be seen is whether Chinese news media can transcend all the limitations of their Western counterparts and bring forth a more constructive alternative to the dominating commercial/professional model.

References

Many thanks to Mr Gareth Davey, Research Assistant on the Global Journalism Programme at Tsinghua University, who helped prepare these references.

Brahm, L. (ed.) (2001) *China's Century*. London: John Wiley & Sons.
Brahm, L. (2002) *China after WTO*. Beijing: China Intercontinental Press.
CCTV (1999–2003) *CCTV Yearbooks, 1999, 2000, 2001, 2002, 2003*. Beijing: China Central Television.
CCTV (2003–04) *CCTV Internal Daily Reporters, 2003–04*. Beijing: China Central Television.

Chen, Xiaoming (2000) 'The mysterious other: post-politics in Chinese film', trans. K. Liu and A. B. Shi, in A. Dirlik and Xudong Zhang (eds), *Postmodernism and China*. Durham, NC: Duke University Press, pp. 222–38.

Chen, Y. (2004) 'Jiaodian fangtan: shinian huiwang' [*Focused Interview*: retrospect on the past decade], *Nanfang zhoumo* [The Southern Weekend], May 6: C17.

Gurevitch, M. (1991) 'The globalization of electronic journalism', in J. Curran and M. Gurevirch (eds), *Mass Media and Society*. London: Arnold, pp. 191–203.

Hong, J. (1998) *The Internationalization of Television in China: The Evolution of Ideology, Society and Media since the Reform*. London: Praeger.

Küng-Shankleman, L. (2000) *Inside the BBC and CNN: Managing Media Organizations*. London and New York: Routledge.

Lawrence, S. (1999) 'Captive audience', *Far Eastern Economic Review*, 8 (July): 70, 72.

Lewis, D. (2001) 'Governance in China: The Present and Future Tense', in L. Brahm (ed.), *China's Century*. London: John Wiley & Sons.

Li, X. (2005) *Chinese Journalism in Transition*. Guangzhou: Southern Daily Press.

Liu, K. (2004) *Globalisation and Cultural Trend in China*. Honolulu: University of Hawaii Press.

Lynch, D. (1999) *After the Propaganda State*. Stanford, CA: Stanford University Press.

Ma, L. (2001) 'Third eye to read China's news', in L. Brahm (ed.), *China's Century*. London: John Wiley & Sons.

Merritt, D. B. (1995) *Public Journalism and Public Life: Why Telling the News Is not Enough*. Hillsdale, NJ: Lawrence Erlbaum.

Pan, Z. D. and Y. Lu (2003) 'Localizing professionalism: discursive practices in China's media reform', in C. C. Lee (ed.), *Chinese Media, Global Context*. London: Routledge, pp. 215–36.

Rosen, J. and D. B. Merritt (1995) 'Imagining Public Journalism: An Editor and a Scholar Reflect on the Birth of an Idea'. Roy W. Howard Public Lecture. Bloomington: Indiana University, no. 5, 13 April.

Rosen, S. (2000) 'Seeking appropriate behaviour under a socialist market economy: an analysis of debates and controversies reported in the *Beijing Youth Daily*', in C. C. Lee (ed.), *Power, Money and Media*. Evanston, IL: Northwestern University Press.

Schnell, J. (1999) *Perspectives on Communication in the People's Republic of China*. London: Lexington Books.

Schudson, M. (1983) *Discovering the News*. New York: Basic Books.

Schudson, M. (2003) *The Sociology of News*. New York: W. W. Norton.

Sun, Yu-Sheng (2003) *Shinian: cong gaibian dianshi de yutai kaishi* [A Decade: Starting from Changing Television Mode of Expression]. Beijing: Sanlian shudian.

Thussu, D. (2000) *International Communication: Continuity and Change*. London: Arnold.

Tong, B. (2003) 'Zhengzhi wenming: xinwen chuanbo yanjiu de xin keti' [Political civilization: a new topic for journalism studies], *Xinwen yu chuanbo yanjiu* [Journalism and Communication Studies] 10 (3): 13–20.

Van Zoonen, L. (1991) 'A tyranny of intimacy? Women, femininity, and television news', in P. Dahlgren and C. Sparks (eds), *Communication and Citizenship*. London: Routledge, pp. 217–35.

Wang, Y. and X. Wu (2003) 'Guanyu Nanjing ling juli de xinwen' [News about *Zero Distance from Nanjing*], *Nanfang Zhoumo* [The Southern Weekend], 23 August: C15.

Weeks, J. (1991) *Against Nature: Essays on Sexuality, History and Identity*. London: River Oram Press.

White, L. (1990) 'All the news: structure and politics in Shanghai's reform media', in C. C. Lee (ed.), *Voices of China: The Interplay of Politics and Journalism*. New York: Guilford Press, pp. 88–110.

World Bank (2004) *World Development Indicators*. http://www.worldbank.org.

Yip, P. (2001) 'How the Internet will shape China', in L. Brahm (ed.), *China's Century*. London: John Wiley & Sons.

Zhao, H. (2004) *The Milestones and Changes of CCTV 1958–2005*. Beijing: Oriental Press.

Zhao, Y. (1998) *Media, Market, and Democracy in China: Between the Party Line and the Bottom Line*. Champaign, IL: University of Illinois Press.

Part IV

Moving media

From the margins to the mainstream?

Chapter 12

Alternative reframing of mainstream media frames

Oliver Boyd-Barrett

Journey from the mainstream

I shall take the unusual step (for an academic work) of introducing my topic with a personal reflection. Given the recency of the phenomenon with which it deals (alternative online news sources, including but not limited to sites frequently referred to as blogs), and the usefulness of direct experience (among other sources) as a contributor to significant research questions, I argue that personal reflection has a legitimate place in scholarship.

Up until the events of 9/11, 2001, my principal sources of news consumption were mainstream print sources (one big-city daily newspaper, one local area daily newspaper), the online sites of two leading national daily newspapers, incidental mainstream television news bulletins, a left-of-center regional radio network, and a weekly left-of-center publication of news commentary. After 9/11, my consumption of print sources declined. I dropped the local area daily newspaper, and the weekly left-of-center publication. I significantly increased the amount of time each day that I spent on alternative online news sites, sites that before 9/11 I had rarely, if ever, visited. I currently spend more time scouring online sites each day than I spend consuming mainstream media. The online sites include some that are ideologically alternative as well as sites of mainstream media and some specialized sites that deal with media issues.

When asked what accounts for these changes, my response is that alternative online news sites have proved rewarding, personally and professionally. At a personal level, some of these sites resonate politically and ideologically in a way that mainstream news sources generally do not – especially important to me during a sequence of international events that have intensified many people's political sentiments. At a professional level, I have concluded that through such sites I often have been informed or educated about significant stories, issues or controversies significantly in advance of seeing these dealt with in depth, if at all, within mainstream media of the USA that I regularly peruse. Such advance intelligence may sometimes be a matter of days, sometimes several months or more. While there may have been times when I was misinformed by alternative sites, I do not believe I was misinformed more often than I may have been misinformed by the mainstream. By the same token, I was as likely to be first appraised of certain stories by the mainstream as often as I was by alternative sites. As I indicate later, advance intelligence from alternative sites may arise from the openness of many such sites to a wider range of mainstream and alternative sources, from the US and overseas, than any single mainstream source typically offers. By contrast, mainstream US media sometimes seem reluctant to build on stories that have first appeared in media with which they have no relationship through ownership or contract.

My list of examples of advance intelligence from alternative sites would include, but by no mean be limited to:

1   GOP (Grand Old Party, aka Republican Party) illegal disenfranchisement of significant numbers of (mainly) African Americans in Florida towards the conclusion of the 2000 presidential election. This story, reported for the BBC by Greg Palast in November 2000, had to wait six months before it was picked up by the *Washington Post* and the *New York Times*, buried in inside pages, and in the context of reports of NAACP investigations of election irregularities (Palast, 2004).

2   A wide range of claims and controversies, and substantiated to varying degrees, surrounding the events of 9/11, contradicting officially sanctioned narratives of those events (see Boyd-Barrett, 2003; best sources on anomalies and distortions in the official narratives of 9/11 include: Griffin, 2004, 2005; Lance, 2004; Ruppert, 2005; Thompson, 2004).

3   Critical dissection, prior to the US invasion of spring 2003, of the credibility of claims that there were significant stockpiles of weapons of mass destruction in Iraq (Rampton and Stauber, 2003; Boyd-Barrett, 2004).

4   Critical dissection of the credibility of significant acts of 'war propaganda' in the lead-up to, invasion, and occupation of Iraq, in spring 2003. These included evidence that the fall of the Saddam Hussein statue, and the rescue of Private Jessica Lynch, were heavily stage-managed events for public relations consumption (Rampton and Stauber, 2003). This extends to a delay of 12 or more days between alternative online reports and coverage in the *New York Times*, *Washington Post*, or the networks of the publication in the British *Sunday Times* in May 2005, of the contents of a 2002 memo from the head of British Intelligence to the British prime minister. This indicated US and likely British commitment to the invasion of Iraq and to the configuration of intelligence to match that policy objective, long before efforts had been made to secure the consent of the US Congress, British Parliament or the UN. It might, in effect, be the 'smoking gun' of conspiracy to war crime.

5   Analysis of dangers and controversies surrounding electronic voting machines, their vulnerability to hacking and their GOP links, covered

from at least 2002 on Bev Harris's site, *Black Box Voting*, and in her book of the same title (Harris, 2004), and belatedly adopted as the theme of at least three *New York Times* editorials during the election year of 2004.

6   Analysis of the implications of the phenomenon of 'peak oil', and the approach, possibly within the next few decades, of a 'post-gasoline' era, and the relevance of this to US wars in Afghanistan and Iraq. This matter had been dealt with extensively from 2001 if not before, by sites such as Michael Ruppert's *From the Wilderness*. The phrase 'peak oil' became more salient in mainstream media from around 2003, possibly in indirect acknowledgment of several books published 2003–05 dealing with that topic (e.g. Heinberg, 2003; Goodstein, 2004; Roberts, 2004; Vaitheeswaran, 2003).

Experience during this time suggested that on at least some matters of grave national and international importance, and as a matter of empirically if only personally validated fact, I was being educated first and sometimes more comprehensively by alternative online sites, sometimes linking to books or overseas mainstream or alternative media, than by US mainstream media. I have weighed some explanations for this phenomenon elsewhere (Boyd-Barrett, 2004), drawing to some extent on Herman and Chomsky's (1988) celebrated propaganda model and its five 'filters', and to which I have added a sixth. These include direct and indirect complicity, intended or coincidental, between US mainstream media and the war and energy policies of the US administration under President George W. Bush.

I should also take into account the likelihood that with or without the Internet, there are always many claims-makers who argue for the truth of one or other claim, with greater or lesser merit. It has always been the role of the press to attend to at least some of these claims-makers and to make judgments as to which claims to adopt for public examination, if not endorsement, and which to ignore. One may argue, therefore, that among the many roles that have been attributed to the press (no press system is likely to undertake merely one role, but will play several, perhaps simultaneously, on behalf of different constituencies and obligations) should be that of validating, through acknowledgment, that some claims and claims-makers have reached a threshold of acceptability if not credibility, while others have not. What is likely different in the age of the Internet is that the claims themselves are now available with much greater facility and convenience than ever before, to those who also consume the news products of mainstream media. Moreover, that such consumers as care to do so, are now better positioned to identify those claims that have not been adopted by the mainstream and to evaluate the merits of mainstream choices in this regard.

I also observed a significant paradox between my experience of many alternative online news sites as sources of new, original, critical information that was ahead of the mainstream, and the fact that many of these sites seemed predominantly to rely on other sources including, to a significant degree, mainstream US and overseas sources. In at least some cases, the appearance of originality was not so much the product of in-house investigations as the result of loaded linking devices, judicious juxtapositions, and summary evaluations, of stories from diverse sources. In this chapter, I shall argue that such juxtapositioning is the outcome of a process best thought of as 'reframing'. I shall also argue that such linkages represent a form of 'borrowing' that was a characteristic of many early newspapers; it has similarities with the principle of news exchange that still contributes to the content of many news agencies (Boyd-Barrett, 1980).

The merit of describing the process as one of 'reframing' as opposed, more simply, to 'framing', lies in the fact that the original stories were constructed with a view to their being the 'final' products in a long chain of news production. Through a process of 'reframing', what was once constructed as a 'final' product becomes a component brick in the construction of a new frame. Common to many online news sites, it happens in many other communication contexts, as when historians make use of diverse published secondary sources to compile, for example, overarching narratives of a given event or period.

From framing to reframing

For Gamson (1992), framing is the 'central organizing idea or story line that provides meaning to an unfolding strip of events', a process that involves, according to Entman (1993), selecting 'some aspects of perceived reality and mak(ing) them more salient' in the media text. Choi (2004) sees framing as promoting 'a particular problem definition, causal interpretation, moral evaluation, and/or treatment recommendation for the item described' (quoted in Dimitrova et al., 2004: 256–7). Frames are differentially located and constructed. For Entman (1993), frames occur at each of four stations of the communication process: communicators, the text, receivers, and the culture. For Pan and Kosicki (1993) frames are constructed through five devices: syntactical, script, thematic and rhetorical structures, and lexical devices. Rhetorical structure, for example, includes 'metaphors, catch phrases, depictions, and naming which can all be used to evoke images and increase the salience or intensity of a particular characteristic' (Choi, 2004: 31).

In practice, most studies of news framing deal with reports as they appear in 'final' form, ready for reader, listener, or viewer consumption. But Bell (1991) demonstrates how in the production process, news stories are crafted from multiple sources, including archived stories, texts of speeches, notes of speeches or interviews, press releases, and so on. Each source contains its own distinctive frame, reflecting its conditions of production, author, and audience. The task of assembling sources into a coherent new story involves multiple actors (including reporters, editors, headline writers), each with their distinctive schemata that they use to make sense of their world. An important part of assembly involves cutting, adding, rearranging or, in short, editing. Bell identified many specific techniques used and discussed their semantic consequences. During assembly there may be modification to the framing of an earlier work, perhaps with a view to rendering it more interesting, relevant, or meaningful for the new target audience. I shall argue that analysis of assembly should take account of the repositioning of the reworked story into a different medium whose history, identity, and ideology may add extraneous color to the interpretations that readers make of individual stories appearing in it.

The process whereby a 'finished' informational product is lifted from the medium in which it was initially presented, then re-presented in a new medium or informational environment, lies at the heart of reframing. In this chapter I focus on reframing that occurs when there is little or no modification to the original article, but the article is inserted into a new, distinctive textual environment, a process that may or may not entail the addition of some form of introduction or discussion, and/or positioning in proximity to textual materials that did not feature in the story's original environment. This also accounts for much news agency news, as when stories are lifted from agency wires by subscribers for repositioning in their own media, e.g. as when AP or Reuters stories appear on Yahoo!News.com or MSNBC.com – distinctive textual environments comprising, among other things, the brand-name signifiers of the hosts' home pages and news menus.

I shall focus on reframing whose purpose is often to give stories a different 'spin' for ideological, propagandistic reasons. In their original information environments the stories may also have served ideological, propagandistic functions, but in order for them to do so, such functions may have been obscured through application of standard reporting practices (e.g. quotations, source identification, multiple sourcing, and balance) that distract readers from 'framing' through the device of commonly accepted indicators of journalistic objectivity and impartiality. By contrast, the process of reframing, in the context of the alternative websites that I examine, openly embraces such functions and in so doing, curiously, exposes the otherwise hidden frames of the originals. This would seem to confirm the observation of Cooper and Kuypers (2004: 162) that 'among the easiest ways to identify frames is through the use of comparative framing analysis'.

My interest arises from the emergence of websites that oppose hegemonic institutions and ideologies, yet also link to significant quantities of mainstream news content. Original news is expensive to gather and produce and alternative sites are rarely well resourced. Many create links to stories in mainstream media that they can then reframe so that the stories work ideologically in support of alternative positions. Reframing constitutes resourceful resistance to the hegemonic meanings manufactured by mainstream media (often in complicity with powerful social institutions; see Boyd-Barrett, 2004).

In this chapter I explore ways in which reframing occurs, some of the devices that achieve it, and their limitations. My original study focused on six websites among those I encountered when tracking non-mainstream media coverage of 9/11, and subsequent wars in Afghanistan and Iraq.

Alternative media

My choices were non-random; the sites were among sources that I found useful during the period 2001–04. I use them here to explore aspects of reframing, with no claim that these sites or their methods are representative of others. The sites were: Antiwar.com, Buzzflash.com, Citizens for Legitimate Government (legitgov.org), Democrats.com, Information Clearing House (ich.org), and Truthout (truthout.org). These opposed foreign and other policies of the Bush administration; five were 'left of center', demonstrated through opposition to corporatism, imperialism, the military–industrial complex, and war; one was libertarian (a conservative philosophy which in the US seeks to minimize government regulation at home and discourage government from unnecessary overseas entanglements). How might such sites, heavily dependent on mainstream news sources, qualify as 'alternative' and/or 'radical' media?

Scholars of alternative media (e.g. Downing, 1983; Couldry and Curran, 2004) typically acknowledge definitional fluidity. Atton (2002) proposed a six-dimensional model or typology of alternative and radical media, manifested through difference, innovation, and transformation in areas of: content, form, reprographics, distribution, roles and social relations, and communication processes. Atton's typology implicitly identifies 'alternity' in terms of a series of continua, but may lack precision in respect to what it is that alternative media are alternative *to*.

Boyd-Barrett (2005) proposed a model across four phases of communication – production, distribution, content, and reception – in terms of a range of continua whose extreme points represent 'mainstream' and 'alternity'. Alternative media are *more* likely than mainstream media to: originate from small, ideologically, or artistically committed groups; employ low-cost production and distribution technologies; exhibit non-commercial behavior; and rely for funding on such sources as nonprofit sponsorships, subscriptions, and users. Alternative media are *less* likely to be component parts of media or other conglomerates, carry advertising, use commercial distribution systems (other than the Internet) or conform to conventional professional rules of operation and job specialization.

In content, alternative media are *more* likely than mainstream to oppose dominant ideologies, agendas, values; represent a wide diversity of sources and perspectives; be considered 'extreme', by the mainstream; promote activism and interactive dialogue between producers and receivers; exhibit innovative, hybrid, and unconventional formulas; demonstrate partisanship and polemic; feature 'non-professional' and 'out-of-house' contributions; and observe 'public sphere' criteria. Alternative media are *less* likely than mainstream to advertise commercial products and services; deliver audiences to advertisers; allow product placement; appear slick, polished and 'professional'.

The audience for alternative media is more likely than the mainstream to be inclusive of politically conscious, activist, working-class, ethnic minorities, intelligentsia and members of ideologically distinctive formations not well represented on their own terms in mainstream media. Alternative audiences are less likely to be addressed as members of a mass, white or middle-class collectivity. Being alternative is not 'either–or', but the product of the aggregate values that a given medium ranks on each of a range of variables. While the sites considered here present themselves as alternative and score highly on many dimensions of alternity (e.g. non-commercial, politically oppositional and activist, cheap and accessible distribution), they score less highly on others (notably, diversity of sources and perspectives) and may even function to consolidate mainstream power.

The sites: principal features

While available globally through the web, the sites all turned out to be based in the US, mainly in the south-west: Antiwar in California; Buzzflash in Chicago; Citizens for Legitimate Government (CLG) in Arizona; Democrats. com in the US, specific location unknown; Information Clearing House in California; Truthout in California. The oldest site (Antiwar) was established in 1995, the youngest in 2003 (Truthout). Each had elaborate home sites, updated at least daily, sending daily news e-mails to subscribers, free of charge. They did not carry conventional, commercial advertising; they appeared to be funded from user donations and site-related product sales, such as political books and DVDs, T-shirts, and posters. Four of the sites appeared to be independent of external institutions. Antiwar was an offshoot of the (Libertarian) Randolph Bourne Institute. Some contributors to the work of Democrats.com declared links to the Democratic Party.

The sites were openly polemical. Antiwar described itself as 'non-interventionist', seeking to get 'past the media filters and reveal the truth about America's foreign policy'. CLG was 'established to . . . expose the coup and counter the Bush Occupation of the White House, and to counter the attempt on the part of the administration, in conjunction with the media, to create the appearance of legitimacy'. Democrats declared itself a 'website for democratic voters and activists'. Buzzflash offered 'news and commentary for a geographically-diverse, politically-savvy, pro-democracy, anti-hypocrisy web audience'. Information Clearing House sought to 'correct the distorted perceptions provided by commercial media', while Truthout offered 'possession of the truth' uncorrupted by advertising-dependent filters of other media.

These sites claimed audience numbers that competed with many main-stream media. Antiwar claimed 500,000 unique visitors monthly and 60,000–90,000 daily visitors in May 2004, and ranked as the thirty-seventh news site in the English-speaking world in November 2004 according to Alexa/Google measurements. Buzzflash claimed 3.7 million visitors monthly in August 2004. CLG did not provide numbers of site visitors, but claimed 25,075 signa-tures to its Petition to Senate to Investigate Oddities of 9/11 (July 2004). Democrats claimed 500,000 subscribers in July 2004. Information Clearing House claimed 1.5 million unique visitors in October 2004.

Only one site conformed to popular notions of 'blogs': namely, regularly updated sites authored and compiled by single individuals. Most showed evi-dence of significant collaboration. In the case of Antiwar, Justin Raimondo was editorial director and principal columnist. Other individuals had assigned roles: web master, managing editor, editor, assistant webmaster/senior editor, associate editor, student coordinator, letters editor, graphics executive editor, outreach coordinator, administrative assistant, accountant. There was one senior researcher, 21 researchers, 18 columnists, and 6 advisors. How many were full-time? In a fundraising letter to subscribers in May 2004, Raimondo referred to 'three guys and as many computers' and to 'a number of very hard-working volunteers', of which one (Raimondo) acted as proof-reader, amongst other things, describing himself as the single member of edi-torial staff. Antiwar was the only site that declared its quarterly costs (in the context of fundraising drives), which in 2005 annualized at $200,000.

The target audience for these sites appeared to be North America. Taking Antiwar as an example, the site was based in the US, significantly targeted its criticism against the US administration, and framed its commentaries with reference to a distinctly American political tradition (Libertarianism). US sources were represented disproportionately on all of these sites.

Framing by the margins

Reframing, I argue, involves the repositioning of existing news copy within a different informational environment to the one in which it originated. This has a potential framing consequence, since the new informational environ-ment represents a unique, purposeful semiotic and semantic universe of meanings likely to influence the interpretations that readers make of indi-vidual stories. For example, I identified Antiwar's informational *environment* of 22 July 2004 as physically framed by:

1   *The title*: this clearly advertised an anti-war agenda;
2   *Margins-top*: list of highlights or main features for the day and a quote. At least two authors listed were identifiably (for the frequent visitor) anti-war and anti-administration;

3 *Margins-left*: mainly a list of links to other areas of the site; five of the links containing the 'anti-war' title;

4 *Margins-right* : contained links to articles many of whose titles suggested polemic, e.g. 'Israel – a rogue state', 'Oops, they invaded the wrong country'. Such titles invited a critical stance towards US foreign policy.

The physical frames embedding the main body of these sites' content signaled preferred ideologies according to which the main content, much of it in the form of links (including linking text) to news stories from external mainstream and alternative sources, should be read. In contrast to the mainstream environments whence many linked stories originate, readers may now find themselves hailed as angry and even activist opponents.

Consider the left margin of CLG (29 July 2004): There are search and advanced search facilities, followed by a link to a 'Yes, Gore Did Win!' selection of articles; a 'Hot Articles' section (same as under 'Bush Occupation' elsewhere on the site); and 'Bushwhacked: The Evidence Mounts', an extensive list of links to articles dealing with various policies of the Bush administration to which CLG is opposed. Categories include: Education and Children; Labor; Healthcare; Women's issues; Social Security and Medicare; World Peace – 'in pieces'; and Constitution threat. Each subsection is substantial – with links to 30 stories alone in the category of Education and Children, for example. Another section linked is 'The Bushwatch Lie Watch', with many subsections, some extensive, including links to chronologies of purported administration untruths; cartoons; press commentaries; feature articles, headlines; columnists and their writings. A 'Bushreport' section links to current mainstream and non-mainstream political stories, including convention.coverage, and four years of links to previous Bush stories. One subsection includes readers' comments and exchanges; a contact-us link. A subsection on media bias includes links organized under the heading 'Tactics and Propaganda Techniques', with examples and editorials related to these issues; relevant dedicated sites; other information, activities and tools useful for activists. Other sections, useful to activists and analysts alike, include an analysis of Senate votes on selected issues and links to a 'complete directory of resources from other sites; news, political websites, anti-Bush material – to oppose the coup'. There are CLG book recommendations for purchase, including, Palast's *The Best Democracy that Money Can Buy*, and a downloadable version of Jackson and Sharon Thoreau's, *Restoring a Legitimate Whitehouse*. Other links connect with copasetic sites and sources, including Al-Jazeera's English site; Uruknet.info, a site dedicated to links that provide critical coverage of events in Iraq; Democracy for America, a site inspired by the earlier candidacy of Howard Dean; Standing Together for Change; Stop the War Coalition (a London activist site, with many links to British sources); Fallout Shelter News (one affiliated with CLG); and Vox News (specializing, among other things, in stories of covert and intelligence operations).

Main body: high volume

A significant feature of the main bodies of content of at least three of the six sites, constituting part of their radical potential with respect to subversion of mainstream frames, was the relatively high volume of coverage of *selected* issues, by contrast with mainstream print, broadcast, or online media. The significance of volume was to diminish, as we shall see, by a less imposing diversity of sourcing. On 22 July 2004 for example, different sections of Anti-war linked to over 130 stories and columns, all of them dealing with significant international conflicts, mostly bearing on foreign policy interests of the US. I did not discern significant overlap; where stories focused on the same topics, they generally provided distinctive perspectives. An additional link to 'more news' went to a page listing a further 65 stories, and connecting successive pages of links to news stories for previous days. Daily monitoring of this site throughout 2004 showed that volume actually increased over time.

Quantity was greater than typically available on these topics in a major newspaper. A *Los Angeles Times* reader on 20 July 2004, would have encountered only ten comparable stories. Indeed, the Antiwar.com site provided daily access to over 13 times as many stories as did the *Los Angeles Times*. A similar conclusion emerges when comparing Antiwar.com with the online edition for the *Los Angeles Times*, in whose edition for 9 November 2004, I found a total of 17 international conflict stories. The site provided free access to stories from the previous seven days (six major stories available each day, including domestic and world). A searchable archive provided access to previous abstracts only; full text versions could be accessed on payment of $2 per story.

Alternative site sources

The overwhelming majority of linked sources on these sites originated from mainstream media, mostly of the US, but also overseas. On 23 July 2004 Antiwar.com carried eight major headline stories. All but one of these stories came from mainstream US media (*New York Times*, *Washington Times*, Yahoo! News, MSNBC, My Way). One was an analysis by an Antiwar.com contributor. And half of these mainstream stories were recycled from the leading US news agency, AP. I also examined the 'viewpoints' section. Of six items, one was an Antiwar.com original contribution. Others linked to the *Washington Post*, *Village Voice*, Salon.com, Common Dreams News Center (an item that had originated in the *Los Angeles Times*) and The Cato Institute. Although these viewpoints did include progressive or libertarian perspectives, they were all American in origin.

Analysis of other sections revealed a similar pattern. In the 'Frontline' section for 23 July there were 13 items, of which only 11 links were accessible. Of these, two were related to the 9/11 report – one a link to a site where the report could be downloaded, another linked to a *New York Times* site Vivisimo for searching the 9/11 report. Of the remaining nine, two came from *Christian Science Monitor*; one from MSNBC (a Reuters story), one from CNN (staffer), and one from the *Washington Times* (a UPI story). The others were from *Asia Times Online*, *Forward* (a New York Jewish paper), TomDispatch.com (a web-blog associated with the left-leaning American Nation Institute). In this section, therefore, could be seen a wider variety of sources, in geography and ideology, although the section as a whole was still dominated by links to mainstream US media. I accessed six other news sections on Antiwar.com. These included:

1 'Violence Continues', comprising five stories, one inaccessible, all dealing with Iraq, from Aljazeera.net, CNN, and Yahoo! News (from AP);
2 'Security', comprising five stories, all of them about Iraq, from Knight-Ridder Washington Bureau, Yahoo! News (2, both AP stories), Wired News, and Information Clearing House (an alternative news site, this story taken, however, from the *Sydney Morning Herald*);
3 'Tales of Torture', comprising three stories, all about Iraq, from the *New York Times*, *Washington Times* (an AP story), and *LA Weekly*;
4 'Saddam' comprising two stories, one from Yahoo! News (an AP story), and one from the British *Guardian*;
5 'Battle of Britain', comprising five stories, of which four were related to Iraq and British involvement in Iraq, and one related to Muslim clerics in Britain, sourced to Yahoo, *Financial Times*, BBC News, UPI, and a local British news site, Manchester.Online;
6 'Global Iraq Fallout', comprising six stories, of which two were from Yahoo! News, one from the *New York Times*, one from AntiWar.com, and two from Australian newspaper sites, the *Herald Sun* and the *Australian*.

On 26 July I explored whether the country-specific or region-specific sections of Antiwar.com were more likely than others to draw on non-US media. There were eight such sections:

1 Afghanistan: two stories, one from Yahoo! News (a Reuters story), and one from the *New York Times*;
2 Pakistan: five stories, of which one was from the *New York Times*, but four were from the *News International* of Pakistan;
3 Asia: three stories, about North Korea, Thailand and Sri Lanka, coming from Yahoo! News (an AP story), the *Observer* (UK), and BBC News;
4 Sudan: eight stories, one from Reuters, one from the *Australian* (comprising AFP and AP information), one from Yahoo! News (a Reuters story), one from the *Guardian* (UK), an AP story, another from the *Guardian*'s Sunday sister, the *Observer*, one from BBC News, and two American, one from CNN, the other from the *Christian Science Monitor*;

5   Israel/Palestine: four stories of which two were from the Israeli news-
    paper, *Haaretz*, and two were from British newspapers, the *Independent*
    and the *Guardian* (an AP story);
6   Middle East: three stories, two on Iran, one on Beirut, coming, respec-
    tively, from Yahoo! News (a Reuters story), one from BBC News and one
    from the *Christian Science Monitor*;
7   Russia and its neighbors: two stories, one from the *Boston Globe* (an AP
    story), and one from Yahoo! News (an AP story);
8   Other: three stories concerning Colombia, Haiti and ex-Yugoslavia, two
    of them originating from the *Christian Science Monitor*, and one from the
    Globe and Mail (Canada) (an AP story).

Did these foreign, geographically labeled sections use a wider diversity of
sources than other sections? Evidence was patchy. There were fewer US
sources, and US sources were less mainstream, with a preference for some of
the 'quality' local papers of the US that have a strong reputation for international coverage, in particular the *Christian Science Monitor*, and for Internet
site, Yahoo!News. Non-American sources were dominated by (relatively
liberal) British sources: the BBC, the *Guardian* and the *Independent*, and other
papers from the English-speaking world, namely the *Australian* and the *Globe
and Mail*. The principal evidence of local overseas media use came from Pakistan and from Israel. No local media were used in linking to stories about the
Sudan or about Palestine. Many stories, regardless of their 'retail' location,
came from Western news agencies, especially AP (headquartered in New
York), and Reuters (headquartered in London): 10 stories out of 30.
    Overall these stories helped to 'reframe' the headline-grabbing stories of
the mainstream US media such as the *New York Times* or the network news
programs, suggesting that important as the war situation in Iraq, Afghanistan, or the 'war on terrorism' was, the role of the US in the world should be
evaluated in relation to a significantly broader range of international
conflicts.
    Similar findings emerged from analysis of all six sites. For example, on
29 July 2004, I examined the coverage of CLG: 69 story-links. Topics
included Iraq (N19, 28 per cent); Democratic Convention (N12, 18 per cent);
Florida election irregularities, 2000–02 (N5, 7 per cent); Michael Moore's
film, *Fahrenheit 9/11* (N5, 7 per cent); 9/11 and aftermath in Afghanistan and
Guantanamo (N3, 4 per cent); Bush scandals (N3, 4 per cent); criticisms of
Bush (N2, 4 per cent); and Patriot Act and security measures (N2, 4 per
cent). There were single stories on: ice-warming in Greenland; investigations
of Riggs Bank. For these stories I identified 34 sources: mostly mainstream
US and western, including: Yahoo!News (8), *New York Times* (6), *Sydney
Morning Herald* (5), *Guardian* (3), *Washington Post* (3), BBC (2), *Miami Herald*
(2), Reuters (2), *Tampa Tribune* (2), *Australian* (1), *Boston Globe* (1), *Boston*

Herald (1), CBC (Canada)(1), *Daily Mirror* (1), *Gainsville Courier* (1), *Los Angeles Times* (1), MSNBC (1), *San Francisco Chronicle* (1), *Toronto Star* (1). Nearly 67 per cent of all the stories came from mainstream sources. Several were local US news media sources, which few readers of the CLG would be likely to access otherwise. Thirteen stories (19 per cent) were non-US: primarily Australian, British, and Canadian. Of 43 mainstream sourced stories, 16 (37 per cent) came from news agencies. In all, the news agencies AP and Reuters accounted for 21 (31 per cent) stories.

Non-mainstream sources included: CLG home site (6 – mainly texts of convention speeches); My Way (3); Capitol Hill Blue (2); Al-Jazeera (1); Counterpunch (1); Drudge Report (1); Earthlink (1); Islam Online (1); Military.com (1);, Letterfromamerica.com (1); Libertyhypermal (1); The Register (1); World Socialist Web Site (1). Six out of 21 or 28 per cent of the stories from these lesser-known sites were actually recycled from mainstream sources, especially news agencies. Only two of the non-mainstream sources were identifiably non-Western. Virtually all sources on Iraq, mainstream or not, were from non-Iraqi, Western media.

Synchronic and diachronic reframing

In relation to some sites, reframing took *synchronic* form: selected mainstream media stories about international conflicts (few for any one medium, any given day) were contextualized by a far greater number of such stories, including stories about conflicts much less frequently acknowledged or represented in at least the front pages of mainstream media, as well as by stories about conflicts that are hardly ever dealt with by mainstream media. Thus quantity and range of representations contribute to the process of reframing.

A *diachronic* dimension of reframing had two aspects, both about 'contextualization', manifested in the site's commentary sections. One aspect placed specific instances of conflict – often the stuff of news stories in mainstream media – within a larger and informed historical context, often reflecting broader narratives about the struggle of the USA for regional and global hegemony. The second aspect had less to do with history and historical significance than with ideas, policies, beliefs, moralities and philosophies that influence policy-makers directly and indirectly – an *ideational* dimension that is sometimes underestimated when history is reduced to narratives of opportunistic grabs for wealth by the already wealthy classes of wealthy nations.

A striking feature of the CLG frame, reflected in many headline-links to what were often mainstream media sources, was the assertiveness as to how key events should be interpreted: for example, that the 2000 presidential election was illegitimate and was tantamount to a coup. This is manifestly different to any interpretive frame commonly encountered in mainstream media. At best, mainstream media might have covered problems encountered during the 2000 election and the unhappiness of interest groups who maintain the election to have been unfair. Almost never, whether in news or in commentary, did mainstream media suggest that the 2000 election was tantamount to a 'coup'. As Palast (2004) notes, it took leading US media such as the *Washington Post* six months even to acknowledge what Palast had been reporting for British media during the election itself, namely the improper elimination from the electoral role of thousands of people (mainly pro-Democratic African-Americans) who had been falsely identified as felons. In the year leading up to the 2004 presidential election, mainstream media like the *New York Times* began to refer to such shenanigans as though they were common knowledge, yet they had done practically nothing to educate readers about such issues at the time. It is a significant step, one that mainstream media never took, to move from accepting that the elections in Florida were tainted by fraud to assuming that this amounted, in practice, to a coup.

Exposing, by contrast, the mainstream frame

CLG's assertive presumption as fact that the 2000 election was a coup helps expose implicit frames of the mainstream: namely that the election, even if flawed, was conducted according to the best practices of the democratic process and in reasonable faith, and that there was nothing sinister about an administration that inherited power in such circumstances. To put it differently, it might be argued that mainstream media framed President Bush and his administration as 'normal' (even 'normally abnormal') and that these activities should be covered in standard journalistic style. To illustrate the point more dramatically by contrast: suppose that mainstream media had framed Bush and his administration as criminals who had seized power fraudulently in 2000 in order to impose a radical, right-wing foreign and domestic policy agenda that would primarily benefit large corporations, the military-industrial complex, and the US plutocracy, and that would later inaugurate an illegal war of aggression, waged on false pretext, for the benefit of large US corporations with whom members of the administration had close ties. Such a frame would not have allowed the mainstream media the luxury of 'business as normal' coverage of the White House; instead, it might have required a 'journalism of outrage'.

When the CLG frame is contrasted against the mainstream frame, the latter is revealed as more protective of special interests than merely neutral. Mainstream consensual US values support morality, are generally opposed to serious crime and criminals, and US media tend to be normatively supportive of such consensual values. Yet mainstream media are cautious in their treatment of US elites. A 'frame of criminality' might have allowed them more scope for expressions of outrage in the face of manifest abuses of power.

Dimensions of reframing

Examination of these six sites does not exhaust the number of strategies which they exemplify in creating some kind of site 'ownership' over the stories to which they create links, strategies which this article has argued constitute a form of 'reframing' of the original news stories. But it can identify significant reframing strategies that are common in the world of alternative Internet news. Where these are articulated in relation to anticipated audience inter-pretations, identification of such strategies should be regarded in part as hypotheses for further research:

1 *New communication environment.* This involves shaping a new textual and visual environment within which to place – by means of linkage and whatever other measure of association that can be said to be achieved by means of linkage – a news story that has originated elsewhere.

2 *Marking alternative site identity and presumed reader.* This associates the original story with an alternative site identity and presumed reader. This textual and visual environment will likely look very different to the environment, whether online or print, in which the story originally appeared. It will be suggestive of a specific identity, of site and reader, that the site organizers presume will be interested in the site; this iden-tity is likely to be very different from that of the original site.

3 *Creating a new proxemic portfolio.* A story that appears on a given page in a newspaper, or whose headline is listed within a given list of headline choices that the reader may choose to click on for further reading on an online site, now appears, in its new location, in proximity to a very different range of other stories, visuals, icons, etc., and this carries the potential for new forms of semantic understanding, association, cross-referencing than previously existed.

4 *Added proxemic value and tunneling.* Coherent, proxemic portfolios are likely to accentuate, broaden, and deepen readers' acquaintance with a topic or issue by virtue of their being presented with stories from a broader multiplicity of sources on the same or similar topics than readers would experience in the original sites of publication. Multiplicity of stories, especially since these are often mainstream media stories, enhances per-ceived credibility. There can also be a tunneling effect because stories will have been chosen for their compatibility with the ideology of the alternative site or with a particular viewpoint that the alternative site wishes to promote.

5 *Linkage as diminution of uniqueness.* In some instances, the link to an·origi-nal story also incorporates links to additional stories about the same or a similar topic. This device may significantly diminish the significance or uniqueness that the story appeared to have when in its original location.

6   *Re-hierarchization.* In being relocated, the degree of importance or significance within hierarchies of significance that are typically established
within any given informational environment may be changed, so that a
story becomes more or less significant or important in a way that may
also affect the perceived credibility, relevance, etc. of the story.

7   *Re-differentiation between news and commentary.* Even where both the original
and the new sites maintain some form of differentiation between 'news'
stories and 'commentary', the original news stories may now be connected
to, or available for association with, quite different commentary pieces
than those with which they were previously associated, thus creating
further potential for radically reconfiguring the semantic universe of the
original story.

8   *Links as framing devices.* Links to stories may now place them within a
completely new text, whether the text is merely intended as an introduction to the linked story, or the link is one of several that is included
within a broader-ranging text or argument. The new text within which
the links are embedded has radical potential, by such means as summary
devices, to emphasize only certain aspects of the linked text, or certain
meanings that the text might invite, or to place the original story within
a significantly different universe of historical, political, ideological,
literary etc., associations.

9   *Exposing cover frames of the mainstream.* Alternative sites frequently reframe
stories by taking them 'outside' of the conventional context of 'neutral',
'objective' or 'balanced' journalism. Through persuasive contextualization, positioning and language, these alternative sites associate them with
a tone of partisanship and emotion which, on at least some occasions,
seems to challenge the claims to 'objectivity' and 'balance' that the original news media would doubtless have used if challenged to defend what
they had produced.

10   *De-legitimating the mainstream.* Alternative sites indicate varying degrees
of distrust of or dissatisfaction with, the mainstream media, on account
of their commercial character and corporate connections, so that it
becomes clear to the conscientious reader who checks out 'about us'
type sections, that he or she has entered an environment that puts itself
apart or keeps a distance from mainstream media sources. Furthermore, these sites regularly create links to stories from both alternative
and mainstream sites that are critical of mainstream media coverage,
including, for example, stories from left-leaning media watchdog sites
such as FAIR.org., whose judgments are frequently based on empirical
research.

11   *Hijacking the mainstream for alternative agenda.* Many alternative sites exist
both to inform and to serve as activist resources. Links to mainstream
news stories may transform them into components of an activist agenda
(or agitative propaganda) for which they were not originally intended.

12 *Democratizing the mainstream.* Though alternative media links exhibit continuing heavy dependence on the mainstream, the spread of their net for mainstream sources is wide, including medium-size provincial and specialist publications. This enhances the national and international influence of these publications in the public sphere and establishes a kind of pseudo-dialogue between them which they would not normally undertake for themselves.

13 *The hijackers hijacked.* Heavy dependence by alternative sites on links to mainstream media stories reinforces the role of mainstream information media as arbiters of what is credible and worthy. Further, dependence on US and Western mainstream media reinforces the hold of Western cultural, ethnic, and philosophical perspectives even on non-Western events, trends, etc.

Conclusion

This chapter has discovered practices of 'reframing' in alternative media and concludes that such practices are likely to facilitate more alternative and radical readings of the news information and commentary than that provided by the mainstream news media (although endorsement for that hypothesis would need to involve empirical inquiries into how these sites are used and consumed by readers). However, the chapter also underlines the considerable importance of mainstream news sources for these sites, suggesting that mainstream sites are more frequently used for reframing than alternative sites of news and commentary. One reason for this is that alternative news sites have only a fraction of the newsgathering resources that are available to the better-resourced mainstream media, and that it therefore makes sense to establish links to the online sites of these media, even if the main purpose is to 'reframe' or redefine the significance of the information and commentary that is thus accessed.

However, one unintended consequence of so doing is that at least some of these sites end up endorsing, further narrowing even as they deepen, the news agenda that is set by the mainstream news media (in complicity with the authoritative, powerful and influential news sources that enjoy most access to the mainstream), so that their dependence on the mainstream may be a significant limitation on their capacity to 'reframe' and redefine. This danger is exacerbated where sites restrict themselves mainly to mainstream Western sources, failing to make the most of the different perspectives that become available on inspection of non-Western sources. While in theory this might seem a reasonable charge, it may be that because these selected sites are themselves Western, they inevitably focus on domestic and international issues of most immediate concern to their (mainly) Western-based, if 'radical' readers and that, in any case, there are relatively few non-Western mainstream sources that offer useful information and perspectives over and above that which is already available in the Western mainstream.

Defenders of mainstream media may view alternative news sites' dependence on mainstream media as a vindication of the mainstream. They may argue that clearly the mainstream is so broad in its range of issues, viewpoints, and perspectives that it becomes possible for sites at various points of the political spectrum to compile selections from the mainstream that suit the ideological and other needs of those sectional political positions. This would be a somewhat optimistic appraisal of Western mainstream media. It is notable, first of all, that the overall range of Western media used by these sites is not great, suggesting that in searching for mainstream sources that are of ideological use to these sites, there is not much to look at: a few leading news agencies that pump out so much news that there is bound to be at least some surplus material of relevance to these sites; a few British sources (almost exclusively the BBC, the *Guardian*, the *Independent*) known to be somewhat more outspoken on US foreign policy issues than the US mainstream; and the print giants of the US mainstream namely, the *New York Times* and the *Washington Post*.

With respect to the latter newspapers, it is not so much that issues significant for radical news sites are not covered (though doubtless many are not covered, or coverage is significantly delayed; see Boyd-Barrett, 2003), but that such issues are marginalized by strategies such as page placement, headlining, source hierarchies, and story structure. All these strategies have been exposed in the context, for example, of coverage by both the *New York Times* and the *Washington Post*, of the issue of weapons of mass destruction, during the lead-up to the US invasion of Iraq (see Boyd-Barrett, 2004). The papers' own ombudsmen as well as their critics have later shown how news that might have cast doubt on the administration's claims that Iraq possessed nuclear, chemical, or biological weapons or was a significant and immediate threat to the US, was deliberately marginalized by editors using such strategies. Indeed, had these prestige media been more openly and aggressively critical of the administration's claims, the invasion might not have occurred. Yet much of the evidence against the administration was well known to readers of alternative news sites such as those explored in this chapter, in part because these alternative sites gave to stories dealing with such evidence the prominence that the mainstream elite press failed to give them.

References

Atton, C. (2002) *Alternative Media*. London: Sage.
Bateson, G. (1972) *Steps to an Ecology of Mind*. New York: Ballentine.
Bell, A. (1991) *The Language of News Media*. Oxford: Blackwell.
Boyd-Barrett, O. (1980) *The International News Agencies*. London: Constable.

Boyd-Barrett, O. (2003) 'Doubt foreclosed (2): US mainstream media and the attacks of 9/11', in D. Demers (ed.), *Terrorism, Globalization and Mass Communication.* Spokane, WA: Marquette Books, pp. 3–33.

Boyd-Barrett, O. (2004) 'Judith Miller, the *New York Times*, and the propaganda model', *Journalism Studies*, 5 (4): 435–49.

Boyd-Barrett, O. (2005) 'Alternative Media Reframing the Mainstream'. Paper presented to graduate seminar, UNITEC, Auckland, New Zealand. 18 April.

Choi, J. (2004) 'The framing of the "Axis of Evil"', in R. D. Berenger (ed.), *Global Media Go to War.* Spokane, WA: Marquette Books, pp. 29–38.

Clair, R. P. (1993) 'The use of framing devices to sequester organizational narratives: hegemony and harassment', *Communication Monographs*, 60 (June): 113–36.

Cooper, S. and J. Kuypers (2004) 'Embedded versus behind-the-lines reporting on the 2003 Iraq war', in R. D. Berenger (ed.), *Global Media Go to War.* Spokane, WA: Marquette Books, pp. 161–72.

Couldry, N. and J. Curran (eds) (2004) *Contesting Media Power: Alternative Media in a Networked World.* Lanham, MD: Rowman & Littlefield.

Dimitrova, D., L. Kaid and A. Williams (2004) 'The first hours of online coverage of "Operational Iraqi Freedom"', in R. D. Berenger (ed.), *Global Media Go to War.* Spokane, WA: Marquette Books, pp. 255–63.

Downing, J. (1983) *Radical Media: The Political Experience of Alternative Media.* Chicago: South End Press.

Entman, R. (1991) 'Framing U.S. coverage of international news: contrasts in narratives of the KAL and Iran air accidents', *Journal of Communication*, 41 (4): 6–27.

Entman, R. (1993) 'Framing: toward clarification of a fractured paradigm', *Journal of Communication*, 43 (4): 51–8.

Gamson, W. A. (1992) *Talking Politics.* Cambridge and New York: Cambridge University Press.

Gamson, W. A. (1993) 'News as framing: comments on Graber', *American Behavioral Scientist*, 33 (2): 157–61.

Goodstein, D. (2004) *Out of Gas: The End of the Age of Oil.* New York: W. W. Norton.

Griffin, D. (2004) *The New Pearl Harbor: Disturbing Questions about the Bush Administration and 9/11.* Northampton, MA: Olive Branch Press.

Griffin, D. E. (2005) *The 9/11 Commission Report: Omissions and Distortions.* Northampton, MA: Olive Branch Press.

Harris, B. (2004) *Black Box Voting: Ballot Tampering in the 21st Century.* Renton, WA: Talion Publishing.

Heinberg, R. (2003) *The Party's Over: Oil, War and the Fate of Industrial Societies.* Gabriola Island, Canada: New Society Publishers.

Herman, E. and N. Chomsky (1988) *Manufacturing Consent: The Political Economy of the Mass Media.* New York: Pantheon Books.

Lance, P. (2004) *1000 Years of Revenge.* New York: HarperCollins.

Lance, P. (2005) *Cover-Up: What the Government Is Still Hiding about the War on Terror.* New York: Regan Books.

Palast, G. (2004) *The Best Democracy that Money Can Buy.* New York: Plume Books.

Pan, Z. and G. M. Kosicki (1993) 'Framing analysis: an approach to news discourse', *Political Communication*, 10: 55–75.

Raimondo, J. (2002) 'Liberal imperialism: war and the soul of American liberalism'. Accessed 15 November: http://www.antiwar.com.

Raimondo, J. (2002) 'Iraq – first stop on the road to empire', http://antiwar.com.

Rampton, S. and J. Stauber (2003) *Weapons of Mass Deception: The Uses of Propaganda in Bush's War on Iraq*. New York: Penguin.

Roberts, P. (2004) *End of Oil*. New York: Houghton Mifflin.

Ruppert, M. (2005) *Crossing the Rubicon: The Decline of the American Empire at the End of the Age of Oil*. Gabriola Island, Canada: New Society Publishers.

Stromberg, J. (2003) 'The crazies who preceded the loonies: The first "new" right'. Accessed 8 February: http://antiwar.com.

Thompson, P. (2004) *The Terror Timeline: A Comprehensive Chronicle of the Road to 9/11 – and America's Response*. New York: Regan Books.

Vaitheeswaran, V. (2003) *Power to the People*. New York: Farrar, Strauss & Giroux.

Chapter 13

Transnational feminism and the Revolutionary Association of the Women of Afghanistan

Lisa McLaughlin

Over the years, transnational feminist mobilization has come to serve as a primary source of inspiration for theorists of cosmopolitan democracy and new social movements. The status afforded to the feminist movement as a harbinger for an incipient global civil society is indicative of the success that women have had in joining across boundaries for purposes of fighting against fundamentalism, militarization, neoliberalism, and various forms of discrimination and struggling for human rights and social and economic justice. In this sense, transnational feminism is key to the social imaginary described as 'globalization-from-below,' an intersection of efforts of various groups to redirect the focus of economic and social development from an economistic market/modernization notion of progress to questions of global justice and equality.

Certainly, it is appealing to think of feminism as one among other emergent forces which are effective in challenging a pervasive 'globalization-from-above,' with its concomitant military-industrial threats to human rights and security and proliferation of public and private institutions embracing market-driven imperatives of neoliberalism. Yet there should also be a sense of discomfiture with the idea that one need look no further than networks of persons working in academic institutions, non-governmental organizations (NGOs), and agencies of the United Nations to locate the bottom tier of 'bottom-up' processes. To do so is to focus on those groups that are already included in the public sphere, those with access to the use of new information and communication technologies, particularly the Internet, for organizing protests, providing information, and mobilizing networks to magnify their influence as aspiring partners in global governance (McLaughlin, 2004).

For heuristic purposes, the 'globalization-from-below' versus 'globalization-from-above' dualism offers a potentially useful and empowering mode of inquiry, for both marginalized resistance movements and for the cosmopolitan theorists for whom they serve as muse. However, heuristic devices simplify complex phenomena by creating opposed categories that are, in fact, intertwined and interdependent. Dualistic and linear concepts of globalization are limited in their capacities to reveal concrete forms of penetration and fusion at various points along categories of scale from the local to the global (Mittelman, 2000: 221). Such is the case with too-linear concepts of 'flow' and 'contra-flow.' While 'circulation' is a more apt descriptor for the contemporary movement of transnational communications than is a notion of 'one-way flow' (Sreberny, 2001: 62), within a global matrix of structural inequalities, issues of North to South and South to North flows are not passé; rather, they become more complex.

In his commentary on the deficiencies of cultural globalization models which essentialize both terms of the local/global couplet, Graham Murdock (2004: 27) suggests that concrete analyses provide a valuable corrective to binary constructions. In this chapter, I follow this advice in order to illustrate that for women – particularly women in the global South – 'reaching out' to the global North to create transnational linkages often involves not only a struggle to overcome the material inequalities which inhibit communicative access but also a struggle to negotiate issues of complicity – or co-implication – with dominant Western narratives of 'difference' and 'otherness,' something which seems to be required in order to become visible and to be heard on the 'global stage.'

I attempt to illustrate this conundrum by addressing efforts to raise awareness of the abuses and material deprivations of Afghan women, before the United States' invasion of Afghanistan in 2001 and in the years following this assault. Specifically, I focus on the campaign waged by the Revolutionary Association of the Women of Afghanistan (RAWA). The Association was founded in 1977 as one of the first political organizations of Afghan women with a humanitarian mission, which included advocating for women's rights to have equal access to health, education, and employment and establishing schools and hospitals for women (http://www.rawa.org). Throughout successive regimes – from the 1978 overthrow of a moderate, left-leaning government by the more hard-left People's Democratic Republic of Afghanistan, throughout a communist-Islamic civil war accompanied by Soviet and American intervention, and the eventual government takeover by the US-supported Mujahadin, to the rise of the Taliban regime in 1996 – RAWA worked to improve women's status within Afghan society.

However, the activities of RAWA and other women's organizations operating in the region, along with the plight of Afghan women, mostly remained invisible to international audiences, including those affiliated with an emerging international feminist movement. Valentine Moghadam (2003) has queried why Afghan women were not 'discovered' by international feminism until 1996, at the time that the Taliban rose to power. Here, I shall pursue a similar but differently inflected question: what is the context in which Afghan women became visible to the global North in 1996? I will link this question to an analysis of how RAWA, whose activities were critical to bringing world attention to Afghan women, came to be 'disappeared,' although not silenced, by the hegemonic mainstream entities which earlier had been so dependent upon the information provided by the organization.

RAWA and communicative access

Afghanistan has long been, and remains, one of the poorest countries in the world, with one of the lowest literacy rates. The country's first Human Development Index (HDI), sponsored by the United Nations Development Program (UNDP) in 2004, places Afghanistan nearly at the bottom of all countries' records in respect to chances of having a long and healthy life, to have access to and make use of knowledge, and to have a decent standard of living. Out of 177 countries ranked by the HDI, Afghanistan falls below all of its neighboring countries on these indices and ahead only of Burundi, Mali, Burkino Faso, Niger, and Sierra Leone. The Gender Development Index (GDI) and Human Poverty Index (HPI) place Afghanistan just above only Niger and Burkino Faso. As the HDI notes, a more recent index, the Gender Empowerment Measure (GEM), which is oriented to calculating the participation of men and women in political and economic life, could not be calculated for Afghanistan because there are no 'indicators' of women's participation available in the form of data. As for access to communication, even the most recent data, as of December 2005, show that Afghanistan has a combined telephone penetration of 3.4 per cent of the population and that 25,000 persons out of a total population of 26,508,694 – or approximately 0.1 per cent of the Afghan population – has Internet access. This is an increase from a percentage previously judged to be so small as not to figure in comparison with other countries.

Against this background, one reason for RAWA's ability to communicate its political agenda is that its membership was, and still is, composed of relatively privileged, educated women from urban environments, notably Kabul. From the time that RAWA was formed at the University of Kabul in 1977, the organization opposed both the Soviet occupying forces and the Islamic fundamentalists who attempted to curb women's rights and deny them the opportunity for social and economic advancement. In a familiar story, both the Soviets and the Islamic fundamentalists used the issue of women's rights for their own political purposes, the first as a sign of the modern advancement of a nation and the second as a sign of the assault on the traditionalist values of a nation. Broadly speaking, RAWA has consistently opposed both the internal fundamentalism of what they refer to as the jihadis and the external intervention of countries, including Russia and the United States, who have strategic interests in the region.

In 1981, RAWA created the magazine *Payam-e-Zan* [Woman's Message], available in Pashto and Dari languages, in order to raise Afghan women's awareness of their rights to equal social status. One of the organization's enduring communication strategies has been to enlist other women to read their communiqués to illiterate Afghan women. Throughout the 1980s, RAWA was nearly alone in working to draw attention to infringements of Afghan women's rights (Moghadam, 2003), and from this decade through the 1990s, it proved to be an important source of evidence of abuses for groups including Human Rights Watch, Asia Watch, Amnesty International, as well as UN development and refugee agencies.

Issues of women's rights have been politicized in Afghanistan since the 1920s; however, RAWA's efforts, along with those of other women's organizations, received scarce international attention until the Taliban rose to power in 1996. Moghadam (2003) attributes this general disregard to anti-communism coupled with a widespread perception in the West during the 1980s that the Mujahadin were heroic freedom-fighters protecting their traditional cultures from Soviet domination. She further attributes this disregard to cultural-relativistic notions that it would be inappropriate to impose Western notions of human rights on Muslim women. Although I cannot lay claim to the vast knowledge of Afghan women's lives that Moghadam brings to her analysis, this explanation seems too conjectural to do justice to the circumstances under which any group becomes (in)visible.

The problem with Moghadam's analysis is three-fold. First, she attributes the views and debates mostly held amongst a literary and scholarly elite to an entire population of feminists, a number of whom were likely to be unaware of what was occurring in Afghanistan. Most of those who were aware of the suffering of Afghan women throughout the 1980s, particularly gender and development experts from United Nations programs and agencies, were more interested in the universal rights of women than in cultural relativism (Basu, 2001). Second, she leans toward defining international feminism in terms of Western feminism, so that the opposition to the Mujahadin by Pakistani feminists, many of whom she notes as having an affiliation with the transnational feminist network, Women Living Under Muslim Laws (WLUML), does not appear to count as a form of international attention. And, third, Moghadam's speculation is contradicted by her more grounded analysis of the Feminist Majority, a liberal feminist entity established in the United States in 1987. The Feminist Majority, in common with most US women's organizations in the 1980s, did have a reputation for being inclined towards parochialism, but never towards postmodern cultural relativism or a discomfort with the idea that saving 'other' women might be a way of enacting privilege. In fact, as Moghadam suggests, judging from its campaign to 'restore' Afghan women's rights and its interactions with RAWA, the organization easily could be criticized for investing too much in the notion of a universalizing 'global sisterhood,' taking a simplistic approach to 'other' women's social histories and life contexts, and overvaluing its capacity to empower other women.

One of the most basic considerations is that a heightened attention to Afghan women in the late 1990s followed circumstances under which educated women who had left the country because of threats to their well-being and lives had moved to urban areas such as Peshawar and Quetta at a time when the World Wide Web first became commercially available in Pakistan in 1995. RAWA, with the technical assistance of some male supporters, began working on its website in 1996. By 1997, it had become one of the main sources for exposing the record of abuses of Afghan women by the Taliban. The women of RAWA maintained the site and were responsible for the frequent updating of its content, available in Urdu and English in addition to Pashto and Dari. Further complicating the analysis, however, is that RAWA's new access to the Internet was consistent with – indeed, indicative of – a time when the Western narrative of discovering and saving 'others,' although challenged by some, was being amended to include the possibility that, due to technological progress, 'previously invisible subjects' might not have to be sought by well-intentioned 'First World' subjects because much of the time 'they' would come to 'us', via the net or the television, requesting salvation.

One impetus for the emergence of a nascent global civil society is the strategic need of marginalized groups to circumvent an oppressive national context by bringing concerns directly to global forums. Additionally, for many feminists with an orientation to making international connections, the United Nations conferences on women, culminating in the Fourth World Conference on Women in Beijing, for better and for worse, have helped to introduce a dynamic in which recognition of political existence seems to require transnational networking as a condition. As Breny Mendoza (2002: 299) ruefully observes, 'Only when indigenous peoples or Third World women and feminists take their struggles to the Internet or the UN do they become politically significant, but not in their local political manifestations of resistance.'

Where transnational advocacy is concerned, it is difficult to quarrel with Manuel Castells' (1996: 312) blunt statement that politics must take place through 'the space of flows' provided by informational networks because 'outside the media sphere there is only political marginality.' This, however, begs a question that is rarely broached in the literature of cosmopolitan democracy (or its companion areas such as new social movement and public sphere theory): how do the politically marginal become visible subjects within the media sphere? Fredric Jameson (1991: 357) notes that, in contemporary times, the privileged, and especially 'First World elites,' encounter what seems to be a new public sphere mobilized by new media developments. People and groups that materialized well before the moment that their existence was registered have become visible and acknowledged subjects because of their emergence in and through the globalizing media. This public sphere is cosmopolitan and ethnocentric all at once. The speaking subject commands 'our' attention both because of a heightened social expectation for awareness of difference and because the voice of the 'other' is heard most clearly if her or his interpretive frame of reference is understood as similar to 'ours.'

Accompanying this phenomenon is the ubiquitous, technophilic assumption that new information and communication technologies (ICTs) – and especially the Internet – are creating a vast, level playing field. How else would it be possible for such a cacophony of voices to be speaking and networking with one another? The privilege hovering over this belief becomes evident in the fact that it fails to take into account the digital divide as an extension of the development divide. Fundamental to the maintenance of this divide is the lack of access to media and communication technologies by the poor, and especially those in developing countries. Access to the Internet, while it enables social movements to publicize campaigns more widely, tends to reinforce social elites' cosmopolitan orientations, along with relations of cultural capital and privilege, rather than to level social hierarchies (Stevenson, 2001: 75).

Of course, people do not simply materialize out of the 'thin air' of the Internet, although it would seem so at times, judging from a range of sources from information technology advertisements, to the business sections and segments of mainstream media, to the writings of some scholars who specialize in the study of transnational social movement organizations (TSMOs) and cosmopolitan democracy. Visibility as a political subject requires access to the means of communications, a neglected issue in the work of cosmopolitan democrats (Calabrese, 1999: 269), however much such words as 'network' and 'technology' are mentioned. Silence and deficient analysis tend to bolster a taken-for-granted-ness toward ease of media access and flow. Despite a definitional grounding in considerations of quality, volume, direction, and movement of content, questions of flow assume access as a precondition. The data in respect to access reveals familiar trends for international communication scholars: for example, approximately 25 per cent of all countries of the world have penetration levels for fixed telephone lines of less than one telephone for every 100 persons, over 80 per cent of all Internet users are located in 'developed' countries, and the US has more computers per capita than any other country (Huyer and Sikoska, 2003).

The structural inequalities associated with gender are key factors in exacerbating information imbalance. The majority of the world's women do not have the opportunity to represent themselves or their concerns, for reasons including poverty, illiteracy, and lack of access to basic infrastructure such as electricity and telephone lines (WomenAction, 2000). According to the United Nations Educational, Scientific and Cultural Organization (UNESCO), women account for approximately two-thirds of the illiterate adult population in the world (UNESCO Institute for Statistics, 2005). Full computer literacy is impossible without basic skills in reading and writing (generally in English, which nearly has become the official language of the Internet). Illiteracy is associated directly with both poverty and women's overall social status, leading to a situation in which poor and illiterate women are unlikely to own, or find much support for owning, communications devices such as radios, mobile phones, and computers. As a recent UN Division for the Advancement of Women (DAW) report recognizes, 'The trend for differentiation in use starts early, as seen in the United States where boys are five times more likely than girls to use home computers and parents spend twice as much on ICT products for their sons as they do for their daughters' (United Nations Division for the Advancement of Women, 2005). In addition, policy decision-making around ICTs tends to favor urban areas, which offer better markets for high-end and expensive communication service and technologies, over rural areas. Moreover, rural women's access to ICTs is limited by poor access to roads and to credit that may be available for women-run small- and medium-sized enterprises (SMEs).

While data help to provide an introduction to questions of who speaks and who does not, this does not ensure recognition in the straightforward manner indicated in Nancy Hafkin's (2003) claim that 'Without data, there is no visibility; without visibility, there is no priority.' However critical is access to the means of communication, there is a risk that orienting oneself to UN-style, data-driven, access-only questions will result in a technological-deterministic approach to representation: they cannot represent themselves, they must use ICTs (with apologies to Karl Marx). As Laura Agustín (1999: 155) has observed in respect to promoting access to the Internet as a tool for empowerment, 'with all of the rhetoric about the need to liberate "unheard voices", we miss an essential point: those voices have been talking all along. The question is who is listening.'

The meaning of 'listening,' in this sense, is akin to that assumed by Gayatri Spivak (1988; 1999), for whom 'speaking' is possible only when there exists a listener, as opposed to someone who takes on the role of ventriloquist after having fit the words and actions of the marginalized into the interpretive frame of the privileged. In her renowned essay 'Can the Subaltern Speak?,' Spivak accuses Western feminists of engaging in intellectual/political practices in which they become 'complicit in the persistent constitution of the Other as the Self's shadow' (1988: 280). In 'speaking for' the subaltern, the privileged feminist substitutes her voice for those who are voiceless in history and erases the investigator's construction and representation of the narrative. 'Western intellectual production [becomes] complicit with Western international economic interests' (ibid.: 271). In her later analysis of postcolonial discourses, she expands her critique to include the appropriation of the 'native informant' position by elite postcolonials who themselves take on the mantle of 'native informant,' speaking in the name of the 'racial underclass' even while distancing themselves from it (Spivak, 1999: 358). In this way, postcolonial intellectuals also become complicit with Western economic and cultural imperialism and neo-colonialism. The subaltern is reiterated continuously as 'difference,' the 'other' of US and European modernization.

The status of so-called 'Third World women' becomes that of a victimized 'object' needing to be saved or 'freed,' thus reinforcing the subject position of the Western feminist as liberated (Mohanty, 2003: 39).

Gender has long been central to 'national body politics,' with nations at times taking on femininized attributes ('the motherland,' 'the rape of Afghanistan') and, at other times, masculinized characteristics ('father of the nation,' 'heroic superpower') (Alarcón *et al.*, 1999: 53). In addition, there is an extensive body of historical literature on the centrality of gender to foreign relations. Rescuing women (and children) becomes a pretext for the 'civilized' world's intervention in the affairs of 'uncivilized' nations. Paternalism takes shape in the form of a narrative in which there becomes an imperative to save innocents from barbaric (usually brown) males (Rosenberg, 2002).

After the 9/11 al-Qaeda attacks on the US, the Bush administration had a historically enduring and politically convenient justification for the invasion of Afghanistan: Muslim women had to be saved from their uncivilized male oppressors. As Lila Abu-Lughod (2003) has written, this narrative eschewed historical and political explanations for women's material deprivations across a succession of gender-repressive regimes in Afghanistan, and instead, highlighted a religio-cultural frame in which an advanced 'First World' had taken on the mantle of savior of invisible, voiceless, burqa-clad Afghan/ Muslim women. Two distant worlds had become united, as suggested by Laura Bush, not only because women everywhere desire to wear nail polish in an atmosphere free from fear but also by virtue of the fact that the wish of the Taliban/terrorists was to 'impose their world on the rest of us' (Bush, 2001).

A number of feminist scholars and activists were quick to address the Bush and Blair administrations' cynical deployment of the 'saving Muslim women' trope as a way of rallying public support for the invasion of an already war-ravaged country. Active feminist debates regarding the obsession with veiling as an imposition of variants of Islamic law, the rhetoric of 'saving Muslim women,' and counter-charges of cultural relativism had been ongoing for some time; however, the 'Afghan women' case post-9/11 intensified the contestation and, in many ways, provoked more nuanced analyses of the Islamic religion and the complex and varied meanings of veiling within forms of Islam. I do not have the space to address sufficiently the subject of veiling here, nor am I able to add a great deal to the many careful interpretations of veiling as a covering practice with religious and political implications.[1] Nevertheless, the meaning attached to the burqa is significant for my analysis in the sense that the garment played a central role in the relations of complicity which I will trace. In the following section, I specifically wish to look at the context in which RAWA's successful outreach to the world necessitated that the organization, at least in transitory fashion, situate itself within a representational framework that would be intelligible to the West. However revolutionary, and however often it has been accused of intransigence in respect to cooperating with other women's organizations (e.g., Moghadam,

2003), RAWA could not overcome the structural inequalities within which their links to Western feminism were forged in order to effect significant change in Western worldviews. As Caren Kaplan and Inderpal Grewal (1999: 358) write, the travels of feminist discourse must be understood as 'produced and disseminated through the cultural divides that mark global inequalities. Such a notion of travel marks asymmetries of power rather than a global cosmopolitanism.'

Complicity as representational strategy

Moghadam (2003) argues that a combination of factors led to the 'discovery' of Afghan women in the mid-1990s. First, feminists finally were able to leave behind misguided notions that women's rights were a Western concept; Western indignation became re-directed from the Soviet invasion to the patriarchal gender practices of fundamentalist Afghan men. Second, the United Nations women's conferences in Nairobi in 1985 and Beijing in 1995 were a turning point in provoking recognition that Western feminists and 'Third World' feminists shared the same set of priorities around human rights. Third, there had been a significant growth in the formation of trans-national feminist networks oriented to the language of universal human rights rather than to that of postmodernism. As I have indicated, I find Moghadam's conclusions in this regard to be speculative and an exaggera-tion of the extent to which the various actors in transnational feminist move-ments had reached a consensus on women's issues or had achieved a high level of worldwide feminist unity. Nevertheless, I would agree that the task of raising awareness of the 'Afghan women question' was aided considerably by the formation of transnational feminist advocacy networks with access to new information technologies, despite my objection to the 'globalization-from-below' versus 'globalization-from-above' dynamic which informs Moghadam's analysis. Women's groups which included Women Living Under Muslim Laws (WLUML), Development Alternatives with Women for a New Era (DAWN), the Sisterhood Is Global Institute (SIGI), the Afghan Women's Network (AWN), the Afghan's Women's Mission (AWM), Women in Development Europe (WIDE), the Women's Alliance for Peace and Human Rights in Afghanistan (WAPHA), the International Women's Tribune Center (IWTC), and Isis International-Manila joined with 'rights watch' organizations and UN agencies and working groups to shed light on the situation of women under the Taliban regime in a way which would grab the attention of UN member-states and UN Secretary-General Boutros Boutros-Ghali.

While operating at a distance from other Afghan expatriate groups, RAWA maintained a high profile internationally (Moghadam, 2003). RAWA formed a close connection with the Feminist Majority, which, for most of its brief history, had concentrated on US-specific issues involving women's rights but which was becoming involved in global outreach. The Feminist Majority joined the National Organization for Women (NOW), RAWA, WAPHA, and the Center for Women's Global Leadership in convincing the US government, under the Clinton administration, to refuse to recognize the Taliban as a legitimate government and in pressuring UNOCAL to withdraw its plans to build an oil pipeline across Afghanistan. The Feminist Majority's Campaign to Stop Gender Apartheid in Afghanistan, launched in 1997, was aided in its efforts by information and images provided by RAWA, although as Shahnaz Khan (2001) suggests, the fact that the campaign's spokesperson was Mavis Leno, spouse of television talkshow host Jay Leno, appeared at times to focus more attention on the philanthropic efforts of a 'Hollywood star's wife.' Khan references a 1998 *People* magazine photograph, taken at a news conference on behalf of Afghan women, portraying a burqa-clad woman standing next to Mavis and Jay Leno; she describes the juxtaposition of the two women, the one liberated and the other veiled and unnamed, as one that reinforces the image of Muslim women as helpless victims who must be freed from their oppression by Western feminists.

While this photograph, as well as many others taken of Afghan women and their liberated American hosts, does reinforce inequalities between women, it is as problematic to assume that the Afghan women who are pictured are dupes of Western feminism as it is to presume that they are dupes of fundamentalism. If Western, white feminism is a hegemon, then it also may be known by its 'others' as a social force whose identifiable set of practices and incentives can be tapped into for strategic purposes. In this sense, RAWA members have tended to 'play to the camera' in a manner that differs greatly from the response to Western exposure exemplified by Sharbat Gula, the subject of 'The Search for the Afghan Girl.' The latter, although not missing, was stalked around the Pakistani border and Afghanistan by *National Geographic* photographer Steve McCurry so that he could find the mysterious girl whose portrait he had taken in June 1985 in order to give her 'the dignity of her name' (*National Geographic*, 2001). The adult Sharbat Gula did not want to be 'found' and was just as angry when photographed by McCurry as she had been as a child. 'The Search for the Afghan Girl' is based on the colonial discovery plot.[2] By contrast, RAWA understands that powerful images are best delivered to the West. Members of RAWA, although they often describe the burqa as a 'disgusting garment' and a 'prison' (Daulatzai, 2004; Zoya *et al.*, 2002), are aware that it is, to a certain extent, an ambivalent form of cover which can be put to strategic use. The burqa is used by RAWA and other groups to hide materials, such as books, that are necessary items for the clandestine schools which they operate. Moreover, they have used it as a vehicle for smuggling still and video cameras in order to survey conditions in Afghanistan and Pakistani refugee camps while avoiding intense scrutiny of their activities.

Although the situation of Afghan women first attracted international interest in the mid-1990s, it was in the years 2000 and 2001 that RAWA enjoyed the most public attention. The succession of news reports concentrating on RAWA's activities during this period suggests that this newfound, however fleeting, fame was initiated by virtue of the fact that RAWA's visual records of human atrocities provided good 'wallpapering' for compelling international stories of abuses committed by the uncivilized men of the 'Third World.' Additionally, in 2000, the organization gained more legitimacy as a consciousness-raising entity influential in the decision-making processes of the UN Sub-Committee on Human Rights along with various governmental committees around the world.

The mainstream news media took a special interest in the melding of burqa-clad Muslim women with technology. The burqa and the Internet occupied center-stage in headlines announcing that 'Women's Rights Groups Use Internet to Fight Taliban Oppression of Women,' 'Afghan Women Unite in Cyberspace Against Taliban Repression,' 'Afghan Feminists Go Online,' 'Afghanistan's Clandestine [that is, techno-savvy] Army,' and 'Web Gives Way to Communicate Internationally.' As with the Zapatistas earlier, the association of the perceived primitive with new ICTs served as inspiration for the postmodern global imaginary – a sort of pleasant surprise that the unmodern were 'catching up.'

When the Feminist Majority invited RAWA to the Feminist Expo in 2000, this also heightened attention to the 'Afghan women question' because visits by leading members of the organization had turned into media events. During the two-year run-up to the US invasion of Afghanistan, RAWA's strategic co-implication with the West became most apparent. The peculiarity of this two-year period of time is that RAWA, which had positioned itself as 'the voice of the voiceless' living under the despotic, patriarchal regime of the Taliban, seemed to participate in the strategic unveiling of women's hidden bodies in a manner that is typically associated with masculine practices of colonial domination and Western-style modernization. Unveiling is performed with the knowledge that there exists an obsession with the question of what is beneath the veil. The clamor for Afghan women to remove their veils is accompanied by the notion that what lies beneath is a restoration project for the West. While veiling is constructed as a wall between terror and 'the civilized world,' the unveiling becomes an entry requirement for the enactment of human agency.

In a transnational campaign which was laudable in many respects, there were two events in particular which provided discomfiting support for US foreign policy in post-9/11 Afghanistan. One of these occurred when the Feminist Majority began selling burqa swatches in 2001, its advertisement accompanied by the entreaty, 'Wear it in remembrance – so that we do not forget the women and girls of Afghanistan until their right to work, freedom of movement, education, and healthcare are restored and they are freed again' (http://www.feminist.org). As Sonali Kolhatkar (2002) has observed, this text treats Afghan women as though they were dead or becoming extinct, reinforcing Trinh T. Minh-ha's (1989) commentary on 'special Third World women' serving as the 'private zoo' for privileged progressives.

The second event occurred at Madison Square Garden in February 2001 at a gathering for women's rights activists. Although specific versions of the story differ, there is a general consistency amongst accounts: at the conclusion of a $1,000 per ticket, star-studded, fundraiser featuring a reading of Eve Ensler's *The Vagina Monologues*, Oprah Winfrey recited Ensler's most recent monologue, 'Under the Burqa,' asking the audience to 'imagine a huge dark piece of cloth/hung over your entire body/like you were a shameful statue.' Zoya, a young and now famous representative of RAWA entered the stage. At this point, accounts differ in respect to the degree of violation. A group of American supporters of RAWA describe a situation in which 'a hushed crowd watched as Oprah helped her remove the burqa.' Noy Thrupkaew (2002) wrote in *The American Prospect* that,

> as [Under the Burqa] wound to a close, a figure in a burqa ascended to the stage. Oprah turned and lifted the head-to-toe shroud. Voila! There stood Zoya, a young representative of the Revolutionary Association of the Women of Afghanistan (RAWA).

Following Zoya's delivery of a 'fiery speech,' Thrupkaew writes, 'Eighteen thousand people leaped to their feet, and New York City's Madison Square Garden rang with cheers' (2002). The event, she suggests, provides evidence of an orientation to radical 'outspoken feminism' and secularity which, although allying RAWA with Western feminism, alienated Afghan/Muslim women who were presumably non-partisan 'moderates.'

RAWA's relationship with Oprah Winfrey was productive, in the sense of attracting support and resources, to the extent that, at one point, its website announced 'Welcome Oprah Viewers!' Nevertheless, in her co-authored book, Zoya eventually would describe the encounter as follows:

> When the time came for me to go on stage, after Oprah Winfrey had read [Eve Ensler's poem] 'Under the Burqa,' all the lights went off save for one that was aimed directly at me. I had been asked to wear my burqa, and the light streamed in through the mesh in front of my face and brought tears to my eyes. A group of singers was singing an American chant, a melody full of grief, and I was to walk as slowly as possible . . . I had to climb some steps, but because of the burqa and the tears in my eyes, which wet the fabric and made it cling to my skin, I had to be helped up the stairs. Slowly, very slowly, Oprah lifted the burqa off me and let it fall to the stage.
>
> (Zoya *et al.*, 2002: 211)

Zoya's story reveals the desire of the privileged to briefly understand and inhabit the world of the 'exotic' and 'strange.' Just as importantly, however, it exposes both the active role of the 'exoticized subject' in processes of representational collusion (Whitlock, 2005) and the necessary disavowal of this role insofar as groups which risk being mainstreamed into official politics use distancing mechanisms in order to maintain their outsider status.

Conclusion

Although the Feminist Majority positioned itself as savior of Afghan women, it burned its bridges to RAWA soon after conservative commentators in the US made accusations that it shared and nurtured the organization's radical (purportedly Maoist) tendencies (McElroy, 2002). Because the Feminist Majority, first and foremost, is a US women's organization with a central mandate to lobby US national leaders, an association with RAWA would create a perception of its activities as too radical, thereby isolating the Feminist Majority from the Congressional leaders who remain a primary constituency for the organization. In addition, the organization's 'global sisterhood' orientation made for a profound discomfort with RAWA's unbending refusal to join other women's groups which felt that it would be more politically expedient to work within Islam rather than against it. The recalcitrance of RAWA's position – which had never changed – became most apparent after 9/11, as evidenced by statements on its website that accused the United States of finding it important to 'work with the religio-fascists to have Central Asian oil pipelines extended to accessible ports of shipment.'

In the end, RAWA could not maintain the role of both victim and savior. The members of RAWA were 'the women who knew too much' and, although they earlier had served as important 'native informants' for the US, the latter would not entertain references to its own political-economic complicity in producing Islamic fundamentalism, the Northern Alliance, the Taliban, and al-Qaeda. Today, RAWA continues to pressure the US, but through words that are no longer meant to 'reach out':

> Immediately after the September 11 tragedy the US military might have moved into action to punish its erstwhile hirelings. A captive, hungry, bleeding, devastated, hungry, pauperized, drought-stricken and ill-starred Afghanistan was bombed into oblivion by the most advanced and sophisticated weaponry ever created in human history. Innocent lives, many more than those who lost their lives in the September 11 atrocity, were taken. Even joyous wedding gatherings were not spared. The Taliban regime and its al-Qaeda support were toppled without any significant dent in their human combat resources. What was not done

away with was the sinister shadow of terrorist threat over the whole world and its alter ego, fundamentalist terrorism.

(Revolutionary Association of the Women of Afghanistan, 2002)

Today most Afghan women, even in Kabul, continue to wear the burqa for a variety of reasons, one being that, particularly in rural areas, failure to veil remains a punishable offense (Brodsky, 2002). When girls' schools are opened, they are regularly burnt to the ground, and teachers of girls continue to be assassinated. The US's pet projects, which generally involve teaching democratic imperatives such as the right to vote, as well as skills for budding Afghan entrepreneurs, are protected in the secure, urban zones of Afghanistan. The US–Afghan Women's Council meets annually to reiterate women's progress in Afghanistan despite evidence to the contrary. The gap between the experiences of RAWA and Western representatives who rarely travel beyond the 'secure zone' of the embassies in Kabul is unfathomably wide, despite the approximately five complicit years spent seeking solidarity. RAWA now spends more time at the World Social Forums than in the halls of the United Nations or the offices of women in the US Senate. This might be viewed as both a form of exile as well as a productive development, suggesting that although complicity may sometimes be an effective representational strategy for the short term, it ultimately may succumb to resistance against the status of the privileged as the final arbiters of who will speak and what will be heard.

Notes

1 See, for example, Abu-Lughod (2003); Ahmed (1992); Shirvani (2002); Sreberny (2002); and Yegenoglu (1998).
2 So also is *Beneath the Veil*, the CNN documentary directed by Saira Shah, which was in production prior to 9/11, but due to synergistic kismet, arrived just in time to expose the atrocities of Afghanistan via videotapes of executions made by the much more intrepid members of RAWA.

References

Abu-Lughod, Lila (2003) 'Saving Afghan women or standing with them? On images, ethics, and war in our times', *Insaniyaat*, 1(1). Accessed at: http://www.aucegypt.edu/academic/insanyat/Issue%201/1-article1.htm.
Afghanistan National Human Development Index (2004) Accessed at: http://www.undp.org.af/about_us/overview_undp_afg/default.htm.
Agustín, Laura (1999) 'They speak, but who listens?, in W. Harcourt (ed.), *Women@Internet: Creating New Cultures in Cyberspace*. London: Zed Books, pp. 149–55.
Ahmed, Leila (1992) *Women and Gender in Islam: Historical Roots of a Modern Debate*, New Haven, CT: Yale University Press.

Alarcón, Norma, Caren Kaplan and Minoo Moallem (1999) 'Introduction: between woman and nation', in Caren Kaplan, Norma Alarcón and Minoo Moallem (eds), *Between Woman and Nation: Nationalisms, Transnational Feminisms, and the State*. Durham, NC: Duke University Press, pp. 1–18.

Basu, Rasil (2001) 'The rape of Afghanistan', *ZNet* (December 30). Accessed at: http://www.zmag.org/basurape.htm.

Brodsky, Anne (2002) 'Inside Pakistan and Afghanistan with RAWA', *Counterpunch* (July 29). Accessed at: http://www.counterpunch.org/brodsky0729.html.

Bush, Laura (2001) 'Radio address by Mrs. Bush', Whitehouse (November 17). Accessed at: http://www.whitehouse.gov/news/releases/2001/11/20011117.html.

Calabrese, Andrew (1999) 'The welfare state, the information society, and the ambivalence of social movements', in Andrew Calabrese and Jean-Claude Burgelman (eds), *Communication, Citizenship, and Social Policy: Rethinking the Limits of the Welfare State*. Lanham, MD: Rowman & Littlefield, pp. 259–78.

Castells, Manuel (1996) *The Rise of the Network Society*. Vol. 1 of The Information Age: Economy, Society, and Culture. Oxford: Blackwell.

Daulatzai, Anila (2004) 'A leap of faith: thoughts on secularistic practices and progressive politics', *International Social Sciences Journal*, 56 (182): 565–76.

Hafkin, Nancy (2003) 'Some thoughts on gender and telecommunications/ICT statistics and indicators'. Geneva: International Telecommunication Union.

Huyer, Sophia and Tatjana Sikoska (2003) 'Overcoming the gender digital divide: understanding ICTs and their potential for the empowerment of women'. INSTRAW, United Nations.

Jameson, Fredric (1991) *Postmodernism: Or, the Cultural Logic of Late Capitalism*. Durham, NC: Duke University Press.

Kaplan, Caren and Inderpal Grewal (1999) 'Transnational feminist cultural studies: beyond the Marxism, poststructuralism, feminist divides', in Caren Kaplan, Norma Alarcón and Minoo Moallem (eds), *Between Woman and Nation: Nationalisms, Transnational Feminisms, and the State*. Durham, NC: Duke University Press, pp. 349–64.

Khan, Shahnaz (2001) 'Between here and there: feminist solidarity and Afghan women', *Genders*, 33. Accessed at: http://www.genders.org/g33/g33.khan.html.

Kolhatkar, Sonali (2002) 'Saving Afghan women', *ZNet* (May 9). Accessed at: http://www.zmag.org/content/gender/kolhatkarwomen.cfm.

McElroy, Wendy (2002) 'The silence surrounding RAWA', FoxNews.com (August 20). Accessed at: http://www.foxnews.com/story/0,2933,60806,00.html.

McLaughlin, Lisa (2004) 'Feminism and the political economy of transnational public space', *Sociological Review*, 52 (1): 156–75.

Mendoza, Breny (2002) 'Transnational feminisms in question', *Feminist Theory*, 3 (3): 295–314.

Mittelman, James (2000) *The Globalization Syndrome: Transformation and Resistance*. Princeton, NJ: Princeton University Press.

Moghadam, Valentine (2003) 'Globalizing the local: transnational feminism and women's rights', *Peuples and Monde* (December 26). Accessed at: http://www.peuplesmonde.com/article.php3?id.article=20.

Mohanty, Chandra (2003) *Feminism without Borders: Decolonizing Theory, Practicing Solidarity*. Durham, NC: Duke University Press.

Murdock, Graham (2004) 'Past the posts: rethinking change, retrieving critique', *European Journal of Communication*, 19 (1):19–38.

National Geographic (2001) 'A life revealed'. Accessed at: http://magma.national geographic.com/ngm.afghangirl/.

Rosenberg, Emily S. (2002) 'Rescuing women and children', *The Journal of American History*, 89 (2). Accessed at: http://www.historycooperative.org/journals/jah/89.2/ rosenberg.html.

Revolutionary Association of the Women of Afghanistan (2002) 'Fundamentalism is the enemy of all civilized humanity: RAWA statement on the anniversary of the September 11 tragedy'. Accessed at: http://www.rawa.org/sep11-02.htm.

Shirvani, Sheida (2002) 'Voice from behind the veil', *Feminist Media Studies*, 2 (2): 268–70.

Spivak, Gayatri (1988) 'Can the subaltern speak?', in Cary Nelson and Lawrence Grossberg (eds), *Marxism and the Interpretation of Culture*. Chicago: University of Illinois Press, pp. 271–313.

Spivak, Gayatri (1999) *A Critique of Postcolonial Reason: Toward a History of the Vanishing Present*. Cambridge, MA: Harvard University Press.

Sreberny, Annabelle (2001) 'Gender, globalization and communications: women and the transnational', *Feminist Media Studies*, 1(1): 61–6.

Sreberny, Annabelle (2002) 'Seeing through the veil', *Feminist Media Studies*, 2 (2): 270–2.

Stevenson, Nick (2001) 'The future of public media cultures: morality, ethics and ambivalence', in Frank Webster (ed.), *Culture and Politics in the Information Age*. London: Routledge, pp. 630–80.

Thrupkaew, Noy (2002) 'What do Afghan women want?', *The American Prospect* 13 (15) (August 26). Accessed at: http://www.prospect.org/print/V13/15/thrupkaew-n. html.

Trinh T. Minh-ha (1989) 'Difference: a special Third World women issue', in Trinh T. Minh-ha, *Woman, Native, Other: Writing, Postcoloniality and Feminism*. Bloomington: Indiana University Press.

UNESCO Institute for Statistics (2005) Accessed at: http://www.uis.unesco.org/ ev_en.php?ID=2867_201&ID2=DO_TOPIC.

United Nations Division for the Advancement of Women (UN-DAW) (2005) *Women 2000 and Beyond: Gender Equality and the Empowerment of Women through ICT*. New York: United Nations Division for the Advancement of Women, Department of Economic and Social Affairs.

Whitlock, Gillian (2005) 'The skin of the burqa: recent life narratives from Afghanistan', *Biography*, 28 (1): 54–76.

WomenAction (2000) *Alternative Assessment of Women and Media Based in NGO Reviews of Section J, Beijing Platform for Action*. Available at: http://www.womenaction.org/ csw44/altrepeng.htm.

Yegenoglu, Meyda (1998) *Colonial Fantasies: Towards a Feminist Reading of Orientalism*. Cambridge: Cambridge University Press.

Zoya, with John Folain and Rita Cristofari (2002) *Zoya's Story*. New York: Harper.

Chapter 14

The Islamic Internet

Authority, authenticity and reform

Musa Maguire

In a February 2004 Olympic qualifying football match, Mexico eliminated the United States with a 4–0 victory. It was redemption for the Mexican team, who had suffered several losses to the USA, including one in the 2002 World Cup. The crowd in Guadalajara felt jubilation and relief. Yet, on that day, the emotional, and perhaps intoxicated fans, displayed more than national pride and passion for the game. They were a focus group, offering crucial insight into world public opinion on the United States. Before the game began, the fans jeered and booed during the American national anthem. After the game, as the US players left the field, fans chanted 'Osama! Osama!' [1]

It is perhaps not surprising that Osama bin Laden could become a Third World icon of resistance. In Guadalajara, and many places far removed from the personal trauma of 9/11, people may see Osama as someone daring enough to take on American might. And Bin Laden articulates the feelings of those touched by US aggression as in al-Qaeda leader's letter to the American people:

> The freedom and democracy that you call to is for yourselves and for the white race only; as for the rest of the world, you impose upon them your monstrous, destructive policies and Governments, which you call the 'American friends'. Yet you prevent them from establishing democracies. When the Islamic party in Algeria wanted to practice democracy and they won the election, you unleashed your agents in the Algerian army onto them, and to attack them with tanks and guns, to imprison them and torture them – a new lesson from the 'American book of democracy'! [2]

Bin Laden's message would not be lost on a Latin American audience, with its own memories of US interventions. It may find sympathetic ears in Guadalajara, or Mexico City, or perhaps even Chiapas, home to another Third World icon of resistance – the Zapatista movement. For successful radical countercurrents in global media, the Zapatistas are the classic case study. Like Bin Laden, the Zapatistas strategically employed media to promote their message and establish a global network. Unlike Bin Laden, they found diverse support in that global network, particularly from progressive movements and prominent intellectuals in the Northern countries.

Let us consider this image as a litmus test. Why does al-Qaeda not receive the same broad-based support from diverse social movements? In a famous recruiting video attributed to al-Qaeda, fighters hold their guns in the air, with only the Qur'an raised higher. The Zapatistas had guns and were willing to fight. Aside from some notorious exceptions, al-Qaeda is known for attacking military targets in areas where people are occupied, facing hostile foreign interests, or living under oppression. So, it is not the guns. But what about the other element in this picture – the Qur'an? The Qur'an represents the ambition of al-Qaeda, along with many other Islamic groups and movements, to establish a society governed by Islamic law. It is through this message that al-Qaeda guarantees its ideological isolation. On the other hand, the Zapatista message was successfully marketed by Subcomandante Marcos, who, 'by diversifying the discourse of struggle,' helped promote the Zapatistas as a movement that 'encompasses a participatory process for social change, one that is concerned as much with social equality, freedom, and participation in decision-making as it is with economic opportunity, women's rights, and reduction of poverty in indigenous communities' (Garrido and Halavais, 2003: 169). Bin Laden, however, makes no effort to diversify the discourse of struggle. His is a plainly Islamist message. Bin Laden calls for ongoing war against disbelief, and the strict implementation of Islamic law. This vision does not mobilize the progressive movement and human rights organizations. There will be no 'shariah now!' demonstrations in the Seattle rain.

But does Bin Laden's ideological isolation apply to the wider Muslim world? Can we segment Bin Laden and his beliefs, perhaps under a label like Islamism, or radical Islam? Whatever its title, does it sufficiently contrast with a safer, mainstream Islam, one digestible to secular humanism, integrated with global social movements, and analytically convenient for interested academics? As these questions burst with controversy and ignite extensive discussion, let me offer my own subject position as a brief disclaimer to what follows. I am an American convert to Islam, and like all Muslims, I believe that Allah, our Creator, revealed the Qur'an to the Prophet Muhammad. I believe that the early generations of Muslims preserved the religion accurately and effectively. Likewise, I trust in the tradition of scholarship that transmitted Islam from that time. To the best of my ability, I apply the shariah law in my private and public life. Moreover, I would love to see shariah law applied extensively and authentically . . . even in Seattle. And concerning these core tenets of Sunni Islam, Bin Laden and I are in agreement. That said, I despise what is attributed to Bin Laden of random violence, targeting of innocent civilians, and certainly the spectacle of violence on 9/11. That disgust is echoed by the vast majority of orthodox Sunni 'ulamā (religious scholars), whether they reside in Britain, Pakistan or Saudi

Arabia. So to the extent that violent extremism abandons Islamic legal rulings on warfare, we can isolate it conceptually. However, orthodox Islam, purified of its radical components, will not simply dissolve into the enshrined ideologies of secular academia. Academic discourse preemptively excludes Islam – as defined by the core beliefs mentioned above – from serious consideration.

No one doubts the importance of Islam as a field of academic analysis. And no one doubts the dramatic political and social impact of such research in contemporary life. Yet, Islam is very rarely addressed on its own terms within academic literature. What follows is an analysis of Islam on the Internet. Yet, the implications are larger. This chapter reflects on the ideological stubbornness of secular academia and its consequences within a rapidly polarizing world. As I intend to show, media scholars often seek to bypass the established beliefs and laws of Islam in favour of a post-modernized 'post-Islam', an ideological bazaar for anyone who labels himself Muslim. This attempted short-cut around the ideological challenge of Islam only short-circuits any meaningful analysis of the Muslim world. Although these scholars offer a useful catalogue of Islamic and pseudo-Islamic activities online, the preemptive refusal of Islamic legitimacy cripples their analyses.

Media Studies, the Internet and Islam

In our established conception of global media, the Islamic Internet certainly represents a profound counter-flow in ideology and information. But is the Islamic contribution consistent with any perceived solution to this imbalance? In her comprehensive analysis of the digital divide, Pippa Norris posits 'postmaterialist values' as a transformative component of online culture. She defines these values as 'concern for environmental protection rather than economic growth, sexual equality rather than traditional family roles within the family, secular rather than religious values, and the importance of individual freedom, self-expression, internationalism, and participatory democracy' (Norris, 2001: 199). Norris invokes dominant state and corporate authority as the 'other' to postmaterialism. Yet, according to her description above, Islam just as easily fits the role. The conflation of orthodox Islam and Western conservatism, based on generally comparable values, is explicitly asserted elsewhere (Castells, 1997, Ch. 1). Even beyond the case of Islam, secular academia leaves little room for religious discourse. John Downing acknowledges that 'religious dimensions of power . . . have had and will continue to have considerable practical import for radical media. Secular research that is blinded by its secularism into neglecting this leaves a significant lacuna' (Downing, 2001: 80). But in this case, the problem extends beyond neglect. Even when scholars turn their attention to the Muslim world, they preemptively disqualify Islam from self-representation.

Focused studies on the Islamic Internet follow a consistent theoretical pattern. First, a refusal to define Islam opens an exaggerated frame of research, levelling all claimants to religious authority. Next, after imposing their own ideological grid, these studies tend to celebrate and scold according to the authors' assumed values. In the end, they produce sound documentation of Islamic activity online, but fail to understand the complex manifestations of authentic Islamic authority on the Internet.

Erasing Islam

The work of Gary Bunt provides a well-researched catalogue of Islamic activity online (Bunt, 2000; 2002; 2003). However, Bunt insistently refuses to accept any clear definition of Islam, leaving his field of research skewed. He claims that 'a single . . . concise definition of Islam can be difficult to provide' (Bunt, 2003: 27) and extends his focus to all 'those who define themselves as Muslims' (ibid.: 5). From the perspective of Islamic orthodoxy, this approach recklessly groups the legitimate and the absurd. For Bunt, Islam is simply an empty claim, with no criterion for validity or soundness. Rather than defining a rough range of legitimacy within the Islamic tradition, Bunt posits a seemingly neutral pluralism, asserting that:

> The term 'Islamic' in this book refers to any influence, for example, cultural, social, textual, political, Divine, in which the primary sources of Islam's formation or interpretation have contributed to an identity label. 'Islamic beliefs' are what an individual who describes him- or herself as Muslim undertakes in the name of Islam, whether that practice is approved by 'authorities' or not. The term 'Islamic environment' does not refer to a specific delineated geographical, historical, or social entity: it is used here in the sense of a place where Islamic beliefs form an identity reference point (however marginal, secular or religious). For example, an Islamic environment could be a mosque, a house or street with Muslim residents, or an individual's sense of place and practice. The rigid criteria defining who is a Muslim utilized by various sources and schools of thought do not apply within this book.
>
> (Bunt, 2000: 7)

Despite Bunt's claims, Islam is not simply a multicultural mêlée of individual interpretations. Islam can be defined around certain core beliefs and established corollaries. By denying these allegedly 'rigid' criteria, Bunt abandons any meaningful understanding of the Islamic Internet. Pluralism, when defined around a negation of Islam, can hardly be considered neutral.

Other scholars offer similar disclaimers of pluralism and refuse to accept any basic definition of Islam. Peter Mandaville, in his analysis of Islam in diaspora, argues that, 'Any analysis of "identity" or "community" can easily stray into an essentialist mode that involves constructing boundaries around some social phenomenon (person, nation, culture, religious community, etc.)

and assigning them certain timeless characteristics or traits' (Mandaville, 2001: 170).

So Mandaville also advocates a brand of pluralism, denying fixed identity at all costs. However, he sees no problem conflating individual and national identity, culture and religious belief. Strangely, this utter flattening of all 'difference' emerges in a critique of essentialism. Islam historically accommodated great varieties of culture. Likewise, within Islam, certain legitimate differences of opinion exist on matters of religious law. However, the core beliefs of Islam – among them the oneness of Allah, the prophethood of Muhammad, and the integrity of the Qur'an – are quite simply timeless and unchanging essentials. Additionally, Mandaville defines 'culturalist Muslims' as 'those whose ethnohistorical roots qualify them as Muslims, but who do not practice their religion or consider it to be a significant component of their self-identities' (ibid.: 172). Again we see a radical conflation of issues. Muslims are defined by certain beliefs and deeds, not by 'ethnohistorical roots.' So even though Mandaville excludes this 'culturalist' category from his analysis, focusing instead on those who assert some level of religious identity, he clearly offers no baseline of legitimacy to speak sensibly of Islam.

Analytical impacts

I must emphasize that both Bunt and Mandaville produce excellent analytical work. Yet, their rigid ideological filter blocks a meaningful discussion of Islam, as they virtually deny that any such thing exists! Instead, both authors chronicle the many claimants to Islamic authority and identify the central issues in circulation. However, without reference to the orthodox tradition itself, we cannot properly say how these issues play out within Islam.

For instance, in Bunt's analysis of the Islamic Mediterranean Internet, he offers an eclectic list of examples to illustrate the online contestation of Islamic authority (Bunt, 2002). With claims of legitimacy as the only criterion for inclusion, Bunt cheerfully bundles the online activities of Algerian jihadists, Hamas, Hizbullah, Sufism, the Druze, individual religious scholars, the Ikhwaan al-Muslimeen, and Mu'ammar al-Qadhafi. Rightly, he often recognizes the specific points of contention between orthodox sects, such as polemics between Sufis and so-called Wahhabis (Bunt, 2002: 181). But only through the flattening lens of secularism could these widely divergent ideologies merge within a single analytical space. Bunt even adds homosexual advocacy sites to his ideological bouquet. He explains that, 'one contentious issue is the notion of "Gay Muslim" identity, which traditional interpreters may see as anathema to Islam, based on their interpretations of the Qur'an and other sources (as well as cultural factors)' (ibid.: 173).

Bunt's relativization of this issue as one of 'interpretation' simply belies the unambiguous, unanimously approved Islamic texts denoting the clear prohibition, even criminality, of homosexuality. Despite the widespread unpopularity of this view in the West, it will not simply melt away from Islam. Elsewhere, Bunt criticizes Muslim websites for excluding the US-based, largely African-American movement 'Nation of Islam' from their online content. He suggests that these websites are limited by their relative infancy, and may in fact 'evolve' in the future (Bunt, 2000: 47). In other words, their development is achieved through the liquidation of Islamic legitimacy.

To his credit, Bunt recognizes authority and legitimacy as central problematic issues for the study of Islam on the Internet (Bunt, 2003, Ch. 1; Bunt, 2002: 165). Likewise, Mandaville recognizes that, 'for the overwhelming majority of Muslims in the West the Internet is mainly a forum for the conduct of politics *within* Islam' (Mandaville, 2001: 182). And even though Mandaville celebrates the idea of a decentralized Islam, he soberly recognizes the endurance of Islamic authority as 'the product of centuries of study and exhaustive research' (ibid.: 179). Similarly, John Anderson emphasizes the transformation of authority in his analysis of the Islamic Internet (Anderson, 2003). Yet, he also engages internal Islamic debates, within the realm or orthodoxy, which highlight another crucial theme – the place of reform in Islamic scholarship. So from these media scholars, we identify the currency of debate on the Islamic Internet – authority, authenticity, and reform. Yet, without a viable frame of legitimacy, based on the established tradition of religious scholarship, the portrait of an authentically Islamic Internet remains blurred.

The Sunni Internet

In Islamic scholarship, the term *Ahl al-Sunnah wal-Jama'ah* means the people of *sunnah* (the life example of the Prophet Muhammad) and the community (those who gather around the truth). In other words, this is orthodox Sunni Islam. And despite the various schools of thought and differences of opinion, Muslims unite around clearly defined beliefs and practices. Certainly, the Internet gives a voice to many individuals, organizations, and governments who openly contest these basic principles. Yet, orthodox Islam also lives on the net. Rather than imposing the filter of secular humanism, and spotlighting those heretical perspectives that pass through, I prefer to engage the Islamic tradition on its own terms.

To focus upon *Ahl al-Sunnah wal-Jama'ah* does not empty our discussion of depth or even controversy. It just establishes a baseline of legitimacy according to centuries of Islamic scholarship. Moreover, by accepting the Islamic tradition on its own terms, we engage a richer span of issues and questions. How does the authoritative Islamic tradition react to and incorporate new technologies? What unique challenges does the Internet pose to the integrity of this tradition? How well do Muslim scholars understand the Internet, its advantages and pitfalls? And returning to a classic debate in communication research, to what extent does the medium of the Internet, with its radical anonymity and decentralization, subvert the best efforts of Muslim scholars to employ this technology on their own terms? Though the vastness of these issues extends well beyond the space of this chapter, I shall offer a snapshot of the authentically Islamic Internet, touching briefly on each of these questions.

Responding to my critique of research on the Islamic Internet, some may retort that I simply ignore difference and only assert my own narrow version of Islam. What I assert, however, is the broad borders of discourse within Sunni Islam. Through my own research as a media scholar, and experience as a Muslim, I classify online Islamic activity within the following clusters.

Radical Jihadists

This group certainly qualifies as the most publicized and demonized among Sunni Muslims. Jihadists may actually mix between various historical schools of thought and even dabble in modernism, but all agree on the primacy of jihad as an Islamic duty in the current age. Some classic jihadist sites are qoqaz.net (covering Chechnya) and azzam.com.[3] Despite its extreme Islamophobic bias, the Internet haganah (haganah.org.il/haganah/) offers a fairly up-to-date listing of jihadist sites. Important to distinguish within this group, are those that advocate and practise jihad within the framework of Islamic law, and those who use jihad as a banner for random violence and acts of terrorism.

Sufi traditionalists

This group claims to represent the continuous tradition of Islamic scholarship along with the spirituality of true Islam. They favour a strict adherence to traditional schools of Islamic law, and consider the Sufi brotherhoods a legitimate pathway to authentic Islamic piety. Many Muslims, however, consider Sufism a dangerous departure from orthodoxy. The Sufi traditionalist view is represented on sites such as sunnipath.com, masud.co.uk, and sunniforum.com.

Religious modernists

For the most part, these Muslims follow Islamic law, but emphasize political engagement and allow flexibility on certain contemporary issues. Their ideological and institutional affiliations usually connect with the major modern Islamist political movements, particularly the *Ikhwaan-al-Muslimen* (a twentieth-century movement founded in Egypt). Religious modernists draw criticism for their lax approach on some shariah issues. Their clear strength is literacy of modern issues and events. Representative websites include islamonline.net, iviews.com, and sites of major Western Muslim organizations, such as the Islamic Society of North America (isna.net).

Conservative Salafis

The Salafi movement strives to uphold Muslim beliefs and practices according to the understanding of the *Salaf-us-saalih* (the pious predecessors, or first three generations of Muslims). Though some modernists and jihadists share beliefs with conservative Salafis, this group tends to favour a grass-roots method of teaching and reform over political activism and revolt. They strongly discourage revolt against leaders, and prefer a strict textual approach to Islamic law. Some conservative Salafi organizations and websites unapologetically attack other Muslims for alleged deviance. Websites representing this view include: troid.com, salafipublications.com, salafitalk.net, and sahab.com (Arabic).

True moderates

When we try to define moderate Muslims, the essential questions is 'moderate, in reference to what?' For many, 'moderate' means those who can comfortably accommodate secular humanist ideologies, abandoning those aspects of Islam deemed backward or medieval. For some Muslims, 'moderate' might mean adherence to the status quo of Islamic societies, avoiding criticism of dominant cultural and social practices that contradict the shariah. However, working within the Islamic tradition itself, without the filters of foreign ideologies and discourses, 'moderate' takes on a different meaning. It represents those Muslims steadfast in adherence to orthodox beliefs and practices, knowledgeable in Islamic law. Yet they understand, appreciate, and tolerate differences of opinion amongst Muslims, within the limits of orthodoxy. And they critically engage contemporary issues without sacrificing religious principles. These true moderates find voices in sites like ibnothaimeen.com, islamtoday.com, as-sahwah.com, and forums.almaghrib.org.

Authority, authenticity and reform: will the real *ahl-us-sunnah* stand up?

Sunni Islamic law is historically composed of four *madhhabs* – or schools of thought. Though many scholars developed schools of law in the early centuries of Islam, only four withstood the test of time, and continue with abundant followers until today (Phillips, 2000). The debate over *madhhabs* forms one of the most divisive and contested issues on the Islamic Internet. The seemingly technical legalistic debate holds major significance, and cascades down to many other controversial issues.

Sufi traditionalists argue the strongest for strict adherence to a classical *madhhab*. They prescribe a necessary deferral to the many scholars, through-out generations, who refined the *madhhabs* from the primary sources of law (i.e. Qur'an, *sunnah* of the Prophet (sallallahu alaihi wa sallam), and some agreed positions of the early Muslims). This, no doubt, is a claim to authority – a cautious and humble submission to the authority of tradition. As one scholar says on the masud.co.uk website:

> To abandon the fruits of this research, the Islamic *shari'a*, for the follow-ing of contemporary shaikhs who, despite the claims, are not at the level of their predecessors, is a replacement of something tried and proven for something at best tentative.

And this quote ignites the controversy. Who are these supposedly under-qualified contemporary shaikhs, forsaking centuries of scholarship for their own shaky interpretations? According to the Sufi traditionalists, it is both the modernists and Salafis. Although these two groups radically differ on interpretations of Islamic law, the traditionalists paint them as one, due to a common ethic of reform in reference to Islamic scholarship.

On conservative Salafi sites, there is strict condemnation of *taqleed* – the process of adhering to a single *madhhab*. This is described as blind-following which privileges an archaic system of law over the primary sources of Islam. An article on therighteouspath.com explains this issue as follows:

> Readers, from the sayings of the four imams [leaders of the four Islamic schools of law] it is clear that blind bigoted following is a forbidden matter. And still to stress on it and to declare it obligatory, and to blame those who do not blindly follow a person, or to say it is wrong, then what kind of justice is this?

From these two positions, the issue seems apparent. Either a Muslim, at any level of knowledge, goes directly to the text himself to deduce rulings, or he follows the schools of law to the letter. In fact, these positions reflect several centuries of debate and controversy among Muslim scholars, centred around the political demise of Islam and strategies for renewal. In this online debate, however, the historical context and complexity are completely lost. More significantly, we see the general character of the Internet – anonymous and decentralizing, disruptive of authority – exerting a deterministic effect on Muslim discourse. On chat sites like salafitalk.net, sunniforum.com, and forums.almaghrib.org, partisan positions on these issues circulate widely. Though each site claims rigorous oversight by people of knowledge, salafitalk and sunniforum enable, or even encourage, grossly biased content according to the respective school of thought. Only forums.almaghrib.org, because of effective supervision, features civil, informed and balanced debates on these issues.

Among 'true moderates,' this conflict can be viewed in its proper context. First, the debate over *madhhabs* is legitimate, but the leaders of those who oppose *taqlid* are themselves scholars, usually deeply trained in at least one *madhhab*. For instance, ibnothaimeen.com features the collected works of Shaikh Muhammad ibn Saalih ibn 'Uthaimeen, an undisputed imam of the Salafi movement. Most Salafi sites link to this website, and would tolerate no ill speech about this scholar. Yet, even the Living Islam websites, a Sufi traditionalist resource, recognize Shaikh ibn 'Uthaimeen as a qualified scholar in the Hanbali *madhhab*.[4] Moreover, Muhammad ibn 'Abdul Wahhab, the eighteenth-century Islamic scholar and namesake of the 'Wahhabi', followed the Hanbali *madhhab* closely (DeLong-Bas, 2004; Abualrub, 2003). So how do we make sense of this overlap, given the simplicity of other conservative Salafi and Sufi traditionalist sites? On this issue, there are two levels of complexity absorbed and warped through the Internet: first, the contested claims to the same sources of authority; second, the conflation of issues in polemics and criticism.

The spirit of reform in Islam dates back to at least the eighteenth century and accelerates during the era of European imperialism in the nineteenth century. Jihadists, religious modernists, conservative Salafis, and the true moderates all connect with this process of reform, albeit with dramatically different interpretations. And it emerges from a valid question – What went wrong? Bernard Lewis asks this question in his book of the same title. Lewis focuses on the decline of the Ottoman empire, the last great Muslim state, and its inability to keep up with European innovation and progress (Lewis, 2002). Despite his guarded remarks of respect for the Islamic golden age (ending in the 1200s), Lewis prescribes secular Westernization as the clear path to a Muslim renaissance. Of course, Muslims do not accept such an answer. But the question remains – what went wrong?

Orthodox Muslims all agree on returning to the authentic Islam – but the definitions of authenticity vary. A quick scan of Islamic websites illustrates the debate. For conservative Salafis, the renaissance of Islam depends on strict adherence to a specific set of scholars, and rabid disavowal of those who disagree with them. Sites like salafipublications.com and troid.org specialize in highlighting the alleged deviance of Islamic scholars and preachers, past and present. However, they do not cope well with differences of opinion that existed throughout the ages. Their claim to purity, therefore, tends to be ahistorical and oversimplistic. Traditionalist Sufis, overtly friendly to the numerous schools of law, offer more historical depth and diverse citations on sites such as sunnipath.com. However, this is where the issues blur. Both sets of Muslim offer a coherent case of authority – the Salafis, by returning to the pure sources; the Sufis, by linking themselves to an established tradition. Yet, the basis of separation includes not only issues of *fiqh*, or Islamic law, framed by the debate over *madhhabs*. A greater, and more fundamental division, exists over the tenets of creed, and the legitimacy of Sufi spiritual practices.

Along with their simplistic position on *fiqh*, the conservative Salafis package a sound position on Islamic creed. Likewise, they loudly and correctly warn against innovation in religion. The Sufis, despite their deeper legal arsenal, promote beliefs and practices that were not found among the early generations of Muslims. Therefore, Sufis link themselves to tradition that crumbles under historical scrutiny. Salafis assert legitimate beliefs through ahistorical claims of authority. Yet, the conflation of issues, propagated and disseminated through the Internet with unprecedented intensity, stages an artificial drama.

Though true moderates share the fundamental beliefs of the conservative Salafis, they shun a distinctive label other than *Ahl-us-Sunnah wal-Jama'ah*. Likewise, when it comes to issues of *fiqh*, they recognize the historical diversity of opinions, and understand the wider scope of Islamic law. The islamtoday. com site, supervised by Saudi scholar Salman al-'Auda, represents this category well. Its non-sectarian labelling, and lack of personal polemics, sets it apart from the conservative Salafi and traditionalist Sufi sites. Islamtoday. com mixes sound religious advice, well-mannered corrections of sectarian errors, and informed commentary on contemporary issues. Likewise, ibnothaimeen.com catalogues the work on Shaikh Muhammad ibn Saalih Al-'Uthaimeen, an undisputed *faqih* – scholar of religious law – of the late twentieth century.

In this contrast, another technological issue emerges. As Diane Saco notes, the Internet can be characterized as a 'social space without faces,' a non-physical space of interaction where anonymity reigns (Saco, 2002: 29). Some conservative Salafi sites are primarily run by small groups of Muslim converts in the West. They make oft-contested claims to represent major scholars in Saudi Arabia. Prominent Sufi sites emerge from committed enthusiasts, such as masud.co.uk or themodernreligion.com. Others, such as sunnipath. com, are overseen by a group of learned, though unflinchingly partisan, Muslims. However, islamtoday.com, supervised by a well-known though sometimes controversial scholar, employs a team of qualified religious experts to author articles, answer questions, and issue verdicts. The trust of Shaikh ibn 'Uthaimeen runs ibnothaimeen.com. Yet, at a superficial level, these sites merge as seemingly equal voices in knowledge and credentials.

Political authority stands as another axis of online Islamic discourse. Historically, Saudi Arabia has provided financial and organizational support for the global Salafi movement. Sufis describe this movement with the pejorative title of 'Wahhabism,' attempting to marginalize its Islamic legitimacy. Using the rhetoric of tradition, Sufis portray themselves as the 'organic Islam,' an alternative to the alleged 'oil Islam' of Saudi Arabia (Winter, 2004). Of course, Sufi authorities often represent state-linked educational institutions in Syria and Egypt, neither of which can claim greater Islamic legitimacy than Saudi Arabia. But beyond this common bickering, issues of political legitimacy animate fierce debate on the Islamic Internet.

The early Islamic community witnessed political upheaval from a group known as the *khawarij*. These rebels rose against the Islamic state, with their own claims of legitimacy, and caused a great deal of bloodshed and turmoil. Although other rebellions occurred throughout Islamic history, some with greater religious justification, the *khawarij* set a precedent of political quietism in Islamic law. For the most part, the corruption and abuse of rulers are tolerated, unless they violate certain core religious principles. In recent history, Muslim states monopolized power and controlled political discourse within their borders. With the decentralizing capacity of the Internet, political dissent, often linked to militant activity, increased dramatically in the Muslim world (Bunt, 2000; 2002; 2003; Fandy, 1999).

Critics of the Saudi religious elite often allege a docile subservience of the 'ulama to the royalty (Abukhalil, 2004). This oversimplifies the Islamic legal issues related to political leadership. According to the Saudi 'ulama, the position of rulers should be honoured, and criticism should be limited to private meetings rather than public denouncements. This reflects established positions within Islamic law, geared to safeguard peace and protect society from turmoil. Conservative Salafis emphasize this political strategy, and rigorously attack those who openly call for sedition against Muslim leaders. In this respect, they scrutinize any hints of political activism, even among those who share their core beliefs. Sites such as salafipublications.com assert almost proprietary rights of the Salafi *manhaj* – methodology – based on these political criteria. Needless to say, for the conservative Salafis, jihadists represent a current manifestation of the *khawarij*.

On the contrary, radical jihadists attack the political legitimacy of all Muslim states, particularly those who publicly promote an Islamic identity, such as Saudi Arabia. Jihadists, too, recognize the traditional Islamic injunctions of obedience to rulers. However, they argue that the wide abandonment of Islamic law cancels legitimacy of leadership. In order for them to operate independently of political authority, and thereby validate their principles of rebellion, they consistently proclaim the apostasy of Muslim leaders. According to their interpretation, this necessitates the overthrow of political authorities. Contributors, mostly Western youth, to the now defunct clearguidance.com forums avidly voiced this perspective. For obvious reasons, websites advocating this position tend to disappear quickly.

Religious modernists demonstrate an alternative approach to political authority. Though they share the pedigree of many radical groups, with roots in the Muslim Brotherhood, these organizations now embrace institutional politics and openly incorporate modern political strategies. The site islamonline.net, for instance, offers extensive current events coverage and commentary, serving as an outlet of Muslim journalism. In the past, the site featured weekly movie reviews, a highly controversial feature, and continues to court popular culture. For their critics, this perspective abandons sound religious principles for perceived political gains. The Muslim political activist group CAIR (Council on American-Islamic Relations – cair-net.org) immerses itself in US politics. Yet, many doubt this strategy, not only for its dubious religious legitimacy, but for past political failures. For instance, in 2000, most American Muslim organizations, including CAIR, endorsed George W. Bush for president.

Within the political sphere, the 'true moderates' offer an interesting balance. The site as-sahwah.com (islamicawakening.com) provides a range of content, from news and commentary to religious lectures. The site forum even offers formal courses in classical religious texts. However, rather than blanket political mobilization, the site grounds its current affairs in religious sensibilities. For instance, in late 2005, the site featured an article entitled 'Why Allah Sends Earthquakes' by one of the premier scholars of recent times, Shaikh ibn Baz of Saudi Arabia. Concerning jihad, as-sahwah.com attempts to articulate an authentic approach, firm against anti-Islamic powers, and cautious of Islamic extremism. In addition, the site allows diverse contributions and discussion, especially in the forums. The widely varying content provides a common location for otherwise segregated viewpoints.

In this snapshot of the Islamic Internet, crucial issues of religious and political authority play out within the bounds of Sunni legitimacy. In many cases, the Internet confuses identity and exaggerates contested claims of authenticity. In others, classically trained scholars employ the Internet on their own terms, creating a unique Islamic media space. The Internet both erodes and extends authority. It offers unqualified individuals an undeserved platform. It also brings the wisdom of true scholars to the global community. But above all, by engaging the Islamic tradition on its own terms, we can understand these issues without ideological distortion. Analysts of Islam in contemporary life must recognize a basic fact. Despite the many claims to Islamic authority, valid or invalid, historically rooted or contemporary, the authentic Muslim tradition survives.

Notes

1 'U.S. Soccer Team Faces Chants of "Osama!"', MSNBC.com, 11 February 2004, http://www.msnbc.msn.com/id/4236314.
2 'Letter from Osama bin Laden to the American people', waaqiah.com (no longer an active site).
3 These sites are no longer active but earlier versions can be viewed on the web archive at www.archive.org.
4 'Shaikhs ibn Baz and ibn Uthaymin', mac.abc.se/home/onesr/h/172.html.

References

Abualrub, J. (2003) *Biography and Mission of Muhammad ibn Abdul Wahhab*. Orlando: Madinah.

Abukhalil, A. (2004) *The Battle for Saudi Arabia: Royalty, Fundamentalism, and Global Power*. New York: Seven Stories Press.

Anderson, J. W. (2003) 'New media, new publics: reconfiguring the public sphere of Islam', *Social Research*, 70 (3): 887–906.

Bunt, G. R. (2000) *Virtually Islamic: Computer-Mediated Communication and Cyber-Islamic Environments*. Cardiff: University of Wales Press.

Bunt, G. R. (2002) 'Islam interactive: Mediterranean Islamic expression on the World Wide Web', *Mediterranean Politics*, 7 (3): 164–86.

Bunt, G. R. (2003) *Islam in the Digital Age: e-jihad, Online Fatwas and Cyber Islamic Environments*. London: Pluto Press.

Castells, M. (1997) *The Power of Identity*. Malden, MD: Blackwell.

DeLong-Bas, N. (2004) *Wahhabi Islam: From Revival and Reform to Global Jihad*. Oxford: Oxford University Press.

Downing, J. D. H. (2001) *Radical Media: Rebellious Communications and Social Movements*. Thousand Oaks, CA: Sage.

Fandy, M. (1999) 'CyberResistance: Saudi opposition between globalization and localization', *Society for Comparative Study of Society & History*, 41 (1): 124–47.

Garrido, M. and A. Halavais (2003) 'Mapping networks of support for the Zapatista movement: applying social-networks analysis to study contemporary social movements', in M. McCaughey and M. D. Ayers (eds), *Cyberactivism: Online Activism in Theory and Practice*. New York: Routledge.

Lewis, B. (2002) *What Went Wrong? Western Impact and Middle Eastern Response*. London: Phoenix.

Mandaville, P. (2001) 'Reimagining Islam in diaspora: the politics of mediated community', *Gazette*, 63 (2–3): 169–86.

Norris, P. (2001) *Digital Divide: Civic Engagement, Information Poverty, and the Internet Worldwide*. Cambridge and New York: Cambridge University Press.

Phillips, B. (2000) *The Evolution of Fiqh: Islamic Law and the Madh-habs*. Riyadh: Islamic Publishing House.

Saco, D. (2002) *Cybering Democracy: Public Space and the Internet*. Minneapolis: University of Minnesota Press.

Winter, T. J. (2004) 'The poverty of fanaticism', in J. E. B. Lumbard (ed.), *Islam, Fundamentalism, and the Betrayal of Tradition: Essays by Western Muslim Scholars*. Bloomington: World Wisdom.

Index

Italic page numbers indicate a table or figure.

Borod, L. 92
Botero, Jorge 28
Botswana 155, 159
boundaries: in context of cultural flows
    45, 59, 79; disturbance of by
    migration and diasporas 33–4
Boutros-Ghali, Boutros 229
Boyd-Barrett, Oliver 7, 116, 153, 154,
    206
brand nationalism 79–80, 81; Korea
    138, 139
Brazil 23, 28–9; Korean Wave 146;
    radionovelas 105; telenovelas 6, 25,
    99, 100–2, 104, 105–7, 107–9, 117;
    under military regime 106, 107,
    108–9
Brazilian bossa nova 54
Brazilian media: television 3, 110,
    111–12; and US business publications
    22
Brazzil magazine 109
Britain: and First Opium War with
    China 169; and globalization of
    Americana 12; historical link with
    Qatar 116–17; as leader in TV
    exports 18; mainstream news media
    used by alternative sites 218; media
    for 'global' Indians 1; proposal for
    pan-African broadcaster 118; soap
    operas 103; Sony film production in
    21; South African programming sold
    to 159; South Asian TV channels 15,
    24
British-Asian films 27
British Asians 14
broadband 13, 29
broadcasting: Africa 155; deregulation
    and privatization 2, 12, 23, 155
Bromley, Roger 60–1
Bunt, Gary 240, 241, 241–2
Burkina Faso 159
burqa: and Afghan women 228, 230,
    231–2, 232, 234
Bush, George W. 63, 249; alternative
    media sites' opposition to 209; and
    Al-Jazeera 121, 124, 126; justification
    of assault on Afghanistan 228;
    mainstream media's complicity with
    203, 214, 218
Bush, Laura 228
business publications 22
business television channels 21

Business Times Singapore 143
Business Week 27
Buzzflash 207, 208

cable television networks 2, 12
CAIR (Council on American-Islamic
    Relations) 249
Cairo 23
Cameroon 159
Canadian Broadcasting Corporation
    125
Canadian Radio-Television and
    Telecommunications Commission
    123
Carlos, Manuel 111
Cartoon Network 21, 22, 158
Castells, Manuel 11, 39, 168, 225
Castro, Carlos 109–10
CBS (Columbia Broadcasting System)
    102, 117, 193
CCTV (China Central Television) 173,
    175; CCTV-9 13, 158, 175; CCTV-
    News 7, 182–9; competition from
    Phoenix TV 182, 183–4, 187, 188;
    and remapping of Chinese
    mediascape 195; success of *Focused
    Interview* 193, 194
cellevision 63
cell phones 50, 58
Certeau, Michel de 190–1
Chaddha, Gurvinder 26–7
Chadha, Kalyani 149, 154, 162
Chalabi, Ahmad 126
Chalaby, Jean 167, 168, 179
Channel Africa 160–1
Channel V 3
chat rooms 61
Chechnya 243
Cheney, Dick 126
Chen, Xiaoming 192
Chiapas 237
Chile 146
China 3, 4, 7, 21, 23, 28–9; approach to
    joint analysis with Russia 166;
    characteristics of journalism 189–92;
    cosmopolitan cities 168–9, 178;
    development of television 171–2;
    globalization of media 6–7, 168,
    173–7; imports of TV drama *174*;
    MultiChoice TV in 156; nationalist
    movement 171; popular market for
    Korean TV dramas 23–4, 135, 137,

27; and movements of people 1–2;
political, economic and cultural
implications 3–4; studies of 19–20,
165
media globalization 167, 168; academic
discourse 4; and CCTV-News 195;
China and Soviet Union 173–7,
178–9; increase in non-Western flows
67; mobilization of new public sphere
225; and outsourcing of media
content 13; and rise of alternative
models 11–12; tabloids in South
Africa 162–3
media imperialism 153–4; and South
Africa media 154, 162; *see also*
cultural imperialism
media in transition 166, 167–8; China
and Russia 178–9
Media Outreach Center (American
Embassy – London) 126
media products: global/transnational
circulation 3, 5, 11; US as leading
exporter of 16, *16*
media programming: theories 51–2
mediation: diasporic communications
33, 39, 42, 45, 46; political process
35–6
Med TV 37
Mehta, R. 60
melodrama: soaps and telenovelas
104–5, 106, 109
Mendoza, Breny 225
Merritt, Davis 'Buzz' 193, 194
Mexican national cinema 90
Mexico: imports of Korean media
products 135, 146; telenovelas (soap
operas) 25, 99, 101, 103, 104, 111,
174; victory over US in Olympic
football match 237
Mexico TV 146
Mexiquense 146
Mickey Mouse Magazine 21
middle classes: emergence in Asia 140;
expansion in Africa 157; expansion in
China 183, 185; global 62; greater
mobility 24; portrayal in Korean TV
dramas 147
Middle East: impact of Al-Jazeera 118;
market for American film and TV 16;
MIH subscription services 156–7;
Western media platforms 21
migrants 41, 50, 117

migration: disturbance of boundaries
33, 58; and transnational networks 2,
5, 24
Miles, Hugh 13, 118, 119
Minbar al-Jazeera (TV programme) 120
Minha Vida Te Pertence (telenovela)
105–6
minorities 39, 43
al-Mirazi, Hafez 119
Mission Kashmir (film) 85
M-Net 6, 13, 22, 155, 156, 157, 158, 159
mobile phones 29
mobility of media 1
mobility of people: geo-cultural markets
14; and globalization of cultural
products 24; and new media flows
1–2; and professional networks 2
modernity: Bollywood 86; in
dependency and developmentalist
theories 51; in Korean TV dramas
142, 147, 149; Western configuration
of 73–4
Modi, K. K. 94
Moghadam, Valentine 222, 224, 229
Mohanty, C. 59
Monjardim, Jaime 100
Moscow 169, 171, 177
Mother India (film) 95
Motion Picture Association 18
Moulier Boutang, Y. 84
Movie Magic 158
MSNBC.com 205, 210
MTV (Music Television) 12, 27, 77
Mujahadin 222, 224
Mukherjee, A. 93
MultiChoice Africa 6, 22, 155–8
Mumbai 23, 92–3
Murdoch, Rupert 3, 21, 103, 125, 182,
188
Murdock, Graham 222
music: in diasporic media culture 39;
East Asian projects 74; Indian film
music channels 1; played by Channel
Africa 161; in urban context 41;
see also pop music
Muslim Brotherhood 248
My Way 210

Nair, Mira 26
Nairobi: UN women's conference 229
Namibia 156, 159, 160
Naregal, V. 88

Korean popular culture 135, 140, 146–7; networks' reporting of Iraq conflict 117–18, 121; platforms for diasporic groups 24; presidential election (2000) 63, 213–14, 214, 249; radio soap model 105; shutting down of Somali ISP 37; soap operas 27, 103; and thesis of Al-Jazeera serving the West 123, 124–5, 126–7; women's organizations of 1980s 224; *see also* American films, etc.
UNOCAL 230
Urdu language 91, 225
US–Afghan Women's Council 234
US Army 58
Al-'Uthaimeen, Shaikh Muhammad ibn Saalih 247

Vale Tudo (telenovela) 111
van Zoonen, Liesbet 191
Variety 108
Varis, T. 103
Vasudevan, R 91
VCDs/VCRs 143–4, 173
Vedomosti (newspaper) 169
Venezuela 13, 25, 104, 118
Viacom 21, 27
Viana, Oduvaldo 105
video games 58, 62, 77
Vietnam 138, 145
violence: attributed to Bin Laden 238–9; as contra-flow 61; mediated terrorism 61–2; and problems of globalization 59, 60
Virdi, J. 86
virtual spaces 61
VIVA Cinema 21
Voice of America 27

Wahhab, Muhammad ibn 'Abdul 246
Wali, Rashid Hamid 121
Walkman 68
Wall Street Journal 22, 27, 136
Wal-Mart 27
Warner Brothers 21, 77, 158
'war on terrorism' 24, 212
Washington Post 68, 202, 214, 218
Washington Times 210
Wasseman, Herman 6
Al-Watan 128
web-based alternative networks 4, 7, 37
Webber, Andrew Lloyd 85

web cams 62
web casting 58
Wei-Lai Drama Channel 144
Western culture: challenge of Korean Wave 138, 149
Western media: circulation in China and Soviet Russia 173; domination of global media 4, 12–13, 20, 73–4, 136; elements in Bollywood 86; globalization of 11–12, 13, 168; and glocalization 20–2; high standard of news channels 184, 188; Al-Jazeera as challenging 118, 123, 129; penetration into Third World nations 191; relative demise of cultural hegemony 67
Western narratives: 'difference' and 'otherness' 222, 225; international feminism 224, 227
Wichita Eagle 193
Williams, C. 56
Winfrey, Oprah 232
Winter Sonata (TV drama) 138, 140, 141–2, 143, 144, 145, 146
women: and structural inequalities in communications 226–7; transnational feminist movement 221, 222; *see also* Afghan women
Women Living Under Muslim Laws (WLUML) 224, 229
World Bank 87
World Social forums 234
World Trade Organization 184, 190

Xinhua News Agency 171, 175

Yahoo!News.com 205, 210, 212
Young & Rubican 28

Zambia 159, 160
Zapatistas 231, 237–8
ZDF 25
Zee TV 14, 15, 24
Zero Distance from Nanjing (TV news show) 194–5
Zhao, H. 186
Zhao, Xinshu 167
Zhao Qizheng 188
Zhao, Y. 189
Zhu Rongji 187
Zimbabwe 159
Zoya 232–3

Related titles from Routledge
Media and Power
James Curran

Media and Power addresses three key questions about the relationship between media and society.

- How much power do the media have?
- Who really controls the media?
- What is the relationship between media and power in society?

In this major new book, James Curran reviews the different answers which have been given, before advancing original interpretations in a series of ground-breaking essays.

Media and Power also provides a guided tour of the major debates in media studies:

- What part did the media play in the making of modern society?
- How did 'new media' change society in the past?
- Will radical media research recover from its mid-life crisis?
- What are the limitations of the US-based model of 'communications' research?
- Is globalization disempowering national electorates or bringing into being a new, progressive global politics?
- Is public service television the dying product of the nation in an age of globalization?
- What can be learned from the 'third way' tradition of European media policy?

Curran's response to these questions provides both a clear introduction to media research and an innovative analysis of media power, written by one of the field's leading scholars.

ISBN13: 978-0-415-07739-2 (hbk)
ISBN13: 978-0-415-07740-8 (pbk)

Available at all good bookshops
For ordering and further information please visit:
www.routledge.com

Related titles from Routledge

Power without Responsibility

Sixth Edition

James Curran and Jean Seaton

'This is a useful and timely book' Richard Hoggart,
Times Educational Supplement

'In a fast-changing media scene this book is nothing less than indispensable' Julian Petley, *Brunel University*

'*Power without Responsibility*, the best guide to the British media' Nick Cohen, *The New Statesman*

Power without Responsibility is a classic, authoritative and engaged introduction to the history, sociology, theory and politics of media and communication studies. Written in a lively and accessible style, it is regarded as the standard book on the British media.

This new edition has been substantially revised to bring it up-to-date with new developments in the media industry. Its three new chapters describe the battle for the soul of the internet, the impact of the internet on society and the rise of new media in Britain. In addition, it examines the recuperation of the BBC, how international and European regulation is changing the British media and why Britain has the least trusted press in Europe.

ISBN13: 978-0-415-24389-6 (hbk)
ISBN13: 978-0-415-24390-2 (pbk)

Related titles from Routledge
Remaking Media
The struggle to democratize public communication
Robert A. Hackett and William K. Carroll

What is the political significance and potential of democratic media activism in the Western world today?

Remaking Media rides on a wave of political and scholarly attention to oppositional communication, triggered by the rise in the 1990s of the Zapatistas, internet activism, and IndyMedia. This attention has mostly focused on alternative media and the 'media strategies' of social movements – i.e., 'democratization through the media'. This book concerns democratization of the media themselves, efforts to transform the 'machinery of representation', as a distinctive field that is pivotal to other social struggles.

Remaking Media takes as its premise the existence of a massive 'democratic deficit' in the field of public communication. This deficit propels diverse struggles to reform and revitalize public communication in the North Atlantic heartland of globalization. It focuses on activism directed towards challenging and changing media content, practices, and structures, as well as state policies on media.

Hackett and Carroll's approach is innovative in its attention to an emerging social movement that appears at the cutting edge of cultural and political contention. The book is grounded in three scholarly traditions that provide interpretive resources for a study of democratic media activism: political theories of democracy, critical media scholarship, and the sociology of social movements. By synthesizing insights from these sources they provide a unique and timely reading of the contemporary struggle to democratize communication.

ISBN 13: 978-0-415-39468-0 (hbk)
ISBN 13: 978-0-415-39469-7 (pbk)

Available at all good bookshops
For ordering and further information please visit:
www.routledge.com

UNIVERSITY OF WOLVERHAMPTON
LEARNING & INFORMATION SERVICES